# THE GARDEN
## OF THE
# GOLDEN FLOWER

# THE GARDEN
## OF THE
# GOLDEN FLOWER
## THE JOURNEY TO SPIRITUAL FULFILMENT

### LONGFIELD BEATTY

SENATE

*The Garden of the Golden Flower*

First published in 1939 by Rider & Co, London.

This edition first published in 1996 by Senate, an imprint of Random House UK Ltd, Random House, 20 Vauxhall Bridge Road, London SW1V 2SA

Copyright © Longfield Beatty 1939

ISBN 1 85958 151 X

Printed and bound in Guernsey by The Guernsey Press Co. Ltd

Where is the root of the Golden Flower?
In the garden of the Two Trees.
And where does the flower bloom?
In the Purple Hall of the City of Jade.

Where is this garden?
In the seed water, the moat of the City.

When does the flower bloom?
At the end of the far journey.
What journey?
From water to fire, earth to gold, serpent to eagle;
from father to mother, mother to son, son to father.
And the cost of the journey?
The blood of father, mother, and son.
Blood, then, is a password?
No, only the Sphinx can teach the password.

# CONTENTS

# CHAPTER NINE

The Complex. Baptism of Jesus of Nazareth. The Drama. Symbols of Œdipus. The Riddle of the Sphinx. Œdipus Christus. Mother distinguished from Destroyer. Titles of the Mother. Symbols of the Sphinx. Conclusion by Quotation.

# CHAPTER TEN

Christ Jesus, Symbol, Power, and Person. The Redeemer and the Individual. The "Dead" bury the Dead. Desire/Love. The Unjust Steward and a Portion to Eight. Marriage at Cana. Mating and Marriage. The Results of Materialistic Morality. The Road from Behemoth.

# CHAPTER ELEVEN

Mystical Experience. Rationalisation. Analysis Physical and Mystical. Prophecy. Thibetan Book of the Dead. The Kabalah. Epilogue.

# THE GARDEN OF THE GOLDEN FLOWER

## INTRODUCTION

*" We moderns are faced with the necessity of rediscovering the life of the spirit. . . . It is the only way in which we can break the spell that binds us to the circle of biological events."*

(DR. C. J. JUNG.)

THE Riddle of the Sphinx is the daily preoccupation of everyone. Consciously or unconsciously we arrange life with a purpose. Failure to be purposeful means failure complete, for upon purpose depends the road, upon the road depends the environment, upon environment life itself. Fortunately it is impossible to be quite without purpose . . . every psychological school concerned with the " unconscious " agrees in that. But the unconscious purpose seems to be bound by this " circle of biological events " in which man cannot find happiness, since what is enough for animals is not enough for him. The Sphinx represents the " biological circle," and her question is primarily concerned with purpose. In that Œdipus answered rightly where so many failed, there is in him the clue to the mystery, the secret of escape from the circle. Yet not in Œdipus alone, but in every such victor.

We are always striving for happiness, and whatever our success or failure, its expression must be in terms of outlook, of consciousness. It is possible to find symbols with which to deal with consciousness and hence to put forward a reasoned answer to the question. But it must never be forgotten that the Sphinx does not appreciate logic, and it is to her and not to the psychologists or philosophers that man must answer. Those gentlemen can indicate the line which an individual should take ; they can point out to him the weapons at his disposal, their use, abuse, and effect; but they cannot answer for him.

Success or failure means happiness or misery, normality or neurosis, sanity or madness. It is terribly important to find the conditions of the question and answer. At the same time there is another warning to be given. Intellectual conviction, however thorough, is not enough for the Sphinx, because character, the " balance of power" in consciousness, is not effected by cold reason.

" To understand mere words intellectually is one thing, but to comprehend the spirit of the words and weave them into the texture of one's character is another."[1]

This " comprehension of the spirit " is intuition, without which all argument is powerless, however competent the proof may be. But intuition is also the basis of mysticism, concerning which it is necessary to exercise very great care.

" Most mystics I have met have been fools, for the very fact that it cannot give an account of itself at the bar of intellect makes mysticism the prey of every crank and every quack who seeks to compensate for his palpable inferiority of common wit by claiming a superiority of private vision."[2]

Man's capacity for self-deception is apparently endless, and the fascination of the supernormal often irresistible. The reality of an intuitive faculty, however, is quite

[1] SEIJI NOMA : *The Nine Magazines of Kodansha.*
[2] C. E. M. JOAD : *The Testament of Joad.*

generally recognised, and some of the greatest names in philosophy support the idea, notably Plato and Aristotle, Spinoza and Bergson. However, it is one thing to admit intuition and quite another to claim for it infallibility. Says the *Britannica* : " The term is often used to cover beliefs and prejudices which one cannot justify or excuse."

Therefore, though intuition may be said with justice to have provided the germ of this book, yet the " intuitive approach " to our problems is relegated to the rôle of epilogue. Intellect, such as it is, must take precedence, but if, through incapacity or oversight, the argument is proved fallacious, I refuse to be confounded. At least intuition remains unaffected by inaccurate interpretation.

The book is really founded on the phrase " consummate duality " which appeared as the climax to a series of sporadic verses. They were, with very few exceptions, written for the usual poet's reason, that there was no peace of mind to be had until the ideas behind them found their way into words. Most of them puzzled me because of their obscure symbolism, and some of them, when subjected to psychoanalysis, revealed an erotic content which severely shook the proverbial poet's conceit. Pride . . . or intuition, still insisted that the verses were not primarily concerned with sex. Freud insisted that they were. Rather than submit to the indignity, I determined to justify my intuition as far as possible *in terms of intellect*. Evidently the Freudian results were quite correct, but they did not go far enough. I remained obstinately convinced that there was something in my mental endowment which was not explicable in terms of lust of one sort or another. It was evident therefore that the orthodox methods must be extended. If, for instance, sex could be shown to have a specific *symbolic* value, then the results of analysis might be expressed in simple abstract terms instead of those derived from the physical relationship, the very focus of which is, of course, the " Œdipus complex " and its " incest dread."

It so happens that there is a very important clue to some abstract reality beyond the sex force, in a most unlikely but well documented locality.  I refer to the sexual *taboos* of primitive races, which have been studied not only by Freud and other psychologists, but also by Sir James Frazer.  It is evident from the works of these unquestioned authorities that most taboos are arrived at in reference to some magical force which is believed to manifest in conjunction with various sexual affairs. This force may - be beneficial or dangerous, and the person through whom it is believed to act is treated accordingly.  In fact the power appears as essentially " electrical " in that people and things become highly " charged " . . . so highly that contact with them may even prove fatal, as in the case of Uzzah, who died from contact with the Ark of the Covenant.  Like electricity, the force can be either " positive " or " negative," static or dynamic, the " sign " depending upon the medium through which it manifests.  If the medium were unclean the force would be dangerous, and it is evident that most people are regarded at least as potentially unclean unless purified by appropriate ritual. The only important exception to this rule is provided by the " priest-king " who was regarded as " pure " by virtue of his position (and/or birth).  Yet such a person had to be surrounded with as much taboo to preserve his purity as would be observed by one through whom the force was regarded as manifesting to the danger of the community.  The former had to be insulated so that he did not accidentally " discharge " and waste the precious force, while the latter had to be prevented from discharging for fear of the consequences for evil. Thus we find the sacred and the profane, the priest-king and the menstruous woman hedged about with substantially the same regulations. On this curious idea hangs the first link in the chain which is to lead us, or so we hope, to an understanding of the real nature of the force, either in reality or as a significant piece of imagination. At all events, primitive peoples have always regarded sexual phenomena as the outward and visible sign of the action of this mysterious force, and not, as might be supposed, as potent in themselves, except in the restricted biological sense. In that respect the Bushmen of Australia are in advance of modern materialists who can see nothing in sex but sex.

Thus provided with a starting-point, the same ideas are traced through the evolution of religion, finding that the same force is recognised at successive stages in more and more abstract or " spiritual " form. The final point in this prelminiary treatment may be said to be reached with the discovery that the Divine " triunity " represents a reality of relationship such that the " physical equation " of the psychologists (male : female : : consummation) is its lowest expression. Between these two " levels," the spiritual and the physical, lies the proper territory of psychology, where it should be possible to do considerable exploration if an adequate link can be found between it and the others. This middle " level " I have labelled the " mystic " because it is necessary to work on a broader basis than would be warranted by the title " psychological level," as will duly become apparent. At all events there are *three levels*, on each of which are *three terms*, such that the first two are " sexed " *opposites*, while the third in some mysterious way includes them. Hence the concept of "triunity" and its significance on levels far removed from theology. Let Dr. Jung speak again:

"I see in all happening the play of opposites and derive therefrom my conception of psychic energy."

"What it (the relationship between the opposites) amounts to is an indeterminable and variable 'x' which stands for the physiological activity of the glands at one extreme and the highest reaches of the spirit at the other."

(*Modern Man in Search of a Soul.*)

Thus the Individual himself appears as the "third term" in relation to the battleground of the 'opposites' which is the totality of his mind, conscious and unconscious . . . though largely the latter. When there is no battle, when the opposites are united, the Individual is "free." In a restricted sense he is free *from neurosis*, but to the mystic the idea of freedom only finds its ultimate expression in Nirvana, where there is no more space or time or desire. And the symbol of freedom is the "consummation," whether it represents only the easing of tension, the contentment which springs from natural physical relations, or some higher concept of which very many can be recognised, culminating in the ultimate unity of Godhead.

"Everything is derived from the first principle, and everything aspires to return to it. But these two conceptions of the divine causality can only be identified if we bring them, both the one and the other, back to a third, which we hold to be fundamental and which alone will enable us to understand, not only why, in what sense, things move in space and time, but also why there is space and time, why there is movement, why there are things."

(BERGSON : *Creative Evolution*, p. 341.)

It cannot be too strongly emphasised that the 'opposites" have no "masculinity" or "femininity" except in physical symbols. They are, however, referred

to (at need) on all levels as " male " and " female," for
the simple reason that there is no adequate substitute.[1]
In order to handle abstractions they must be labelled.
On every level except the physical all three terms are
abstract, and so it is reasonable to use the physical
symbols which correspond to abstractions according to
the plan of our three " equations." Then gradually it
may become possible to discuss the abstract in special
terms. For the time being, however, the primary
necessity is to keep our feet firmly planted on earth.

The burden of our task is evidently to discover as
much as possible about the " indeterminable ' x ' " of
Dr. Jung, and to that end we may summarise the present
data as follows :

(1) Two complementary terms exist whose relationship
    is as male to female.
(2) These terms represent forces in the psychology of
    the individual who himself represents the third
    term.
(3) The highest expression of this relationship is that
    of the spiritual " triunity."
(4) The lowest expression of the relationship is that
    of the sexes.
(5) The sexual relationship, being written as an equa-
    tion, represents the relationship between the
    terms at all levels ; male : female : : consum-
    mation is thus the basic equation.

" It is shameful or exalted just as one chooses that the
divine longing of humanity, which is really the first thing to
make it human, should be brought into relation with erotic
phantasy."                    (*Psychology of the Unconscious*, p. 51.)

Clearly our next link is to be forged when these ideas

[1] The Chinese " Yin " and " Yang " suggest themselves, but
it is judged that our own terms are less apt to cause confusion.

are applied to communities rather more advanced than those ruled by primitive systems of taboo. We should, in fact, apply the concept of three terms and three *levels* to the evolution of religious dogma and ritual. Broadly speaking, it is apparent that the growing theological system has alternative lines of development in this respect ; either sex is to be regarded as a divine mystery, or else ignored as far as possible on the ground that its whole territory is essentially evil. What tragedies have followed both choices ! For the first, human nature is apt to degrade the doctrine until there is nothing left *but* the physical ; while the rejection of sex can only lead to a faith out of touch with reality. Indeed I hope to show that where sex has been repudiated religion is dead, because the keys of even the highest abstractions are hidden in the physical equation. The modern Christian Church may well be suffering from such a malady. Certainly her teaching has largely lost that evident reality which the worshipper reasonably requires of any faith. The meaning of the Bible has been overlaid with layers of learned commentary, based for the most part, and where such a distinction is possible, on the rejection of the physical to the supposed greater glory of the spiritual. Though prominent divines have been known to rhapsodise over a clover-leaf as a symbol of Godhead, they would regard with horror the suggestion that the most vital symbol of all is the relationship of the sexes. Yet, not only is the " consummation " the pre-eminent symbol of " triunity " ; it is the first clue to the nature of " spiritual " reality. Let us anticipate boldly so as to obtain a clear foundation which will prove its solidarity later on.

It is asserted that the idea of trinity is our most vital clue, and for the following reasons :

(1) Developed religions recognise a triple Godhead, of whose three terms, the Son is a human hero.

(2) Psychology recognises two opposing forces such that the Individual is only *free* (from neurosis, complex, etc.) when they are neutralised (sublimated or transferred).

(3) All systems of traditional mysticism speak of *liberation from the opposites* as the ultimate goal.

(4) Psychology, mysticism, and religion are unanimous that the *force which tends to unite the opposites is love*.

For reasons which will appear later, the fact that Spirit is symbolised as male, and Matter as female, provides our second major clue, leading to the identification of the third term with *Consciousness* . . . a supposition which is easily checked.   We are thus able to arrange our three equations as follows :

|  | 1 | 2 | 3 |
|---|---|---|---|
| *Cosmic Level* | Spirit | Matter | Consciousness |
| *Mystic Level* | Father | Mother | Son |
| *Physical Level* | Male | Female | Consummation |

Of these the first equation should be immediately applicable to religious symbolism (e.g. the New Testament) ; the second to the psychology of the individual, and the third to myths, taboos, and so on.   Obviously it will be almost impossible in practice to recognise a clear dividing line between the *levels*, and the foregoing example of how the classification is applied is therefore not unduly complicated, but actually simplified.   For instance, in one way or another myths, fairy stories, legends, and religious tradition are all susceptible to psychoanalysis, as were even my own poems.   But we need not stop there.   The materialist, not possessing the necessary tools, is forced to conclude that there is nothing higher than the physical reality which alone his method can reveal. Nevertheless he must recognise that even the psychological terms of his equation imply a reality beyond the " libidinous " territory of animal instinct. But he has no means of dealing with such a " beyond," and therefore falls back on the comforting assumption that even if there is a higher reality it must be *reducible* to his own terms.

" I believe that a large proportion of the mythological conception of the world which reaches far into the most modern religions is nothing more than psychology projected into the outer world."

(FREUD : *Psychopathology of Everyday Life*, p. 309.)

If only the quotation had been expressed the other way round it would have been possible to agree with the statement unconditionally ; for to say that religious and other abstract ideas are *symbolised* in psychological terms is no more (and no less) true than to say that the Divine Trinity is symbolised in copulation. Yet Divinity is not *reducible* to such terms ; on the other hand, the abstract becomes more and more comprehensible as the terms are expanded away from the physical. Nor is it reasonable to suggest that such a concept as the Divine Trinity is essentially inconceivable (save, of course, in its entirety). Indeed, we shall find before long that Father, Son, and Holy Ghost are transformed, with the aid of the equations, into precise concepts ; primarily with regard to the evolution of consciousness as expressed in the symbolism of Genesis.

It would be pleasant to leave the matter where it stands without putting further strain on the reader's sense of proportion, but, fortunately or otherwise, the greatest symbol of all . . . at least the greatest personified

symbol, is yet to be introduced. Fortunately because
there is hardly anyone who will not take from it some
sense of the underlying truth ; unfortunately because
it may, in some cases, tend to confuse the issue. To be
warned, however, is to be armed. The " new " concept
is that of the Consummator, the symbolic figure of the
God/Man.

" Both philosophy and psychology should start neither
with God nor with Man, but with the God/Man."
(NICHOLAS BERDAEV : *Freedom and the Spirit*.)

It is impossible to over-emphasise the importance of
this symbol *which occurs on all three levels as the personified
third term*. There is a Cosmic Christ, a Mystic Christ,
and a Physical Christ . . . the last being the traditional (or
even historical) human being in whose life were included
the symbols by which the universal abstractions could
be read. Undisputed chief of these " personifications "
is Jesus of Nazareth, though it is idle to deny that in
varying degrees of perfection each and every hero is a
Christ. . . . Ultimately of course each individual is a
Christ, but not, regrettably enough, to any considerable
degree of perfection. Yet there are heroes in plenty in
whom the symbols read true enough to confirm them as
leaders of no common order. Such as Zoroaster,
Buddha, Krishna, Osiris, Attis, Adonis, Hercules,
Quetzalcoatl, and even Susa-no-o, the " Impetuous Male "
of Japanese mythology. Nor should we forget Arthur
Pendragon of the Round Table, to whom, even in such
illustrious company as these, there attaches a peculiar
interest.

But how comes it that the Consummator is represented
on all levels ? The answer is to be found in terms of the
evolution of consciousness, to which certain clues are

provided by traditional symbolism. Thus the Christ is represented as Fish/Man (Icthus), Man, Son of Man, Son of God, and " Very " God. If these titles are considered successively in the light of the " sign of the prophet Jonas " our feet may thereby find themselves upon a road. For Jonas is identified with Oannes, the Fish/Man of Nineveh, from whose symbols a great deal can be deduced. Indeed, it is hardly an exaggeration to say that Jonas stands for the keystone of an arch between science and religion. If Jonas is the only sign which " this generation " shall be given, there is yet every indication that it may be sufficient.

" An evil and adulterous generation seeketh after a sign ; and there shall no sign be given it, but the sign of the Prophet Jonas."

(Matt. xii, 39.)

Yet Jonas is not alone significant for his relationship with Oannes. The importance of the adventurous prophet lies chiefly in the fact that his symbolic associations are sufficient, even by themselves, to establish the essentials of the identity of the " Triple " Christ. Jonas, in fact, is the interpreter of the Christ in general and of Jesus of Nazareth in particular. As such he may be said to provide the key to Dr. Jung's " indeterminable and variable x."

But Jonas is only the first link of a long chain, a chain of heroes whose significance increases as their symbolism is rationalised. Following such links we reach at length the focus of them all. We arrive at a cliff edge beyond the walls of Thebes and take part in that famous drama of the Riddle. Œdipus is no longer a classical hero, or even a psychological cipher, he is you and I and all humanity. And not only humanity, for he is also the potentiality of God.

# CHAPTER ONE

## TABOO

" Civilisation, culture, work, business, routine, philan-
thropy, art, philosophy, scholarship, religion, and crime are
third directions growing out of the sexual pattern."
(DICKINSON AND BEAL : *A Thousand Marriages*, p. 358.)

WHILE bearing in mind that under no circumstances can our subject be neatly pigeon-holed,
we shall do our best to follow a logical method,
so that the argument grows naturally to a point where
it is hoped the reader will suddenly find himself inside
a circle of evidence which he cannot choose but accept.
Once " inside " there should be no further difficulty.

To begin with, we shall endeavour to establish a solid
basis of physical analogies, and only when these have
been firmly set, go on to the more tenuous realms of
" mysticism," remembering, however, that the subjective
is quite as " real " as the objective, even if the latter
is not, as asserted in the Orient, an " illusion," a
" vanity."

The first subjects of investigation are primitive communities wherein the principles we are investigating are
recognised only in their gross sexual form. It is therefore
curious to find that such people have moral codes whose
strictness is astonishing in the eyes of modern civilisation. Contrary to present-day experience, which may be
summed up as a case of familiarity breeding contempt,
the savage often submits to a system of sexual control

23

far more rigid even than that of our hypocritical grandparents.

In *Totem and Taboo* (p. 3), Professor Freud says :

" We would surely not expect that these poor, naked can-
nibals should be moral in their sex life according to our ideas,
or that they should have imposed a high degree of restriction
upon their impulses.   And yet we learn that they have considered it their duty to exercise the most searching care and
the most painful rigour in guarding against incestuous sexual
relations.   In fact, their whole social organisation seems to
serve this object or to have been brought into relation with
its attainment."

We shall see later why *incest* is particularly dreaded . . .
because the " sin " of that relationship is due to the
extreme sanctity of it !   But our present concern is with
the savages' point of view, which must be regarded
(hypothetically) as recognising sex and all that pertains
to it, *primarily as the vehicle of magical power*.   It is in the
hope of throwing some light on the nature of this
power that we pursue the subject.   I believe it no
exaggeration to say that in every country and every age,
from the glories of Greece to the caves of pre-history,
from the fetishes of aborigines to the ceremonial incest
of Pharaoh, the central mystery of all ritual and belief
was sex. . . . Yet not sex in itself, but the " electrical "
force of which it is the physical vehicle.   Certainly the
symbolism of sex has always been recognised (inevitably,
since it derives from the unconscious) ;   sometimes, as
in Greece and Rome (Hermes and Bacchus at their best),
raised to lofty spiritual heights, at other times degenerating into bestiality and black magic . . . but never regarded
as " just sex," a mere biological phenomenon.   Indeed,
the more primitive the community, the more insistence
seems to have been placed on the *magical* quality, an idea

which has been explained by the assumption that to
primitive man anatomy in itself is so mysterious as to
be a fit object of worship ; hence the universal phallic
cult. Yet primitive society generally, and even prehistoric society, appears to have regarded sex not only
as a vital factor in their daily lives (fertility), but also as
something magical and *symbolic*. That this is true of the
Bronze Age is shown in the numerous phallic ceremonies
represented in pictographs upwards of 2000 B.C., several
of which are illustrated in Cleland's *Our Prehistoric
Ancestors*. One of the drawings shows a boat-load of
gesticulating warriors presided over by a great, horned,
ithyphallic figure reminiscent of the medieval Devil.

But pictographs are not enough, and we must turn to
better documented communities, where it is found that
virtually everything connected with sex is wound round
with a mass of taboo which at times appears absolutely
incomprehensible in its severity. Thus the widespread
custom of the seclusion of girls at puberty for a period
during which they may neither set foot on earth nor see
the sun. Sometimes each is shut up in a small, dark
cage for as much as five years (New Ireland), or in a
room where no sunlight can enter, for seven years
(Borneo). In Alaska the wretched maiden was confined
" in a small hut where she had to remain on her hands
and feet for six months ; then the hut was enlarged a
little so as to allow her to straighten her back, but in
this posture she had to remain for six months more."
(*The Golden Bough*, ab. ed., p. 596.)

Now what mentality is this which can enforce such
cruelty, not upon enemies, but upon children ? At first
sight the evidence is simply staggering ; it seems
impossible that parents could tolerate such customs
under any circumstance whatever. And yet the evidence

is there, an illustration of the extremes to which the degradation of an idea may be pushed by credulous and fearful people. It stands as an awful warning of the necessity for a just sense of proportion. The parents of these women, being human, suffered with their daughters, only allowing the imprisonment because it was sanctioned by the custom of many generations, backed by the authority of the priest.

In the foregoing examples the girls were " insulated " to prevent them discharging the magic force to the detriment of the community. Thus they were " unclean," and this very condition must have included the symbol of the power which was held to be manifest in them. Further, they became unclean from the first menstruation. There can be little doubt that it was the menstrual blood which constituted the essential symbol of the power's presence, and that it was regarded as unclean from the manner of its appearance. Hence it was assumed that the woman was unclean . . . i.e. the medium through which the power acted ; but the power itself was neither clean nor unclean, being " electrical," the same force which, in the priest-kings, made them the divine " batteries " of their peoples. Blood was *their* sign, for such kings were doomed, from the day they took office, to death at the hands of their subjects, either at the end of a fixed term, or when their powers (sexual powers) actually began to fail. Only a violent death could atone for the weakening of the magic power, just as only the " blood of atonement " is sufficient to redeem humanity from the " fall." Blood, in fact, and suffering are the signs of all those in whom the magic force becomes manifest, whether they be heroes, kings, priests, mystics, or those unfortunates in whom popular credulity detects the symbol of such power in an unclean medium. . . .

" Write in blood and thou shalt find that blood is spirit."[1]

From the Blood derives that element of cruelty which characterises not only initiations, properly speaking, such as circumcision, but also in the deaths of kings and, of course, of heroes. Suffering is the only purge for uncleanness. Thus Jesus is crucified " for the sins of the world," Osiris is nailed in his coffin, " living and with open eyes," Attis castrated himself, Adonis and Diamid are gored to death by boars, Odin is hanged upon a tree. Indeed, Frazer gives sufficient information concerning some of these relatively civilised cults, for instance that of Attis, to put them into line with Moloch or the fiendish cults of primitive India and Central America. The chain of blood . . . the blood of the sacrifice, is unbroken, alike in the world's history and over the earth's surface.

But what is it which inspires the sacrifice ? Surely the gaining of a victory, whether of the reappearance of vegetation (Cults of the Corn Spirit), or the forces of good over those of evil (Taboo), or *the triumph of Spirit over Matter*. It is this last which now holds our attention as the highest expression of the symbol of *blood*. All the heroes just mentioned are personifications of the " triple " Christ (q.v.) and their message is immortality. . . . Spirit over Matter, the victory of blood. The faithful are redeemed by the blood of the Christ, and even their robes are " washed in the precious blood." The Eucharist conveys the same saving principle to the worshipper of Jesus as the degraded cults of Mexico conveyed at a lower level through the excision of the living heart. To attain spiritual power (immortality) the hero must become the victim. He must suffer and die.

[1] Nietzsche.

And the symbol of his victory is blood, for he himself has become blood . . . that which was mortal has become immortal. So menstrual blood is now easily recognised in its " uncleanness." . . . No wonder the unfortunate woman had to suffer, since it must have appeared a great sin indeed to manifest the divine power in such a singularly *un*-spiritual fashion.

But we have digressed from the broad considerations with which we are most concerned. The symbolism of blood is at present only valuable to illustrate the way in which the same magical properties are everywhere recognised as attaching to sex, especially in regard to functions of that symbol. It is, however, important to bear in mind how blood and pain are inseparable. Masochism and sadism both derive symbolically from a natural law which Christians are brought up to recognise in the doctrine of Atonement. The crimes of such maniacs as Gilles de Rais, who tortured and murdered some hundreds of children, derive, whether we like it or not, from the same immaculate abstraction which hanged Odin upon the tree and nailed Jesus to the Cross ; while between these extremes sadomasochism is asserted by Stekel to be the essential basis of all neuroses.

To one school of thought taboos derive solely from the necessity of protecting society as a whole, which otherwise might disrupt under a sexual theory of " each man for himself." The likelihood seems that such a disruption would be less probable than that the community would perish from a falling birth-rate ; the reason being that in the absence of artificial inducements such as are provided by conventions, ceremonies, privileges, and taboos, stable marriage would be almost an impossibility. I stress this point because the absence of the magical " aura " of marriage would tend to reduce society to the animal level. If our own civilisation appears to be far removed from that condition, there is at least a chance that we may be deluded.

It has been suggested that there is an almost universal practice to regard women as " unclean " at a time when the magical force is first believed to become active through the symbol of the blood. They are accordingly segregated until " purified," or until the force ceases to manifest. In the same way youths are made to undergo elaborate " initiation ceremonies," the object of which is undoubtedly the same as that which dictates the seclusion of girls at the same period of life. Moreover, the same element of cruelty is present to ensure that the subject is completely " purified " by the " blood of atonement " and dedicated to the community so that force acting through him may thereafter be to the benefit, and not the hurt, of his fellows. The force must be canalised, as it were, to the common good, until a fresh manifestation necessitates further ceremonies to the same end.

Now since the " consummation " is the most potent of all abstract symbols common to all three " levels," including as it does the whole mystery of " triunity," it is natural that customs connected therewith should reflect this pre-eminence. They will, in fact, be found as well documented and distributed as those connected specifically with adolescence and " initiation." For instance, seclusion of both bride and groom is a widespread taboo, and elaborate precautions are taken to ensure that the magic force is not misdirected. Ordeals have to be gone through and great care exercised to purify the " atmosphere." In fact an examination of typical ceremonies makes it quite clear that in marriage we are dealing with a fresh manifestation of the same force which was first thought to become active at puberty. Perhaps it will be as well to give a few illustrations taken from *The Mystic Rose* (Vol. II) :

" In British Guiana a young man before marriage . . . is wounded and sewn into a hammock full of fire ants."

" The first ceremonies (at a Malay wedding) consist in fumigating the bride and groom with incense, and then smearing them with " neutralising paste " which averts ill-luck.  When a Matabele bride arrives in the bridegroom's house she pours water over him."

" The practice of throwing rice originated in the idea of giving food to the evil influences to induce them to depart."

" In the county of Durham men with guns used to escort the bridal party to the church.  The guns were fired at intervals over the heads of the bride and bridesmaids."

But perhaps the best example of the power liberated at the consummation is that set out in the book of Tobit (vii and viii), where it is described as having caused the immediate deaths of six successive grooms on the wedding night.  Only when appropriate magical ceremonies had been conducted in the bedchamber was the force overcome, neutralised, or sublimated.  I use *three* words to describe the effect of the ceremony because it should be emphasised that though the primitive imagines the evil to be " put to flight " (sometimes in visible form, as in the case of Tobit), others imagine the force to be *neutralised*, and still others that it is *sublimated* into a higher and beneficent force.  This latter idea still seems to rest at the bottom of the Christian attitude.

As to seclusion, though for practical reasons the periods must be shorter than in the case of adolescents, they are nevertheless sometimes long enough to partake of the cruelty element.

" Again, both bride and bridegroom are secluded within the house.  It is said that among the Bedui the wife may not leave the house for three years, nor touch any work."

" At Fez she must remain inside the house for two months, or at least six weeks, not even being allowed to go on to the roof. At Tangier she was formerly obliged to stay at home for a whole year, but this period has been reduced to three or four months."

" Amongst the Beduins the bride stays in the tent for a fortnight."

Now it seems to me that these taboos against leaving the house are fundamentally directed against " touching the earth or seeing the sun," which will be recognised in due course as particularly important because Earth and Sun represent the two (cosmic) poles of the " electric battery " with which the tabooed person (in this case the bride) is thought to be connected. Nor are specific examples lacking where the acknowledged object of seclusion is to insulate the subject from the two " poles," adolescents having to wear special hats, or to live in a house raised above ground. . . . Frazer provides many examples in *The Golden Bough*. But the practice is most conspicuous with the king rather than the adolescent, the " holy " rather than the " unclean " ; though it is evident that either type is equally to be " insulated," though for opposite reasons. Incidentally, I would suggest that the only reason why women have to undergo more prolonged seclusion than men (even if they avoid the more agonising " male " forms of initiation) is that the men, especially where culture is very low, simply cannot be spared by the community. Warriors and husbandmen are too valuable to be shut up, otherwise they would, no doubt, suffer with their sisters.

But if the male adolescent was lucky in comparison with his sister, the king may perhaps be regarded as worse off than either of these, his subjects. He only reigned so long as the magic force acted through him, and while this occurred he had to be " insulated " as nearly as possible in the same way as the maiden. Moreover, when his power was thought to fail he was killed . . . usually with every sort of cruelty.   And his subjects often thought it safer to give him a fixed term rather than wait for his actual enfeeblement (impotence), an arrangement which was clearly more convenient than the other.   Finally, it is to be remarked that as with " initiation " and " consummation " the accession of the king was frequently an occasion for magical ceremonies, again likely to partake of cruelty, as in the following example taken from *The Golden Bough* :

" The savage Timmes of Sierra Leone, who elect their king, reserve to themselves the right of beating him on the eve of the coronation ;   and they avail themselves of this constitutional privilege with such hearty good will that sometimes the monarch does not long survive his elevation to the throne."

No doubt if his magic force was in full working order a mere beating could not do much harm ;   and if he were a mere pretender to the divine office, then his death could hardly be other than deserved !

Once in office, the king's " purity " was preserved at the cost of considerable personal inconvenience, even among highly civilised races. . . . With primitives it must often have meant a most wretched existence.   Thus the environment of Pharaohs, Mikados, and, I think, of certain Central American dynasties, was hardly less trying than seclusion at adolescence.   The king was highly dangerous to any ordinary person with whom he came into contact, however indirectly.   For this reason his articles of daily life were regarded as " charged," and in extreme cases might even kill the unfortunate who touched them, even without the knowledge that they were " taboo." It would be wearisome to go into many details, because the ideas are exactly the same as those connected with the other taboos already dealt with; therefore I will quote only one example, that of the Mikado, who is referred to by Frazer as typical of such monarchs. The account quoted was " written about two hundred years ago."

" He (the Mikado) thinks it would be very prejudicial to his dignity to touch the ground with his feet, and for this reason, when he intends to go anywhere, he must be carried thither on men's shoulders. Much less will they suffer that he should expose his sacred person to the open air, and the sun is not thought worthy to shine on his head."

In this short paragraph are comprehended the two great prohibitions of all such " insulation " . . . prevention of " discharge " to Earth or Sun. In the case of one unclean, such discharge would blight the earth, while kings would in the same circumstances lose their sanctity (become magically impotent). As for the Sun, which is the primary symbol of the *source of power*, contact with it could only result in the unclean becoming more so . . . and therefore more dangerous ; while the king might lose what power he had by having it withdrawn to the source (or perhaps so much power would be given that the " insulation " would break down and disaster result). In cruder language this means that the " devil " in the person unclean has his home in the Earth, while the " angel " in the king comes down from the Father Spirit in the Sun. In such terms it is clear enough how contact with either of these great " poles " of the cosmic battery would upset the condition of such sensitives as the " unclean " and the " holy." But to continue with the Mikado. . . .

" There is such holiness ascribed to all parts of his body that he dares to cut off neither his hair, nor his beard, nor his nails. However, lest he should grow too dirty, they may clean him in the night when he is asleep. . . .

" In ancient times he was obliged to sit on his throne for some hours every morning, with the imperial crown on his head, but to sit altogether like a statue, without stirring hands or feet, head or eyes, nor indeed any part of his body, because, by this means, it was thought that he could preserve peace and tranquillity in his empire. . . .

" His victuals must be dressed every time in new pots and served at table in new dishes : both very clean and neat, but made only of common clay. . . . They are generally broke, for fear they should come into the hands of any laymen, for they believe religiously that should any layman presume to eat his food out of these sacred dishes it would swell and inflame his mouth and throat."

This instance should suffice to make the nature of the " charged " condition clear enough for the present, and should also give some idea of the potency ascribed to it, not only among savages but in highly civilised communities. It is not so long ago that the kings of England used the " royal touch " for the cure of the " King's Evil " (scrofula). Charles I is said to have healed a hundred sufferers at one time in the year 1633.

Perhaps this little circle of evidence may be said to close with the custom of treating newly-weds as though they were king and queen. Here the magic force has been fully canalised, and the man and woman, hitherto unclean, have become beneficent " batteries " *just as though they were divine rulers*.

" The Malay wedding ceremony, even as carried out by the poorer classes, shows that the contracting parties are

treated as royalty, that is to say as sacred human beings . . .
the bride and bridegroom are even called ' Raja sari ' (i.e. the
' sovereigns of a day ')."

All taboo, therefore, is, strictly speaking, the ceremonial recognition of an occult force, which invests its
media with power and therefore with extraordinary
importance to the community. There are two main
groups of tabooed objects, according to their purity or
otherwise, but in all cases the force itself remains
immaculate. It may be found surprising that such
difficult ideas should be embodied in the customs of
primitives, and yet we find among the most backward
races of Oceania, Australia, and North America, not
only the superstitions of fear, but also an adequate
conception of the abstraction itself, the " magic force."
As the Polynesian " mana," the potentiality of the
force is believed to be inherent in everything and to
become manifest at such occasions as we have indicated,
when it is insulated or canalised by taboo.

" *Mana*, then, is, as Freud would say, an ambivalent notion ;
it cuts both ways, implying alike divine and diabolic effects
as possible manifestations of the awful power lurking in the
occult. It is thus equally the root idea of religion and black
magic, since both equally use rites, that, duly performed by
an expert, bring *mana* into play ; and the procedure will
electrify or electrocute according to the will of the operator."

(*Encyc. Brit.*, XIV, 771.)

The idea that the force may be called into play by the
will of man, independent of any physical event whether
sexual or otherwise, is a step further than was implied
by the previous examples. Yet it is a step which is really
inevitable since, granted that the force is manifest
through the symbols of sex, it follows that the wit of

man would soon claim to liberate the force through his own artificial symbols. This, to my mind, is the root of all magico-religious ceremonial. Having observed the sexual symbols of " mana," the priest devises a ritual using equivalent symbols ; and from the ritual the *mana* is liberated *under controlled conditions*. Such an interpretation would go a long way towards rationalising such a widespread ritual as the making of fire by friction, which is at once notoriously sexual and inviolably sacred. The fire which springs from the friction of the male-female pieces of wood is *divine* fire, just as the tabooed King who is raised up between Earth and Heaven (female-male) is also divine. In all cases *the force is only liberated through the interaction and union of " sexed " opposites in some form or other*, a judgment which will be justified more fully in the next chapter.

And now to confirm our reading with two final authoritative quotations.

" The uncleanness, as it is called, of girls at puberty and the sanctity of holy men do not, to the primitive mind, differ materially from each other. They are only different manifestations of the same mysterious energy, which, like energy in general, is in itself neither good nor bad, but becomes beneficent or maleficent according to its application."

(*The Golden Bough*, p. 607.)

" They (the priest-kings) are credited with extraordinary magic powers, contact with their persons or their property is therefore feared, while on the other hand the most beneficial effect is expected from these contacts."

(*Totem and Taboo*, p. 81.)

# CHAPTER TWO

## BASIC SYMBOLS

" The more abstract the truth you wish to teach the more must you allure the senses to it."

(NIETZSCHE.)

LET us now consider the lines along which a system of belief is likely to develop out of the fundamental recognition of an "electrical" force. There are two alternatives, one of which leads to phallicism, the gross cult of virility and fertility, while the other is a process of " spiritualisation." In other words, granted that sex can be " magical," the magic can be refined to reach its highest symbolic expression or it can be degraded. We are already in a position to maintain that whatever the advancement of a community, the central mysteries are probably sexual. But in every discussion it is as well to deal with a particular example, and for the present purpose the religion of the Israelites occupies a unique position.

Here was a people, who, when their records begin, were in the act of emerging from the animistic state, of which the taboo attitude is typical. Onto this base was then grafted the conception of the One God, Jehovah, superseding the more restricted rôle of the same divinity as a tribal god.[1]

[1] The evolution of belief is, of course, more complex than may appear from such generalisations as this, but I believe the presentation to be true so far as it goes. To take it further would

37

The broad upward movement of the Israelite religion
is too well known to require elaboration; suffice it that
from the primitive root was finally developed a faith
which includes some of the highest conceptions yet
reached by mankind. What I want to emphasise is the
operation of the opposite tendency, towards degradation,
resulting in the cult of the One God having to fight a
series of battles against reversion to more primitive
faiths, typified by the name of Baal, and chronicled,
among other places, in 2 Kings xvii. The significance
of the backsliding of the Israelites lies for us in the fact
that Baal is essentially the *male principle*, whose complement is Baalat.[1]  In other words the reversion was
towards gross phallicism. The various tribal gods were
personifications of the Male, restricted to their own
area and their own people. Thus the god of Sidon was
Baal-Sidon, that of Lebanon, Baal-Lebanon, and so on,
all of them more or less on a par with one another, and
closely connected with the fertility of the ground, of
beasts, and also of humans, personified in their consorts
the Baalat.

Their worship was thus diametrically opposed to that
of the One God, omnipotent and omniscient Spirit.
Therefore the leaders of the unitive faith opposed Baal
as the Devil . . . which, in a sense, he was, not only

confuse the main issues without assisting conclusions. For Jehovah
as a tribal god see Reinach : *Orpheus ;* also Frazer : *Folklore in
the Old Testament ;* Robertson Smith : *The Religion of the Semites ;*
and Blavatsky : *The Secret Doctrine.* I will quote from the last
two works respectively.

" Broadly speaking, the land of a god corresponds with the land
of his worshippers ; Canaan is Jehovah's land as Israel is Jehovah's
people " (p. 91).

" Of *tribal* gods there were many. . . . ' Thou shalt not revile
the gods,' says one of them (Jehovah) in Ex. xxii, 28."

[1] Robertson Smith, *ibid.*

because of the moral degradation involved, but because retrogression would be continuous and cumulative, inevitably reducing the nation to its original barbaric state. For wherever sex-worship predominates in the absence of corrective ideas, there follow all the abuses which find their climax in Satanism . . . that is, in the state of *inverted values*, where good seems evil and evil good. Cruelty runs riot, sorcery and necromancy flourish, ethics fall back into a state where only taboo stands between man and beast. And these abuses are in the last analysis the effects of materialism carried to its logical extreme, for sex can only be worshipped as such when its symbolic rôle is forgotten. And if it is suggested that the materialist doesn't worship anything, I feel sure that within everyone's memory is material to refute the contention. Judging by the cheaper press and the cinema, the Western world worships sex and money, but history provides more dramatic instances. When the French Revolution enjoyed its early triumph over Christianity, was not " sex appeal " enthroned in Notre Dame as the " Goddess of Reason " ? The lust for money is recognised everywhere as a modern cult, but not everyone realises that it is closely connected with coprophilia, which, in turn, links it with Satanism. One of the most authoritative psychologists says :

" Pleasure in the intestinal contents (coprophilia) becomes enjoyment of money, which, however, after what has been said, is seen to be nothing other than odourless, dehydrated filth that has been made to shine."

(FERENCZI : *Sex in Psychoanalysis*, p. 327.)

I may seem to share something of the character of Pickwick's " fat boy." But these instances are not primarily to make flesh " creep," they are to impress the immediate practical importance of the theme. There seems to be a big gap between us and the Baal-worshippers. We have no Golden Calf set up in a public place, nor do we cause sons or daughters to pass through the fire ; yet :

" To the ordinary man Satanism often seems incredible, or at any rate a myth of the remote dark ages. He does not realise, and he is happy in his ignorance, the devil's fires that burn just a little way beneath the thin and crumbled crust of our boasted modern civilisation."

(MONTAGU SUMMERS : *A Popular History of Witchcraft*.)

And here is the retired Prime Minister, Lord Baldwin, broadcasting on the 16th April, 1936 :

" Materialism means slavery, slavery of the mind to the things of the body, and *slavery in the end means destruction*."

I am not suggesting that the modern English or American materialist is in the least likely to fall victim to necrophagy or focus his faith on the physical functions of goats . . . though Jung asserts that the goat-cult still exists and necrophagy is by no means unknown ; but I do suggest that modern society derives its culture from social compulsion rather than from a natural sense of proportion which alone can save it when the social mechanism cracks. Our civilisation runs on an artificial ethical system which has become largely divorced from its mental focus, and in consequence lacks a point of balance . . . which is particularly essential in machinery moving at high speed. I think the point will be admitted in view of the following statements :

" Dr. J. A. Hadfield, Lecturer in Psychology and Mental Hygiene at London University, said that it had been computed that there were in this country 4,000,000 persons who required treatment for neurotic disorders."

(*Morning Post*, 4 Jan., 1937.)

" According to C. W. Beers, one person out of every twenty-two has to be placed in an asylum at one time or another. In the whole of the U.S. the hospitals care for almost eight times more feeble-minded or lunatics than consumptives."

(ALEXIS CARREL : *Man the Unknown*, p. 154.)

And now to return to Israel, whose ascendency over the neighbouring peoples was due to the cult of the One God. Jehovah was regarded as the Father and Mother of his people, in other words, the Creator self-sufficient, androgyne. That is to say, when thinking anthropomorphically, such a *unity* must be personified as androgyne. Jehovah included in himself both the Baal and the Baalat, and it is easy to see that it could hardly have been otherwise. First the fertility cult had made phallicism the natural focus of primitive magic, then, with the conception of the ruling spirit, came the tremendous cult of the Great Mother, the Creator's " other half," from whom were born all things. At all events, the idea of the Creator-Unity requires that *in physical terms* he must be bisexual, otherwise the " giving birth " of the universe becomes impossible. Translated into mystical symbols " When the One becomes Two, the Threefold appears " (Book of Dzyan). Unity gives place to Duality (Father-Mother), which, in turn, gives rise to the Son who is " one with the Father," forming the cosmic " triunity." And the Son is himself " threefold " since he functions on all three levels :

(1) As " Light," the " Lord God " of Genesis (*q.v.*).
(2) As the Mystic Christ, the " divine spark " in the Individual, the spirit or " overself." In abstract terms " Individuality," or " Self-Consciousness."
(3) As the Historical Christ of whom Jesus of Nazareth is the Archetype.

The foregoing involve certain ideas which have not yet been dealt with . . . but no matter, for all that is required here is to get the sense of the third term, which is not only existent (active) but *personified* on all three levels.

The One God is Father/Mother regarded as an un-differentiated unity—though the preponderating sex is usually represented as masculine for reasons which will be dealt with later. To be more explicit, a " Causeless Cause " . . . Unity, should be regarded as producing Father and Mother . . . Duality, who in turn produce the Son . . . Trinity. Thus for ordinary purposes Unity is equivalent to Father/Mother undifferentiated, and it is therefore unnecessary to introduce the " Causeless Cause." Perhaps the foregoing ideas will become clearer in the light of some ancient symbols. For instance, it is said of Amen-Ra :

" He had no Mother by whom his name was made, he had no Father who begot him, saying : ' It is even myself.' He shaped his own egg, he mingled his seed with his body to make his egg come into being within himself."

(BUDGE : *From Fetish to God in Ancient Egypt*, p. 17.)

Compare the Hindu Father/Mother, Prajpati, " Lord of Creation,"

" ' I will procreate myself, I will be manifold.' He per-formed Tapas ; after he had performed Tapas he created these worlds."

(*Rigveda*, X, 121.)

On the above Dr. Jung comments as follows, having quoted it on page 228 of the *Psychology of the Unconscious* :

" The strange conception of Tapas is to be translated, according to Deusen, as ' he heated himself with his own heat,' with the sense of ' he brooded, he hatched.' Here the hatcher and the hatched are not two, but one and the same identical being."

Or, in our own terms, Amen-Ra and Prajpati are Father/Mother, conception taking place with an internal " heating " or *movement* which we shall later identify with the Word, which is equivalent to the Chinese K'ien, " Creative, unceasing energy," or, in Christian terms the (cosmic) Word of God. Thus a fairly clear picture is beginning to emerge, which answers some problems in regard to the Creator and the One God. In the particular rôle of Genesis we shall have a good deal more to say, but for the time being it is essential to generalise as far as possible. We may, however, summarise the *very beginning* as follows :

*The Word moves (heats, conceives) within Father/Mother and the Son is born* (the cosmic Christ).

What all this amounts to is that Jehovah, as the Unity which marked such a great advance over gross phallicism, nevertheless is *based upon the physical equation*, and the focus of his worship is still the " consummation," albeit raised to a higher plane than that reached by the animistic peoples. If confirmation of this were needed, we have only to cite the famous Ark of the Covenant, the most holy object in all Israel. Uzzah, it will be remembered, was struck dead when he attempted to prevent the Ark from falling (2 Sam. vi). Obviously the Ark was strongly " charged " with the " electrical force," and Uzzah was not ceremonially pure.[1]

In fact, Uzzah was destroyed by that force which we

[1] (Lev. xv and xvi, 1–3, gives a very straightforward account of the precautions to be taken in order to avoid the harmful effects of the force, especially in the case of menstruous women and men in an equivalent situation. After the two sons of Aaron died from contact with the Ark, the Lord warns Moses of the necessary ceremonies and institutes the " scapegoat," presumably that the force may discharge only after the worshippers' impurity has been *transferred*. In this last respect compare the miracle of the Gadarene swine.)

have already learnt to recognise under the symbol of the (physical) consummation . . . the sex-force. He might equally have met disaster (though presumably not quite so thoroughly) by contact with some other medium of the force, an " unclean " person or a " holy " one; or even by contact with something which was (or had been) in magical contact with the " tabooed " person, as the following example illustrates :

" On one occasion a (Maori) slave ate his chief's dinner by mistake; when told of what he had done, and when he realised that he had a tabooed person's ' sacredness,' he was seized with convulsions and cramp in the stomach and died at sundown."
        (CROWLEY : *The Mystic Rose*, I, 191.)

The very fact that the Ark was thus " charged " makes it virtually certain that it was a sex symbol ; and probably, for reasons already given, that it was associated with the " consummation " *as representing the androgynous divinity to whom it was dedicated.* Thus we are not surprised to learn that the contents of the Ark were in fact " a perfect bisexual emblem, or symbol of Y (e) H (o) V (a) H, the male and female symbol." (BLAVATSKY, *S.D.*, ii, 460.)

" The priests said, See, God loves his people as a man loves a woman. The Cherubim embraced one another like man and woman."
        (RÓHEIM : *Animism and the Divine King.*)

But we have still to confirm that Jehovah was *essentially* a " sex " god, and the enquiry will take us for the first time into the realms of abstract symbols. It is a universal belief that the magic of anything resides in its name, at least to some extent ; as is indicated in one of the recent quotations concerning the Creator, " He had no Mother by whom *his name* was made." Thus the gods especially were credited with " names of power." Indeed, in many cases it was death to pronounce the sacred name. A good illustration of this is provided by the story of Isis, who persuaded Ra to tell his secret name that she might have power over him . . . and he was the Creator ! In other words, even the omnipotence of the Unity is " in a word." We have already indicated that this may be so in one particular sense; now it is seen that this Word, in a different sense, is a *name*. We have already cited " In the beginning was the Word " (John i), and it is interesting to note that in Tyndale's first translation of the Bible into English, verse three, which now reads, "All things were made by him," was rendered " All things were made by *it* (the Word)." (Copy in British Museum.)

Then there is the " new name " of Jesus upon which so much emphasis is placed in Revelation (e.g. ii, 17): Oeaohoo, the mystery name of the power of God ; Ôm, the word by which the worlds were made :[1]

" Ôm, essence of the Wedas, revealed in the Wedas, revealed in the world, sprung from immortality !

" Ôm is spirit. Everything is but Ôm.

"Ôm permits, Ôm gives the signal. Ôm begins the ceremony. All chants begin with Ôm. All hymns begin with Ôm. The Priest begins with Ôm. His commands are in the name of Ôm. The sacrificer offers the oblation with Ôm. The teacher begins with Ôm. The pupil begins with Ôm.

" The pupil murmuring Ôm seeks for Spirit ; in the end he finds Spirit."

Compare the words of the Psalmist :

" That they may seek *thy name*, O Lord,
    That they may know that thou alone,
  Whose name is Jehovah,
    Art Most High over all the earth."

(Psalm 83.)

[1] *Taittireeya-Upanishad*, Books i, iv and viii. SHEE PUROHIT WAMI and W. B. YATES : *The Ten Principal Upanishads.*

We are at all events justified in regarding the names of gods as particularly significant, so that a further investigation of Jehovah from this point of view can hardly be anything but helpful. First, we are confronted with two mystical alternatives, JAVEH (Yahwe) and IHOH, with JAH as a contraction of the former; and this is in turn linked with RA, whose rôle in Egypt may well be compared to the highest conception of Jehovah. Thus it is said of the Egyptian Unity:

" He was self-created . . . no other being existed, there was no god before him, there was no god with him to declare his form. His unity was absolute. He was a Trinity, i.e. he had three persons or characters. His name is more helpful to a man than hundreds of thousands of helpers. *The man who utters the secret name of Amen (Amen-Ra) falls down and dies a violent death.*"

(Quoted from BUDGE : *From Fetish to God*, p. 17.)

Compare again the Christian attitude :

" I will not let thee go, unless
Thou tell thy name to me."

(A. & M. 248.)

The identity of Ra and Jehovah may seem very specious on the basis of name alone, but I do not, in fact, emphasise the resemblance primarily on that score. Their symbolic rôles are identical, as will appear in due course ; the consideration of names is only introduced here as a parallel of some interest. Incidentally, a difficulty arises when considering written names, for their power is thought to reside in the sound rather than in letters. The " name of power " must be properly pronounced in order to be effective, and even then the force liberated is conditioned by other matters, such as the knowledge

and purity of the worshipper. But always the force is
that same " electricity " with which we have been dealing,
*and the name of the medium through which it acts (in this case
Father/Mother) is the symbol of its power.* What this really
amounts to is that *sounds* are " sexed," at any rate when
attributed to such mysteries as the name of the Unity.

In this light Jehovah is IHOH, the Hs being normally
mute so that the essential word is IO, symbol of physical
union (psychologically) and symbol for god-names the
world over.

"Iaccus (Bacchus) is Iao or Jehovah, and Baal or Adon
was a phallic god."

Moreover, Bacchus bore the same mystery-name as
Jesus, i.e. ICHTHUS, the *Fish*, of which we shall have
much more to say later on. At the moment we only
stop to note that IO is also a Moon symbol, and is found
as such on the Rosetta Stone, from which : " it is concluded that the god-name Jehovah (IO) was designative
of the moon as *causative of generation.*" (*S.D.* ref. " Iao.")
Now the Moon is linked with Water (e.g. tides, but a
deeper connection is due to the fact that both are
essentially " female "), and hence with " fish " ; so the
relationship between *god* and *fish* is symbolically that
between Spirit and Matter. To emphasise the basic
" femaleness " of the Moon is impossible now except in
physical symbols, though for other reasons, chiefly
connected with Sun and Moon as Father and Mother,
there can be no reasonable doubt in the matter (cf.
Aradia and Diana). In physical terms, however, it
should be remembered that the Moon is in myths nearly
always assigned to a Goddess, and that as a matter of
scientific knowledge the Moon regulates periods of
fertility and gestation.

But if the Moon is " female " how can it be equivalent to IO ? We shall find in due course that the waxing of the Moon stands for physical growth and the waning for decay ; in this respect the latter is sometimes regarded as " male " . . . the destroyer as opposed to the creator (physically). Thus, loosely speaking, the Moon has a male " aspect " (the " Man *in* the Moon ") in confirmation of which it may be noted that Soma, the " magic " drink of the Hindus, which has been psychologically equated with the fertilising fluid, is nevertheless identified with the Moon. In fine, though fundamentally feminine, there is a male aspect which is sufficient to justify the portrayal of the Moon as androgyne, and therefore as a fit symbol of IO, in respect of physical generation.

Another relevant development of the idea comes from the fact that the " J " sound is " unknown in any other important language "—other than English, (HANNAY : *Rise, Decline and Fall of the Roman Religion*), becoming, therefore, " I " according to pronunciation. Thus JESUS becomes IEUSUS, or, better IESU . . . I (es) U. Similarly IOseph, IOshua, IOnas, IOrdan . . . all names with outstanding significance in regard to the " consummation " or the Consummator. Turning to the pagan traditions where the same ideas are represented, IUpiter, IUno, IAO, IO, come at once to mind. Indeed, IO as a god name is very widespread, being found in North America and Polynesia, besides being of necessity connected with the Ankh of Egypt, which, reduced to its symbolic essentials as the " sign of life," becomes the *male* (I) supporting the *female* (O). In fine, the Ankh, symbol of life, is basically a sexual symbol, and the written (or diagrammatic) representation of this is the " consummation " sign of male/female, which in turn is *sounded* as IO. Hence IO is a god-name which we would expect to find universal were it possible to discount the corruptions of history and fashion in favour of a childlike *naïveté* in such matters. . . . But the point is clearly outside my own province, belonging, if it can be said to belong to anyone, to those psychologists who are concerned with that " unconscious " which is common to all humanity.

A further interesting sidelight on the " sex " of *sounds*, especially in relation to the IO god-name, is provided by the Druidic mystery word OIV of which it is said :

" The three original letters were obtained by Menw the Aged from the *voice* of God himself, which manifested itself in rays of light, thus $/\!/\backslash$. The sense of ' O ' was given to the first column, ' I ' to the second, and ' V ' to the third, whence the mystery word OIV which *may not be pronounced*. As a bardic poem says :

" The Eternal, Origin, Self-existent Distributor.
Holy be the lips which canonically pronounce them ;
Another name in full word,
Is OI and OIW, the *Word*, Ieuan Rudd sang it."

(LEWIS SPENCE : *Mysteries of Britain*.)
(For further details see *Barddas*, I, 21.)

We are immediately reminded of the opening of St. John's Gospel and the ancient tradition which was before it, expressed as follows by A. E. Waite :

" According to that wise King (Solomon) and the Kabalists, the primal manifestation of God originated in a first movement of Eternal Being. This movement was represented by $\backslash$ ."

Thus we may assume that the " first movement " was the Word, and that it " came forth " from Unity which had become Duality, to produce the Trinity of FATHER/MOTHER, SON.

At all events it should now be clear that in at least one sense OI (or IO) represents the " Word of God," which is the *secret name*, so powerful that it may instantly kill those who make contact with its vehicles. For the medium, whether a symbol like the Ankh, or a person tabooed, or a name, represents one and the same force . . . that which unites the opposites. God is love. Yet not love as we understand the word in ordinary speech, for this " electrical " force is an abstraction to which we dare not attach any attributes save that already mentioned . . . the tendency to integration, *spiritual* integration. I say " spiritual " because otherwise the fact that Uzzah and others were " disintegrated " might seem inconsistent; there is no reason, however, why physical death should " come into the picture." But it is too early in the day to trouble with definitions. Does this demonstration of the widespread power and paramount significance of the consummation symbol take us far enough ? What of Christianity, which is the development of the faith of IHOH?

Running right through the New Testament is the same symbolism. Christ is the Bridegroom, cities are virgins or harlots, gardens are sisters and wives, the Father is the husbandman; and above all there is the Cross, whose essential meaning is the same as that of the Egyptian Ankh, the prolongation of the vertical beyond the horizontal conveying the same meaning as the " loop " above the horizontal. For, if the horizontal is "female" and the vertical "male," it is also true that the former represents the forces of Matter, while the latter represents the forces of Spirit. The ultimate victory of the latter is demonstrated by the continuance of the vertical in one way or another. Thus the Tau cross is a

simple consummation sign, while the Calvary Cross and
the Ankh have an added mystical significance. The
former is static, the latter dynamic, representing a
*process*. Hence the metaphor " to take up the Cross,"
which means the seeking of the mystic consummation,
which is the victory of the spirit (immortality); and the
condition of success is to " abolish in the flesh the
enmity " (Eph. ii, 15, 16), in other words, the individual
must become *free of the opposites*.

But what other consummation symbols are there in
the New Testament? First should be mentioned that a
man's attainment is conditional upon his being " twice-
born," of " water " and of the " spirit " (fire). He must
" enter again into his mother's womb," which is the
psychological equivalent of incest. Thus the crucifixion
is itself an incest-symbol *when regarded as the equivalent of
physical death*. For the Christ, who is born of Mother
Matter, enters again into the " womb of Earth," to be
" reborn " victorious and immortal. Again, " male and
female " are " one flesh " . . . the psychic duality is a
potential unity, with the realisation of which comes
freedom. Christ is born of a Virgin (who must symbolically remain *ever*-virgin). The first " sign " is at a
*marriage* where water (Matter) is transubstantiated into
wine (fire . . . Spirit). No sign is given to " this generation " (humanity as at present constituted) " save the
sign of the prophet Jonas," which is the sign of the
Fish, Ichthus, Iacchus, Oannes. Moreover, Jonas
was swallowed by a whale, which is psychologically
equivalent to the re-entry into the womb of Mother
Earth . . . in other words, *death*. And Jonas came safely
out of the whale . . . he was " born again." The great
saviour of Israel in battle is IOshua, who is the Son of
the Fish (Nun).

Marriage is the theme of the entire book of the Song of Songs . . . physical symbolism certainly, but also a mystical sermon which has little connection either with Jesus or with the Church. Nevertheless, even the latter symbolism " rings true " so far as it goes. Finally, the " last day," the end of the cosmic plan in space/time, is called the " Marriage of the Lamb," " which was slain from the foundation of the world " ; but this latter point involves several ideas with which we are not yet ready to deal.

We should do well, however, to consider the " sign of Jonas " a little more closely, since so much hangs upon that cryptic phrase. To start with, Jonas is clearly a symbol of the historical Christ, which would account for the direct reference of Jesus to the *prophet* Jonas. But his rôle is less controversial as a symbol not of Jesus but of the Mystic Christ, in which sense the sign is applicable to all men, and will, therefore, have an " unconscious " basis, which should be recognisable by ordinary psychological methods.

Now Dr. Jung shows that the monster (whale) which every Hero has to overcome in some form or other is in reality the " destroying mother." And this " mother " is identified with the " dragon," the " serpent " which guards treasure, and with the " giant." Fairy tales as much as genuine myths abound in the story to such a close type that it is even possible to draw a simple diagram to represent the action. Without introducing the diagram itself, which, for all its essential simplicity, introduces some terms not germane to the present issue, we may say that the scheme is as follows :[1]

The Hero sets out on a journey to attain Treasure. He meets with difficulty (Monster), which he overcomes

---

[1] For diagram see *Psychology of the Unconscious*, p. 131.

(kills). He attains the prize (Treasure). Alternatively he is killed (swallowed or captured) by the Monster and subsequently escapes. Perhaps it will be as well to translate the foregoing broadly into mystical terms (which, however, still remain to be justified). The Individual sets out on life (quest, way of the cross) to attain immortality (evolution, extension of consciousness, sublimation, transference). He meets with difficulty (materialism in the widest sense, he is *dominated by the opposites*). He is killed (dies, re-enters womb, incest), but in that act (crucifixion) unites the opposites in *marriage*, thus attaining the Treasure.

Very mixed metaphors, but no attempt is yet made to sort out these ideas into precise meanings. All that is required at present is a general sense of what is meant by " mystical " as opposed to " physical " interpretation of symbols. Thus the foregoing abstract ideas are confirmed when we find in the majority of cases that the Treasure is a woman or a woman symbol, more especially a Virgin or Apple. (Cf. Eden and Hercules.) In the former case the consummation (immortality) is represented as a marriage, where, for instance, the King gives his daughter to the Hero who has saved her from the Monster. In the latter, however, the attainment is more usually represented as conferring some special magical power upon the hero (e.g. Siegfried), indicating that he has attained a new and higher level of consciousness. Thus in all its forms, the myth can be reduced to an allegory of the spiritual destiny of man which involves the conquest of the forces of Matter (the world and the flesh) and especially of death (the destroying Monster, Mother Earth) by the power of the *integrating* force (love). Only after this is achieved comes the state of liberated consciousness which is immortality.

Thus Jonas is literally the "only sign," since it includes all others. Jonas, the Fish/Man, stands for the basic idea which runs through every faith concerned with immortality and the conditions of its attainment. Even Fuh Yi, "the chief guide and civiliser of China in olden times," is represented as a *merman*. It was he who is regarded as the author of that profound metaphysic embodied in the Yih King,[1] in which it is evident that the principles of the "equations" were recognised, together with much learning calculated to remove the vanity of modernity. Not that present-day savants are still plated with the arrogance of Victorian materialism, on the contrary, a tendency to humility is becoming more marked. The arrogance, however, is not wholly lost, for it has found at least a temporary home among exponents of "popular" science. In such company the "typical myth" which we have been considering would have found a *reductio ad absurdum* for each of the great analytic schools as follows. The Freudians would explain it all away with the Œdipus Complex, the followers of Jung with the "battle for deliverance" (from the Mother), and the Adler school with the "will to power." I doubt very much if Freud, Jung, and Adler ever subscribed to such final judgments, but the illustration is adequate for its purpose and should appear reasonably true. After all, if the relative nature of the physical "level" is not clear now, it is obviously waste of time to go back into gross symbolism beyond which the natural tide of the enquiry has already taken us. Besides, Jung, who has treated the "typical myth" in great detail, inevitably brings in certain considerations which are not immediately relevant. Nevertheless, I refer the reader directly to him for the meaning of the Mother Monster.

[1] See MEARS : *Creative Energy.*

This " destroying mother " . . . what is she ? Obviously, since the prize is Life, she must represent Death, but there should be a more accurate sense as well.

Basically, that is to say, from her place in the equation, the Mother is the female principle, which is Matter, i.e. that which is subject to death. The hero thus has to *overcome the Mother* in order to earn immortality ; death *need* not come into the picture at all. The hero becomes immortal when he (his consciousness) has risen above Matter . . . *immortality is a state of mind*.

And so we reach the very threshold of the " mystic level," properly so called, where " male " becomes the " spirit in man," the Mystic Christ ; while in place of " female " we have the *dual* principle of Matter ; and, finally, in place of intercourse appears the mystic consummation which frees the Individual from the dominance of " the world and the flesh." But though the way now lies open, there remains a certain amount of necessary work to be done among the basic symbols, especially from the viewpoint of the *forces* which they represent. The " electrical " or " integrating " force which we have been dealing with so far is too vague a designation, and those adjectives must now be restricted to *the sum of the forces operating throughout the equation*. This has already been recognised in respect of the Cosmic Level (Genesis) as the Word of God, but it has now to be considered on other levels, i.e. as love in its various aspects.

Dr. Jung recognised the " destroying mother " for the very good reason that he also recognised a " creating mother " : the full antecedents are given by him in a way which admits of no misconception. There exists beyond doubt a psychological force to which he has given the name of Mother, and which acts in two different ways. The question now before us is the nature of this dual force, not so much in the relatively restricted field of orthodox psychology, but on all three levels with which we are dealing. Is there such a force recognisable in nature? Obviously. It is that which causes *growth* and *decay*, anabolism and katabolism. These are two forces, two " mothers," one " creating," the other " destroying," but together they are still symbolised as Mother, which then corresponds neither to " ana . . . " or " kata . . . " but to *metabolism*. In its widest sense *anabolism* is that which builds up substances from an atomic condition of space, and from this vacuum gives rise to molecules and aggregations of molecules, nebulæ, stars, planets, and all the host of heaven. Katabolism, on the other hand, is that which causes worlds, men, and all things physical, in due time to grow old and die ; finally reverting to that former condition of existence where there seems to be no difference between matter and energy. For these two forces what better symbol is there than the dual Mother ?

And so we find that the second term in our equations has *in practice* a dual nature. But Dr. Jung, though he saw clearly the dual *mother*, presumably failed to find evidence for a dual *father*, probably because the mechanistic theory propounded in the *Psychology of the Unconscious* is inconsistent with the concept of *spirit* other than as an aspect of the psyche reducible to the territory of the *mother*. But suppose that the first term is also dual ? At least such a hypothesis is logical enough, our recent quotation from Bergson guarantees that, and it may well yield useful results. We make a beginning by writing our basic equation as follows :

| First Term | Second Term | Third Term |
|------------|-------------|------------|
| FATHER | MOTHER | SON |
| | | (Consummator) |
| *Dual* | *Dual* | *Triple* |

Jung has already provided us with names for the two aspects of the second term, i.e. the Creating and Destroying Mother. Can we find any such names for the first term? It has already been suggested that Father is equivalent to Spirit, and it must be apparent that two aspects of the traditional rôle of Spirit can, in fact, be separated. Thus there is a *descent* of spirit into matter, symbolised physically as the Incarnation, and a corresponding *ascent* expressed in the Ascension. Here, then, are two expressions which will suit our purpose, the Father differentiating into the *descending* and *ascending* aspects of spiritual evolution. We shall find before long that a very great deal hangs upon these concepts, which have profound significance at all three levels, but for the time being we should endeavour to make the position still clearer by personifying them. Now the idea of *descent* is clearly associated with the Father, while *ascent* equally is the rôle of the Son. In the same way we might regard Mother as dividing not into two more Mothers, but into Mother (Creator) and Daughter (Destroyer). We may now re-write the essentials in equations :

| *First Term* | *Second Term* | *Third Term* |
|---|---|---|
| FATHER | MOTHER | SON |
| Spirit | Matter | Man |
| Father/Son | Mother/Daughter | Son |
| Descending/Ascending | Creating/Destroying | Consummator |

Note that there is no inconsistency in the arrangement since two *levels* are represented, the Mother (*sic*) is as it were a " generation " later (lower) than MOTHER, the latter being Cosmic, the former Mystic. It would perhaps be preferable to use different words to indicate these complementary rôles, but on the whole it has been found

easier to keep them as they are.  In actual practice
FATHER and MOTHER, let alone the Unity which is
behind them all, are too high for ordinary purposes.
We seldom have to consider the Cosmic Trinity, except
in the early stages of Genesis.  The same applies to that
other apparent inconsistency, the Son who appears in
two places.  How can the Son be an aspect of the first
term when it is already the third term ?

In order to understand the position it is necessary to
realise that the Unity *exists outside space/time*.  Thus
beyond space/time the third and first terms are identical,
" I and my Father are One."  And in the same way the
second term is also absorbed into Unity, for Matter is
inconceivable except in relation to space/time.  Let us
try to imagine all this in relation to a cosmic scheme of
evolution whose origin rests with the Unity . . . the
" androgyne."

Unity produces FATHER/MOTHER, who conceive
(Word).  From FATHER derives all that we call " Spirit,"
while from MOTHER " falls " the universe of Matter.
With Matter arise also space and time.

From this point, which may be called *Alpha*, the
beginning of the scheme, *the Father descends ; and this
Father is the Son of* FATHER/MOTHER, recognised in
Genesis as the " *Lord* God," and more generally as
*Light*.  I am sorry to introduce these complications,
especially as the unavoidable use of capitals smacks
somewhat of that popular saccharinity, which, as Mr.
Joad suggested in the quotation which headed our
Introduction, is the " prey of every crank and every
quack."  Believe, please, that I have no desire to take
refuge in vague generalisations : there is no such need.
The foregoing " genealogy " had to be mentioned even
at this early stage because it is necessary to visualise

*processes* rather than static symbols. These processes begin at " Alpha," and are summarised below :

(*a*) Spirit (Father) into Matter (Mother).
(*b*) Matter gives birth to the Son (Consummator) who *ascends*.

In Christian terms (*a*) clearly represents the Immaculate Conception, while (*b*) is symbolised in the Virgin Birth and subsequent " Ascent into Heaven " of Christ the King. Indeed, the whole question provides a good example of the great difficulty of dealing with abstractions *by* abstractions rather than symbols. Yet such meanings do represent considerably more of the truth than can be grasped intellectually from the bare allegory. For instance, the short excursion into the *processes* represented by Father and Mother in their dual aspects, has opened up a scheme of evolution of consciousness. Nevertheless, on the same symbols hang other meanings. . . . We have indicated " A, B, C " of the cosmic level which concerns all humanity, and there is still the *individual* to be considered before dealing with the physical level.

But let us sum up as simply as possible.

(1) Unity *disintegrates*. (Alpha.)
(2) The universe " visible and invisible " comes into being in space/time.
(3) The diversity *reintegrates*. (Omega.)

This is very close to the form of expression used by Bergson.

Now what is the symbol which causes reintegration? Surely the third term, which is the Triple Christ (consciousness). And he must be the perfect vehicle of the integrating force which is the Word and Love : " And

the Word was made flesh and dwelt among us."
(John i, 14.)

No doubt such a series of deductions would have
taken Dr. Jung very much further than he wished to go
when writing the *Psychology of the Unconscious*, indeed,
they may even seem to take us too far . . . or, at least,
too fast. However, it is really necessary to formulate a
bold hypothesis now for later justification, rather than
to attempt to build one brick at a time. Not that the
reader is required to " swallow " the whole tale of
universal evolution as it has just been set forth . . . even
in the bare essentials. On the contrary, he is only asked
to accept that there need be no inconsistency in the
Father/Son relationship as we have set it out in the last
equations.

We can now go back to the " typical myth " well
armed for further battles with the symbols. Thus it
should be evident that the Monster is properly the
Destroying Mother (Daughter) . . . in fact *Antichrist*
(cf. Aradia), and it should also be clear why she or it is
properly connected with *water* while the Hero is associated
with *light* and *fire*. Then, too, the Hero emerges as a
personification of the Sun, while the powers of the Moon
are those which he has to overcome . . . otherwise the
" powers of darkness." Not for nothing is the Christ
referred to as the " Sun of Righteousness." Fire, is,
in fact, an important link between the highest abstract
metaphysics and the grossest materialism, finding its
appropriate expression at every level.

Thus, the power of the Creator is *light* both in Genesis
and in the Christ, the " Light of the World." Psychologically this concept evidently corresponds roughly to
" grace," " faith," or even " intuition " . . . " If the
light that is in thee be darkness, how great is that dark-

ness." At any rate, fire and light are respectively symbols of spiritual power and wisdom, but they in themselves, the physical " elements," are not spiritual powers. . . . Obvious ? Of course, and yet the error is a common one. It is of the greatest importance not to mistake the reality which is abstract for the symbol which is concrete. An agonised man upon a wooden cross must not hide the keys of the purpose of life, the truths for which he died.

Admittedly among peasants there is a deal to be said for emphasis on the human element, but it cannot reasonably be doubted that among educated people, especially where emotional instability is marked, it is fatally easy for such an object of devotion as the *body* of the Crucified, to become, not the focus of a philosophy but of eroticism. If confirmation of this is required, we have only to turn up the histories of great mystics. And I feel sure that any practising psychologist will be able to give examples of the attitude to which I refer.[1] To become united with the Ascending Spirit is one thing, to be identified with a tortured body is another. . . . And yet how much asceticism is the result of the latter, especially in such sects as the flagellants ? And how many women have been physically in love with the Crucified ?

Apart from the harmful effects of emotional attachments as such, the main reason why the tendency should be strictly regulated is because it conceals more important meanings of the theme. The worshipper, obtaining emotional satisfaction, looks no higher, not even to the intellectual conception of the relationship between Matter and Spirit. God is love on all levels : if men insist on using the force at its lowest what is that to Him ?

Such observations are by no means irrelevant to our

[1] See Postscript.

main theme because we have recognised the " electrical "
force associated with taboo as " love." Yet how often
does history witness of cults wherein the worship of gross
fertility has predominated over all other considerations.
Sex ceased to be a symbol and became a slogan. Yet
whatever the orgies, it must not be forgotten that they
were not degraded *because* they were sensual. Uncleanness is not inherent in any act, least of all in the sexual
act, but exists, if at all, in the minds of those concerned.
Even ritual prostitution, an integral part of many cults,
can be raised to a state where it is not only devoid of
shame or dishonour, but is a sacred duty . . . a duty
which might well represent a very high spirituality.
Thus in the cult of Adonis at Cyprus,

> " All women were formerly obliged to prostitute themselves
> to strangers at the sanctuary of the goddess, whether she went
> by the name of Astarte, Aphrodite, or what not. Similar
> customs prevailed in many parts of Western Asia. Whatever
> its motive, the practice was clearly regarded, not as an orgy
> of lust, but as a solemn religious duty."
>
> (*Golden Bough*, p. 330.)

> " If we survey the whole of the evidence on this subject,
> some of which has still to be laid before the reader, we may
> conclude that the great Mother Goddess, the personification
> of all the reproductive energies of nature, was worshipped
> under different names but with substantial similarity of myth
> and ritual by many peoples of Western Asia ; that associated
> with her was a lover, or rather a series of lovers, divine yet
> mortal, with whom she mated every year, their commerce
> being deemed essential to the propagation of animals and
> plants, each in their several kind ; and further, that the
> fabulous union of the divine pair was simulated, and, as it
> were, multiplied on earth by the real, though temporary,
> union of the human sexes at the sanctuary of the goddess for
> the sake of thereby ensuring the fruitfulness of the ground to
> man and beast."
>
> (Ibid., 331.)

In fact, the " magic force," which is seen to have its focus in the act of union, was *personified* as far as possible, in order to make it " real." If eroticism entered into the worship, it was more likely to have been due to the traditional " weakness of the flesh " rather than to the cult itself. For the underlying idea is the essence of purity, like the " immaculate conception." It is nothing less than the sign of the interaction of the two great terms, of Spirit and Matter, of the birth of the God/Man out of Matter. It represents the abstract reality behind the " Lover of the World," the Bridegroom who is the Triple Christ, whose sister-wife[1] is the ever-immaculate Virgin, otherwise the Great Mother. She like her Son is a symbol on all three levels. On the *cosmic* she represents the universe of Matter, on the *mystic* she is the Ever-Virgin, on the physical " Mother Earth " (or the human mother).

Some idea of the antiquity of the cult of " Mother Earth " may be gained from that little statuette known as the " Venus of Willendorf," a " great mother " of some 15,500 B.C. The date given is approximate for the beginning of the Upper Paleolithic period, which lasted between five and seven thousand years, and which was separated by about eight thousand years from Menes, First Pharaoh of Egypt. Between Menes and the present day, a third period of nearly the same duration has passed. Nevertheless, from the Venus of Willendorf to Mary of Nazareth the cult of the Mother stretches unbroken and unweakened. And the cult of the Mother is essentially the cult of love . . . or of lust, or of the Word, according to the perception of the observer. The focus of the cult is the symbol of the consummation,

---

[1] " A garden enclosed is my sister, my spouse." *Song of Songs*, iv, 12.

personified as the union of the Son with Father/Mother, expressed physically as the act of union, and in a special and very important sense, as incest. Incest is the highest mystery as well as the lowest crime, even as Freud years ago discovered.

I would have avoided dealing with the physical aspect had it been possible, because of the unfortunate associations which have accumulated round the subject in the course of the last few generations. But it is essential to deal with sex directly. . . . One has to lay bricks to build a bridge, however ethereal the design may be. Therefore I make a plea that all sense of shame or eroticism be put away. Sex has an inner and immaculate significance, and when this is fully grasped, many of the problems which beset us will begin to solve themselves. . . . We shall find among other things that there is nothing at all which is " evil " save in the eye of the beholder, and that the evils of the world are the effect of darkened eyes and not their cause ; however convenient it may be to think of them the other way round. And the new and clearer vision seems likely to come not first from the churches, but from the consulting-rooms : already the revolution has begun. But in time we shall speak less of psychoanalysis than psychosynthesis, for therein lie the Keys of Peter . . . if only man will look up instead of down.

# CHAPTER THREE

## ABSTRACT SYMBOLS

" To the Christian conception of the Trinity the Jesuits have added one which is expressed by the formula J.M.J., that is to say, Jesus, Mary, Joseph. It has practically superseded the other. God is too lofty, and the Holy Spirit too immaterial; the people must have white idols with plenty of gold, pink and blue."
(REINACH : *Orpheus*, p. 418.)

**B**ECAUSE it concentrates attention on the physical equation, such an example as the above is very striking, and makes us wonder how such a system as Buddhism with its doctrine of the " passionless path " could ever have had even a chance of popular success. Is it that the Eastern mind is able to grasp abstractions which are out of reach for the West ? At least such a state of affairs is a possibility, well supported by so great an authority on the Western mind as Dr. Jung in his comments on *The Secret of the Golden Flower*. If true, it should make us very chary of condemning the symbolism of Eastern religious thought as a mere playing with words ; still less are we entitled to be patronising. There is a small nineteenth-century work on Hinduism which refers to Krishna in the following terms :

" And yet this dreadful being is extolled by the author of The Bhagavad Gita, a man of high intellectual culture, as the god of gods. . . . How can we explain this ?

" A French writer, M. Jacolliot, has been capable of the stupendous blunder of maintaining that in the history of

Christ we find much that has been borrowed from the history of Krishna.  No Oriental scholar can tolerate such an idea. . . . The fierce warrior turned into the Prince of Peace; the debauched cowherd into a being of every moral excellence ! By what process of moral alchemy could such a transformation have been wrought ?

"But it is, alas, easy enough to show, how, from such muddy sources as the *Gospel of the Infancy*, the Hindu poets, in a time of great moral debasement, might gradually evolve the pestilential tale of which we have ventured to quote only the less disgusting portions."

(MITCHELL : *Hinduism Past and Present*, 1897.)

Our investigations of the equations have shown already that there need be no inconsistency with the general truth if physical symbols are used in place of those more abstract; for instance, J.M.J. is just as true, so far as it goes, as FATHER:MOTHER:SON.  May it not be the same with the symbols of Krishna ?

Primarily Krishna is the god *of love*, and sensual imagery is piled on extravagantly to emphasise this very point. The " Oriental scholar " might have said to himself : " That Krishna had sixteen thousand concubines is a physical impossibility, therefore these tales refer to something other than physical love."

He might even have gone further, and discovered why there were just sixteen thousand, no more and no less.

It is undisputed nowadays that Krishna is far older than Jesus or even Gautama Buddha, and yet Hannay (who believes in nothing *but* the physical) lists no fewer than seventy-five parallel circumstances between the lives of the two Heroes.  Of these I will quote a selection to indicate that they are mostly symbolic.

1. Born of a chaste mother.
2. Real father spirit of God.

3. Of royal descent.
4. Deity in human form.
5. Angels hail virgin.
6. Birth announced by star.
7. (Six brothers (Krishna); four brothers, two sisters (Jesus).)
8. Born in humiliating circumstances (cave, inn, farm).
9. Costly jewels, precious things, given him by Magi.
10. Preceded by Forerunner.
11. Father warned in a dream that the king or ruler sought to kill babe.
12. Slaughter of the innocents, babe's life preserved.
13. Tempted of the devil.
14. Transfigured before disciples.
15. Crucified.
16. Pierced. (Krishna by an arrow, Jesus by a spear.)
17. Descended into hell.
18. Rose from the dead.
19. Ascended into heaven.
20. Will come again, warrior on a white horse, sun and moon darkened.

All these, except No. 7, which is my own interpolation, are quoted more or less verbatim from Mr. Hannay's list. Owing to the fact that I have had no opportunity of checking references, I cannot claim these instances as definite correspondences. But they do illustrate the point, and, after making all allowances, it seems somewhat ridiculous either to accuse the Hindus of copying the history of Jesus, or to reduce Krishna to the spiritual status of a " debauched cowherd." On the contrary, if the reader cares to return to the quotation which now follows *after* the symbolism of the various phrases has been cleared up in the course of our argument, he will agree, I think, that whatever else Krishna may have been, he was nevertheless a personification of the Christ.

" ' They who trust in me,' said Krishna, ' know Brahm : I am the victim, I am the sacrifice, I am the worship, I am the road of the good, the Creator, the Witness, the Asylum, and the Friend.' "[1]

So the gross loves of Krishna give point to my argument that the doctrine of " triunity," found wherever religion has reached any considerable height, is nevertheless expressed fundamentally as the sexual relationship. It may appear as though this idea is inconsistent with the first duty of the saint and mystic. Whether from Buddha, Lao T'ze, Jesus, or Hindu Yoga, the first steps on the " path " are concerned with the subjugation of the emotions of which sex is the source and power. But a moment's reflection shows that no inconsistency arises. The mystic has little use for physical sex as such, though his whole life is " one-pointed " in relation to the *sublimated* sex-force which is the " ascending spirit." He recognises, whatever the verbal expressions of his order, that the force which gives sensuality its extraordinary range and power, whether expressed directly or indirectly, is the same as that of the Christ which performs miracles. It is love.

If love is used exclusively in the grosser forms, not only does it prevent the requisite development of character which must precede any extension of consciousness, but it proves dangerous for the aspirant, in whom,

[1] Cf. Tammuz : " The holy one of Istar, the shepherd, the wise one, the man of sorrows, the child, the lord of knowledge."

by the very fact that he is aspiring, it manifests more powerfully than in other people. Insistence upon chastity is based upon this fact. It is not a question of the destruction of the emotions, but of sublimation. Within reason, sex should be excluded from the consciousness of the mystic, but the force that *was* sex is used by him and greatly extended. And this leads to the consideration of an important point. In the service of an androgyne divinity, the priests and even the worshippers should themselves become symbolically androgyne, that is " perfect." The priest must be as like his god as possible. At the same time his aspirations are concerned with the " triumph over the flesh " which is equivalent to becoming " dead to the world." Seen in this light, strange customs become intelligible. Of special interest is the ritual of Attis described by Frazer in *The Golden Bough*, p. 347 ff.

That unfortunate divinity was driven to self-castration under a pine-tree, and it appears that his devotees were in the habit of emulating him, but without fatal consequences. Such self-made eunuchs lived thereafter as women, presumably dedicated to the god. There seems no doubt that the cult was much debased, and that the mutilations were usually the result of hysteria on the " Day of Blood " . . . the vernal equinox whereon was celebrated the death of the god.[1]

" Now the death and resurrection of Attis were officially celebrated at Rome on the 24th and 25th of March, the latter being regarded as the Spring Equinox. . . . But according to an ancient and widespread tradition Christ suffered on the 25th of March, and accordingly some Christians regularly celebrated the crucifixion on that date without any regard to the state of the moon."

(FRAZER : *Attis and Adonis*, i, 306.)

[1] See *The Cult of the Sun*, Chapter VIII.

Attis will be found in due course to represent the Consummator with some completeness ; being miraculously born of a virgin, he was the husband and son of the Great Mother. The focus of his cult was death and resurrection in the mystical sense, and the gross rites to which Frazer witnesses must in the end be regarded as the practical degradation of an immaculate abstraction.

But let us consider the particular question under review, after discounting certain minor aspects of the evidence. First, the natural reduction to the status of women of effeminate, impotent, or aged men, as occurs among primitives ; and second, physical modification which takes place without volition. Both these classes are obviously outside our field, and further, it is advisable to confine our attention to changes from man into woman. There are obvious practical reasons why a woman might wish to become a man, but very few " the other way round," especially in communities of low culture. This makes the change all the more remarkable when it does occur, for while there are cases where a man who becomes a " woman " is looked down upon by the rest of the tribe, it seems more usual that " she " is thereafter treated as though of unusual importance. This is specifically the case where the " woman " is dedicated to temple service or is supposed to be psychic.

Thus in the Attis cult, the temple was served by such " women," while the " bearded Venus " of Cyprus, like Cybele, demanded only that her priests should masquerade as women : all the worshippers similarly adopted the clothes of the opposite sex for ceremonial occasions. A similar practice obtained in the worship of Aphrodite and was even carried to the extreme of mutilation . . . which hardly seems consistent with the popular rôle of that goddess as the source of voluptuousness. The underlying principle . . . that the devotee should rise above physical love in pursuit of the divine, is even echoed to-day in the robes of Christian priests and bishops, a form of clothing which has been ridiculed in some quarters with considerable short-sightedness. After all, the argument is clear enough. God is a spirit and the spirit is above sex ; so therefore are the priests also above sex. But the genuine mystical sublimation is very rare and always has been . . . the " frailty of the flesh " almost guarantees that the priest be " above sex " only as regards his vestments and profession of faith. In cults below the level of Christianity it is even natural that the symbolic inversion of sex should be interpreted in widespread homosexuality and even ritual pederasty ; but that is a question which may be explored at leisure by those who regard it as of sufficient interest. For the time being it is enough to get a clear idea of the underlying " unconscious " requirements in response to which such cults come into being. Once these fundamentals are understood there will no longer be any difficulty in recognising the symbolism of evolved religion, or in realising how such customs as homosexuality and prostitution could have been features of religious foundations all over the world, in Europe, Asia, North America, Yucatan, Tahiti, and even Old Japan.

Speaking generally, it is evident that inversion is more apt to be regarded as a gift of god than as perversion. Even when not regarded as peculiarly the mark of divine favour, the invert was certainly not looked down upon.

It remained for the present age to treat inversion as criminal. Of course there is what might be termed " perverted inversion," and there is also that form of the attitude which is not characterised by one sex

" becoming " to all intents and purposes the other sex, but rather of normal sexuality transferred from the opposite to the same sex. If we call the latter *object* homosexuality and distinguish it from *subject* homosexuality, the former is out of the present territory altogether ; indeed, when I use the word " invert " it refers not to the homosexual but, in so far as current psychology provides an exact parallel, to the *eonist*. In this state the individual feels " a male body to co-exist with a female soul " (or *vice versa*) and it has nothing in common with desire directed to the same sex. Whether or not eonism can be regarded as antisocial is a matter into which I need not enter, for it is our concern only to point out that there is a stage of mystical development which has been recognised, and, deliberately as well as instinctively, simulated in those terms. Even among the ancients it is very necessary to make this distinction between homosexuality and inversion in the mystical sense. The former was, of course, an accepted social phenomenon in classical antiquity, and has continued down to the present day, although driven more and more underground—and thereby degenerating. But in any case and always, it is different from the much rarer *identification with the opposite sex*, whether the change is a mere gesture, religious or otherwise, or, on the other hand, the effect of a deep-seated psychological link which insists that the sex of the subject, in spite of all physical evidence to the contrary, is not that to which he or she would appear to belong. And further, the highest development is where, as in the case of priests, the " liberated spirit " signifies by psychological " change of sex " and in transvestism (wearing the clothes of the opposite sex) its freedom from the domination of desire.

To sum up this digression, I regard *inversion* as identification with the opposite sex, and quite distinct from homosexuality. Inversion is expressed as eonism (transvestism) in various degrees of crudity, of which the grosser forms are frankly psychopathic, while the higher derive their significance from the idea that such identification with the opposite brings about a psychological neutralisation, which eventually sets man upon the level of his androgyne divinity.

At present it is only necessary to consider the mystical forms of inversion, and then only in so far as the symbols assist our argument. But in a later chapter (X) we shall have the subject again under review from a different angle; in preparation for which it may be remarked that, quite apart from the psychological attitude which insists upon eonism as essentially innocent . . . or at least as innocent as any other form of sexual expression, historical evidence tends to show that the whole field of homosexuality and inversion is *potentially* moral and by no means necessarily antisocial. It is the conventional morality of modernity which has been responsible for turning what was at most a curiosity into an " *a priori* " criminal who is likely to adapt himself to the implication by *becoming* antisocial. Society, in fact, is responsible for real perversion. I am thinking here particularly of the cases cited by Krafft-Ebing, against which the following may be contrasted :[1]

" A Chuki boy at the age of sixteen will often relinquish his sex. He adopts woman's dress, and lets his hair grow. It frequently happens in such cases that the husband is a woman and the wife a man. These abnormal changes of sex appear to be strongly encouraged by the Shamans, who interpret such cases as an injunction of their individual deity."

(*Mystic Rose*, ii, 111.)

[1] See also BLOCH : *The Sexual Life of our Time ;* and HAVELOCK ELLIS : *Studies in the Phychology of Sex.* 4 vols.

Such cases are clearly traceable to the supposed sublimation of the sex force, and the same origin may be suggested for the meritoriousness sometimes accorded, as we have seen, to castration. It is significant that this last is recognised as the psychological equivalent of intercourse.

" Just as coitus is, in a certain sense, a castration, death appears as the final coitus or final castration of life."

(RÓHEIM : *Animism and the Divine King*, p. 26.)

But *why* does it so appear ? Because the act represents the *mystic* consummation which is the " overcoming of the world and the flesh," the Treasure (immortality) obtained after the slaying of the Monster.

To put the whole question shortly, we may say that change of sex, castration, crucifixion, are all symbols of the mystic consummation. This would explain the teaching of Jesus regarding eunuchs, which is nonsense unless read mystically ; for actual castration is psychological suicide. Instead of grappling with his problems, the misguided devotee destroys the physical symbol of the very power in whose service the sacrifice is supposed to be made. For the phallus is obviously the physical symbol of the " ascending spirit," hence its tremendous symbolic value and psychological power.

The mystic must sublimate sex by an effort of will. There are no short cuts. If castration . . . the physical act, were anything but degrading, the one modern sect which practised it at least would not have provided such a black record of bestiality and inverted values. I refer to the Russian " Doves " (Skopzi). (Goldberg : *The Sacred Fire*.) Nevertheless, it is natural that people who *appeared* to have become " masters of sex " (androgyne) should have been regarded, at least by primitive society, *as though the change represented the mystical victory.* Such people would be recognised as above the common run of mortals, even if such claims rested on no more than a physical anomaly. But Isaiah and Jesus of Nazareth do not refer to such people, they adopt the mystical attitude and refer to the mystic consummation.

" Even unto them will I give in mine house and within my walls a place and a name better than of sons and of daughters : I will give them an everlasting name that shall not be cut off."

(Isaiah lvi, 5.)

This is as much as to say that he who has succeeded in the sublimation of the sex force[1] stands on the threshold of immortality. He has " overcome the world and the flesh " and receives a new *name*, i.e. an androgyne name " in the image of god." . . . He becomes, in fact, the Son of God.

" All men cannot receive this saying, but they to whom it is given. . . . And there are eunuchs which made themselves eunuchs for the kingdom of heaven's sake. He that is able to receive it, let him receive it."

(Matt. xix, 11 ff.)

It has probably already been remarked that the symbolism of inversion seems to be connected with that of the " magic " force first manifest at adolescence and investigated in the chapter on Taboo. At least it seems that the " change of sex " usually takes place at that period, and one cannot help surmising that inversion represents the complement of seclusion. We saw that

[1] It should be noted that mystical " sublimation " involves more than the ordinary person would associate with the phrase, and is more far-reaching than the same term as understood in psychology.

adolescents were secluded that they might be "insulated" until purified, but clearly, where an adolescent "changes" his (or her) sex so as to become "androgyne," then the young person ranks as a "clean" or "holy" one who is tabooed, not for impurity, but because he is regarded as the precious medium of divine power. In one case the force is regarded as dangerous, in the other, by virtue of symbolic identification with the androgyne divinity, it is made beneficial, and the medium is venerated accordingly. Such a supposition, though hardly capable of direct proof, finds a measure of confirmation in the practice of inversion at marriage ; for we saw that marriage is the next great occasion when the magic force is supposed to manifest. If, as we suggest, inversion indicates the sublimation of this force into that with which the priest-king is "charged," then at marriage the contracting parties would pretend androgynity *to show that they were not unclean but holy*. It has been noted already that the bride and groom are sometimes treated as king and queen, which is one way of indicating this successful sublimation, so that if we can find inversion practised as a "taboo" ritual, the case will be a strong one.

As a matter of fact, the inversion of dress at marriage appears to be quite widespread. The Masai groom has to wear woman's dress for a month. In the Bombay district the bride wears man's clothes for two hours while riding through the village. The Spartan bride wore a man's cloak and shoes, while in Eastern Europe she simply puts on her husband's hat. In ancient Cos the groom wore woman's clothes when he received the bride, and in Argos she wore a beard.

So I think we may claim, thanks to psychology, that all such instances probably stand for the same idea, finding unconscious expression in apparently meaning-less, or at best, superstitious, custom and tradition. And further, this idea is based upon the mystic consummation.

Now what have we discovered so far ? Sex and its phenomena derives universal significance from the fact that they are concerned with an abstract force which is " brought down " both in kind and in potency according to the " purity " of the individual through which it acts. At one end of the scale this force has been recognised as the Word, and at the other as lust, while the " purity " of the medium has become equivalent to the state of his consciousness . . . whether " spiritual " or " bestial." Moreover, the terms of the equations have shown them-selves to be capable of subdivision, and they and their derivatives also represent *processes*. Again, these processes are each animated by a *force*, so that the " electrical " energy with which we started evidently includes several subsidiary powers. Love, in fact, is the *integrating force* which represents the sum (or neutral-isation) of all derived powers. Love is the expression of Unity, at once All and One.

" Hesiod conceives Eros not merely as the god of sensual love but as the power which forms the world by inner union of separated elements ; an idea very prevalent in antiquity, especially among the philosophers."

(NETTLESHIP : *Dictionary of Antiquities*.)

With this concept of Eros may be compared on the one hand the Christian dictum " God is love," and on the other the general Oriental conception of the integrating force which in Buddhism is recognised as love, though in other systems, from Thibetan Buddhist eschatology through Hinduism to the Chinese " Tao," it assumes a form which at first sight is very difficult to identify with human love. Thus Tao, the Middle Way, is the harmony of Yin and Yang under all their myriad forms of manifestation, but he who " knows Tao " finds in himself the omnipotent power of Tao, so that *by himself* all contradictions are harmonised and he " receives all things under heaven," returning " to the state of the Uncarved Block." (See later quotations.) This state, which is also " returning to the state of infancy," is connected to Christianity on one side and the ultimate abstraction of Nirvana on the other. There is, in fact, complete continuity of symbolic expression—though there is at present no point in elaborating the position as we are hardly sufficiently established upon the symbolic basis of the whole structure. Yet we have at least established that the sex-force with which we began has grown into an abstraction which is for the time being beyond the reach of our intellectual tools ; and that in the world-wide ramifications of its symbols, which have no respect for the passage of time, there is an " unconscious " harmony which becomes apparent when interpreted in the light of the " key " provided by our equations.

And so, from such by-ways as eonism and Jehovah, Krishna and " J.M.J.," we are enabled to speak more accurately of those energies designated by Dr. Jung's " indeterminable and variable " x." Briefly " x " has been merged into an abstract force with various derivatives, which, in its entirety, is a continuous attribute of consciousness. It rules equally in the genitalia, in the head, or in the heart, and we shall find eventually that the same force holds the balance of the stars and regulates the fantastic dance of the ultimate constituents of matter. In due course we shall seek to justify these somewhat far-fetched generalisations, which are useful at the present juncture because what is required is emphasis not so much upon diversity as upon harmony, not so much with superficial detail as with the depth of the whole. What matter how the " opposites " are labelled, whether they are recognised as Positive/Negative, Good/Evil, Yin/Yang, Pleasure/Pain ? The careful use of such verbal distinctions is sometimes of great importance, but it is even more important to appreciate in the first instance their origin from a common abstraction. With this qualification we may attempt a classification of the powers appropriate to the basic symbols. They consist of :

(i) *The Integrating Force.*

Love, the Word, the "electrical" sex-force, libidinous energy.

(ii) *The Derived Spiritual Forces.*

(*a*) The *descending* power of the Father. Light, Lord God, Cosmic Christ.

(*b*) The *ascending* power of the Son. Evolving consciousness, the Mystic Christ, the "redeeming symbol."

(The phrase "redeeming symbol" is derived from Jung, who says : " the immediate effect of the redeeming symbol is the reconciliation of the pairs of opposites." From the context it is clear that the " symbol " is that of the Christ, having, of course, various forms of expression psychological and otherwise. See *Psychological Types*, p. 334, and cf. the present Chapter IX, " Œdipus Rex.")

(iii) The derived *Material Forces* comprising :

(*a*) *Anabolic force* (birth, growth, increasing density, increasing fertility, the Mother, Creating Mother).

(*b*) *Katabolic force* (death, decay, decreasing density, decreasing fertility, the Destroyer, the Daughter).

Thus we have two pairs of forces for two pairs of primary symbols, derived from two Terms which are " opposites " ; and all these are derived from and included in the Unity, and its totality of forces.

" Thus look upon all the works of the Most High two and two, one against the other."

(Ecclus. xxxiii, 15.)

Having now filled in the main features of the country through which we are to travel, we are at liberty to outline more heavily the chief symbols which have been recognised. It has been emphasised that the main thing is the *relationship* between Terms, but it is hardly less important to value the symbols of those Terms correctly. Divorced from an appropriate context, one word can occupy several positions having even mutually contradictory meanings. *Serpent*, for instance, could probably be made to represent the first and third terms on all three levels, and occasionally it may also appear as second term (female). For instance, as a phallic emblem, familiar in the literature of psycho-analysis, the snake is *male*, i.e. first term on the physical level, but its close association with Monster (whale) and Fish (water) make it *female* on the mystic level. Then, as the winged or fire-serpent (Dragon) it is associated with the third term as a sign of immortality. Possibly this idea originated in the primitive belief that because the snake changes its skin and goes on living, it is potentially immortal. At all events, when Dr. Jung asserts, " Christ is also a serpent," there is no cause for surprise. We know that Iesu is ICTHUS, the Fish, and that the same word stands for Iacchus (Bacchus). Now the chief symbol of the Bacchic rites was a consecrated serpent, and the cult must be connected with the serpent-god

Abraxas-Iao, of whom an ancient gem says : " Abraxas is the one Jehovah." Plutarch writes : " The men of old time associated the serpent most of all beasts with heroes," and we shall see, on analysing myths, that true heroes are always personifications of the Christ in one way or another, usually with a serpent among their symbols. Thus the " plumed serpent " indicated the famous Quetzalcoatl of Central America, and was equally the sign of whatever faith flourished in the ancient city of Ankhor in Cambodia. The dragon of China is too well known to require comment, but the significance of Arthur of the Round Table is apt to be missed unless he is recognised primarily as " Pendragon." He was, as we shall see, closely identified with Osiris on the one hand and the Holy Grail on the other.

Being a Christ-symbol, it is not surprising to find the serpent standing for the *ascending spirit* in its abstract or cosmic sense. Thus Jung cites, " a series of medieval pictures in which the communion cup contains a dragon, a snake, or some sort of small animal." An interesting example of the dragon is to be found in a small chapel in the North wall of Hereford Cathedral. A relief in the form of a shield shows a feather beside a chalice and, rising out of the latter, a typical heraldic dragon. I think the significance of the feather comes to us from Egypt and Asia Minor, where it seems to have signified *spirit* as opposed to *matter*, and especially *truth*, i.e. spiritual truth. Its relation to the rest of the design seems to be in the nature of a musical clef. . . . " This design is concerned with the spirit." Thus we are already prepared to read the dragon in the chalice as the " plumed serpent " of the Christ, and one might go further by associating the chalice with the Great Mother (cf. the Grail and Cauldron of Keridwen), and the wine, which

presumably fills the chalice, with the " blood of atonement." Thus a complete message appears somewhat as
follows : " Out of the womb of incarnate experience is
born the extended consciousness which is immortal
(born not of water but of blood)."

The Book of Numbers (xxi, 8 ff.) provides an excellent
example of the serpent in a dual rôle, for it is the bite of
the reptile which dooms the Israelites to die, and the
sight of the same reptile which prevents that death.
Clearly the former is the Destroying Mother—(serpents
are the classical messengers of the wrath of the Goddess
Hera), while the latter is the fire-serpent or plumed
serpent of the Christ. For this reason it is referred to as
made of *brass* and set upon a pole. For brass can be
equivalent to *gold*, and the serpent on a pole corresponds
to the Ankh. Moreover, the reptiles in this passage are
referred to as " fiery serpents," which is another clue.
Surely " fire " here plays the same rôle as *feather* in the
last example ; as much as to say . . . " Don't take this
literally, it is an allegory of spiritual truth." Again, the
pole upon which Moses set up his brazen serpent is
drawn in my nineteenth-century Bible as a Tau, while in
the Revised Version this pole is referred to as " standard,"
indicating that the whole thing is a mystic sign rather
than a mere support for the magic reptile. Thus, as in
the previous case, an inner meaning may be distilled from
the incident, which has very much the same significance.
The Israelites stand for humanity (" this generation ")
which is caused to *fall* through the agency of their lower
nature (cf. the serpent of Eden). They thus become
subject to death through the " bite " of the serpent.
But even their lower nature cannot destroy the immortal
spirit within them. . . . Even the serpents of materialism
are " fiery." So, although mortal, they are potentially

immortal, being " saved " by the Divine Serpent, the
Ankh, the Christ. In fact this biblical incident describes
how Moses gave out the essential idea of the Christ in
the form of an allegory. . . . I don't mean to say there is
no actuality behind the tale, quite probably there is, but
symbolic meanings are in addition to and not instead of
the " actual " facts. Or, more correctly, actuality is only
the embodiment of abstraction.

Then there was the famous Orphic Eucharist of the
Serpent, where the living reptile crawled over the Host
as an act of consecration. As can be imagined, this
Orphic cult never became very widespread, but, by the
substitution of the Fish for the Serpent in a Eucharist
such as that held in connection with the Holy Grail, the
ritual became less instinctively repulsive and no less
significant. For the Fish is perhaps the most important
of all thermiomorphic symbols. We have seen already
that the Christ is expressed as Fish/Man//Man/God, of
which the first pair of terms identifies him with Vishnu,
Jonas, Oannes, Fuh Yi, and others. The Gnostics
" identified the radiant and perfect serpent with Jesus
Christ," but the Church recognises him as *the Fish*. . . .
" This latter practice was adopted by the early Christians,
who went so far as to identify Christ with a very large
fish, and to call themselves ' little fishes.' ' We are little
fishes,' says Tertullian, ' born in the waters of baptism,'
and a Christian inscription of A.D. 180 speaks of Jesus as
' the Great Fish.' "[1]

ICTHUS, which now reads Iesu, Christos, Theou,
Uios, Soter (Jesus, Son of God, Saviour), is of paramount
importance, and one cannot help wondering, since
Bacchus bore the same title, whether the original reading
were not " Iacchus Christos, etc. . . ."

[1] REINACH : *Orpheus*, p. 21.

Then Oannes, the Merman, is identified with Hea, one of the Babylonian Trinity who was symbolised as a serpent and whose name was written " with two signs signifying ' house ' and ' water.' " (*Encyc. Brit.*, VII, 821.) Traditionally, Oannes was a god/man who appeared, as did Fuh Yi, in the form of a fish and taught the people wisdom, especially arts and crafts . . . true heroes always seem to be craftsmen, particularly workers in wood and iron. But the more important rôle of Oannes is only understood in the light of the following quotation from the New Testament :

" The men of Nineveh shall rise up in judgement of this generation and shall condemn it : because they repented at the preaching of Jonas, and behold a greater than Jonas is here."

(Matt. xii, 41 ; also Luke xi, 30.)

Can there be any doubt that Jonas and Oannes are one and the same ? Here is an interesting comment taken from a plaster cast in Tewkesbury Abbey, said to have come from some other ecclesiastical foundation. A *mermaid* is represented holding an X (Greek Cross) against a background of grapes and vine leaves. Now, " mermaid " is equivalent to Oannes :: Jonas :: Christ. The rôle of the Christ is always the demonstration of immortality . . . the ascent of the spirit following the descent of the Father at the Incarnation. These two movements are symbolised in the Greek Cross, the upper " arrow-head " representing the *descent*, and the other " arrow-head " the *ascent*. A similar symbolism is found in the " Arrow of Ra " and the " Seal of Solomon."

Then, as to the *vine* and *grapes*. Jesus says : " I am the true vine " (John xv, 1), and that immortality is conferred by his *blood*. " Whoso eateth my flesh and

drinketh my blood hath eternal life " (John vi, 54).
Now the blood of the grape is wine. So he who drinks
the wine of the Christ is immortal. Bacchus was the
god of wine. Jesus also instituted a sacrament of wine.

But let us turn to wider conceptions of the *fish*.
The Gospel references are, presumably, already appreciated. . . . " Fishers of men," miracles of fishes and
fishing, even the risen Christ fishes with his disciples and
eats bread and fish with them. The true Papal ring is
" Annulo Piscatorio," bearing the device of a *fish*,
which was used to seal Bulls, a mark now made with
ink. The King of the Castle of the Holy Grail was the
*Fisher* King, and the symbol of the quest (spiritual, quest
of the Grail) is the fast of *fish*.

In mythology fish-heroes are legion and need not
detain us, since the method has already been adequately
illustrated by more important personalities. Indeed,
we have gone far enough to begin the analysis of myths ;
then, once the method has been firmly established, we
shall be free to enter the more tenuous realms of mysticism. At least we have already established the Triple
Christ as a paramount symbol, and the evolution of
consciousness as the central theme of the Christ. He
stands primarily for consciousness . . . evolving consciousness, and is the Archetype of all men. Behind the
personal power of the founder of every cult stands this
great abstraction, which can only become visible when
the proper methods are used to " materialise " it. Yet
whether recognised or no, it remains the most tremendous
reality, the most all-embracing reality which can enter
the consciousness of man. It is almost trite to remark
that this truth has always been available for those
" with eyes to see," yet it has seldom been described,
except in fantastic terms. This is not *because* there was

no apparatus, no scientific method whereby the abstract could be brought down into the realm of intellect. Yet it is true that there could hardly have been such apparatus until materialism had reached its climax and in that climax the necessary methods were produced. I refer, of course, to the conception of the " unconscious " and the psychology which derives from it. Materialism has, quite unintentionally, played the rôle of the Prophet : " I have declared unto them thy name, and will declare it."

" In very truth the myth is truth, symbolic truth, while reality is error. The man who learns to see the symbol will laugh at the talk about a Reality Principle, even if he honours and loves Freud as I do. So far from being irreligious, psycho-analysis offers us a way to religion that is its greatest gift to man. Neither the Virgin Birth, nor the Death on the Cross, neither the Walking on the Sea, nor the Raising of Lazarus, neither the Resurrection nor the Kingdom of Heaven, neither good nor evil, sinning nor salvation, does the analyst find incredible ; on the contrary, all these things to him are self-evident reality. He makes bold to interpret them, but he knows their meaning is equivocal ; nay, all-embracing, for God and the world are in the symbol."

(GRODDECK : *The World of Man*, p. 268.)

# CHAPTER FOUR

## GENESIS

" Life as a whole, from the initial impulse that thrust it into
the world, will appear as a wave which rises, and which is
opposed by the descending movement of matter."

(BERGSON : *Creative Evolution*, p. 284.)

IT is reasonable to suppose that all communities have
some tradition to account for their origin.  Mankind
has too much pride to be content with an undis-
tinguished genesis.  But, quite apart from motive, there
is always the possibility of a common source for such
stories, immeasurably far back in prehistory.  Such an
idea gains support from the fact that there is a great
deal which is common to creation myths the world
over, but the resemblance is more easily accounted for
by the assumption of a " world unconscious," from
which the symbolic expression of basic ideas wells up
irrespective of locality or antiquity.  Fortunately it is
not our business to go into the question, but only to
note that there is, in fact, a good deal common to most
accounts of man's origin, and that the variations which
occur are usually attributable to local conditions, and
are not of such a nature as to weaken the symbolic
significance of what we may regard as the " standard
account."

Obviously anthropogenesis offers a very valuable
source of symbols, for in that " high and far-off time "

conditions must have existed which could only be dealt with traditionally by means of symbols.

> " 'Ere earth and sea and covering heavens were known,
>      The face of nature, o'er the world was one ;
> And men have called it Chaos ; formless rude.
>      The mass ;  dead matter's weight, inert and crude ;
> Where, in mixed heap of ill-compounded mould,
>      The jarring seeds of things confusedly roll'd."
>
> (OVID : trans. Elton.)

This Chaos, in one form or another, may be said to be common to nearly all creation myths, except, perhaps, in the case of very primitive peoples whose imagination could not take them so far.  With Chaos begins the world Genesis story . . . a " watery " mass, boundless, self-existing in darkness, from which in due order arise gods, dry land, and men.  Often one finds some expression of " spirit " differentiated from " matter," as the " bird " or " light " against " water " or " darkness."

But comparisons do not really concern us, since in the Bible we have a story in itself so remarkably complete that it is quite unnecessary to go further afield.  It need only be pointed out that the biblical Genesis is linked with a world-myth on a similar basis, and especially with Mediterranean cultures.  And it is interesting, but no more, to find the same sort of tale from Mexico to China, and back to the Red Men of North America via Scandinavia.  Our concern is with meanings, not with origins.  In the first place, we are on the look out for " dualities " from which to infer important relationships. Genesis is packed with such dualities in a very orderly manner and on all three levels.  The primary one is obviously Heaven/Earth, and thereafter a series of others are easily recognised.  Only one major concept, that of the Firmament, refuses to fit in with the abstract scheme of *duality* and *trinity* outlined in the previous chapter. For this reason the idea of the "firmament" is of peculiar interest. Being neither a Term nor assignable to any *level*, it is evidently in the nature of a *boundary*, in spite of Genesis i, 8: "And God called the firmament Heaven," which is inconsistent with verses 6 and 7:

"And God said, Let there be a firmament in the midst of the waters, and let it divide the waters from the waters.

"And God made the firmament, and divided the waters which were under the firmament from the waters which were above the firmament: and it was so."

Now "water" is, as we have seen, equivalent to *matter*, so that if we read "matter" or, better, "creation," instead of "waters" we may get a clearer picture. "And God divided the creation which was above the firmament from the creation which was below." It has been suggested that the only reason why we are not aware of the universe on the higher levels is because our consciousness is limited to the physical, and if this is accepted, we can define the firmament as *that which separates one form of consciousness from another*. Or, like the equator, as "an imaginary line," but separating two levels *of consciousness*. According to our method there would then be at least two firmaments, one between the *cosmic* and *mystic*, and one between the latter and the *physical*. Have we already met symbols by which these may be identified? I think so, for entry into the mystic consciousness is gained by *the re-birth*, so that "to be born again" means "crossing the line" into the mystic level. Similarly "union with the Father" may be recognised as entry into the *cosmic* . . . the crossing of another and higher firmament.

But in that case, surely the word ought to have been used in Genesis in the plural? Admittedly that is a significant point, and one which makes us think there must be a more fundamental meaning than the one already put forward.

It has been suggested that "firmament" divides level from level, but there must also be a dividing line between Term and Term. On this hangs a very important point which will be appreciated when we come to consider the Individual in his relation to the environment as a whole. It means that the three levels are, as it were, a *vertical* arrangement of the Terms. The physical level corresponds to the second term, the mystic level to the first term and the cosmic level to the third term. Thus both Terms and *levels* are equally comprehensible only as " two and two, one against the other." *The opposites are the fundamental of all creation and the firmament represents the " line " between them wherever and however they or their subdivisions may occur.*

And one of the most fundamental pairs of opposites is that of Spirit and Matter, corresponding to the cosmic and physical levels respectively, *in which case the level between them constitutes the Firmament*. As a particular case, therefore, the mystic level *is* the firmament, and we shall see in due course that it is this level which is the " scene " of Eden and of the New Jerusalem and the Marriage of the Lamb. In fine, the mystic level is the " kingdom of heaven " . . . the firmament is heaven. Then the " waters above the firmament " are on the cosmic level, and the " waters below the firmament " are on the physical level. So from a very simple application of the method a clear meaning has been distilled from apparent inconsistency . . . the statement that there are " waters above heaven." Not that I put forward this concept of the firmament for immediate acceptance, obviously the evidence has hardly been sufficient for that, but the point had to be covered, since reference to the firmament is obviously an important part of the Genesis story as a whole, and hence of the present argument.

Now the primary duality of Genesis is obviously Heaven/Earth, then come a series of more particular pairs, culminating in Adam and Eve. Without reviewing the verses in which they occur, these may be written down immediately as corresponding roughly to the three levels as follows :

*Cosmic* : Light/Darkness ; Spirit/Matter ; Heaven/ Earth.

*Mystic* : Male/Female.

*Physical* : Sun/Moon ; Adam/Eve.

As to the Creator, it will be found that the abstract " generations " already worked out are personified in the narrative in such a way that we have a Creator for each of three distinct cycles. The first of these is " God," the second " Lord God," and the third the Serpent, and their essential symbolic connections are as follows :

### THE THREE CYCLES OF CREATION

| Cycle | Agent | Opposites | Effect |
|---|---|---|---|
| 1. | " God " WORD | Heaven/Earth | Spirit " in the image of God " |
| 2. | " Lord God " LIGHT | Male/Female | Soul " a living soul " |
| 3. | " Serpent " LOVE | Adam/Eve | Body " of the dust of the ground " |

Nor should it be forgotten that the Individual has the same constitution as the Triple Christ, whose special rôle on each of the three *levels* may be summarised as under :

*Cycle or Level*

1. (WORD)  " the Word was God . . . and the Word was made flesh."
2. (LIGHT)  " the light shineth in darkness."
3. (LOVE)  " to them gave he power to become the sons of God, even to them that believe *on his name*."   (John i, 1–14.)

As to the ultimate UNITY, which is not represented in the foregoing arrangement, it may be imagined as the totality of the three Agents, just as the Triple Christ is the totality of the three " Sons."  In fact, as Man is one person, so is God one person ;  but both Man and God are also *three*.  To this point I would add only that Man . . . the ordinary man self-conscious (i.e. recognising his own unity) does not include much more than the physical ;  the remainder " of himself " is still " unconscious," a point which will, perhaps, seem clearer after consideration of the four *elements* at the end of this chapter.

Before going on to the body of the Genesis story, let us briefly recapitulate the initial stages of the cosmic process. At " Alpha " the latent power of the Word becomes active and the Unity of FATHER/MOTHER begins to separate by fusion as in the case of biological cell-division. From FATHER devolves the universe of Spirit (Father/Son), while from MOTHER devolves Matter and its metabolic processes (Mother/Daughter).

Clearly the scope of Genesis is with the *descent* rather than the *ascent*, the gradual emergence of physical humanity differentiated into sexes, and the real constitution of that humanity. It is a tremendous theme. I would willingly have postponed the analysis of it until later on, but have been convinced by the necessity of beginning, literally, " at the beginning," although what now follows is more complex and speculative than any other section of the argument.

The first twenty-four verses of the book Genesis describe the first (cosmic or spiritual) cycle of seven " days," while the remaining two cycles are recognisable by their symbolism in the next few chapters, in spite of a certain amount of confusion, especially in the sequence. And this idea of sequence is necessary to the general narrative, though when we come to consider the Individual, as his identity is revealed through the Genesis symbols, we can afford to dispense largely with the time element.

Taking the general first, each cycle of *descent* produces a humanity of its own level. . . . There is a " spiritual (divine) " man, a " mystic man," and a " physical man," and these are *successive* evolutions.

The culmination of the *first cycle* is Man " in the image of God," which we have to conceive as a spiritual order of evolution composed of the " Sons of God " who are " brothers of Light." Oriental conceptions agree with this idea as do most religions ; for instance, the Hindu idea of the " Selves," so aptly termed " Overself " by Mr. Paul Brunton (*The Quest of the Overself*), corresponds closely, as does the idea of " Sparks " incorporated in *The Secret Doctrine*. Obviously the altitude is one at which we are more or less helpless ; but may we accept as hypothesis that there is such a " spiritual " order of beings, and indeed, that, from the particular point of view, we ourselves partake of that nature . . the nature of the " Spark." Although that highest constituent of our individuality must inevitably remain unconscious for an unknown period, yet such a " divine " constituent is a necessity if we are to face the symbolic correspondences fairly.  In practice it is probably as well to regard the Individual as connected to his true Self the " Spark " by a sort of thread, up which his consciousness slowly climbs : " Where the Id was shall be Ego," said Freud.  " Where the unconscious was, shall be consciousness," would be a parallel expression.

The first cycle ends at ii, 3, where God is represented as " resting," and the following verse initiates the second cycle of the " Lord God " (Light), who made the *mystic* Heaven and Earth.  That no physical creation is intended is shown by verse 5, wherein the Lord God makes :

". . . every plant of the field before it was in the earth, and every herb of the field before it grew."

And the *Lord* God made Eden, which is thus not a physical but a mystical environment in which exists Man the " living soul."  In other words, the Sparks exist on their own level, but on the mystic level Man is more complex ; he is not only a Spark, but a " living soul." This does not mean that he is superior to the Spark as such, but only that the former is free of certain limitations imposed upon the latter by the progressive *descent*. The mystic man is a mystery except in the barest essentials . . . as must be perfectly obvious.  But it is with those essentials that we are concerned.  For instance, we are compelled to regard " mystic " man as androgyne . . . male/female.  He is not Light, i.e. a Spark, a part of Light of the same " generation " ; but he is the " children of Light."  Now these individuals, conscious on the mystic level, correspond on the *ascent*

to those who have been " crucified " in accordance with
the symbolism already established, which insisted that
such a person, who had " overcome the world and the
flesh," must *ipso facto* have become " androgyne " . . .
must have become neither man nor woman (psychologically).

But physical man is said " in his generation " to be
" wiser than the children of Light," which can only
mean that the former has more experience than the latter,
*who do not descend into incarnation.* Thus we are already
prepared in the *third cycle* to find that the final " fall " is
characterised by eating the fruit of the " tree of knowledge." It is evident that the *descent* generally is
equivalent to the " fall," which thus represents *progressive
limitation of consciousness,* just as the *ascent* represents, as
we have already indicated, sublimation (extension) of
consciousness.

As might be expected, the *third cycle* is treated in more
detail than the other two, having the self-contained story
of Adam and Eve as its basis, with the Serpent in the rôle
of the Agent. Now the Serpent stands for desire,[1]
especially sensual desire. The best idea of the concept
is perhaps conveyed by the Buddhist phrasing, " Briefly,
desire is all that by which a man clings to (physical)
existence." Thus the Serpent may be said to *attract*
Man away from the mystic into the limitations of the
physical environment. In fact he leaves Eden as his
consciousness becomes limited and the " heaven-world "
fades from his sight. In Greek mythology this would
correspond with the end of the " Golden Age." Yet
in the " fall " itself is the source of that knowledge which
is to make Adam " wiser than the angels." One more
idea must be added . . . a speculation which is relevant

As opposed to love. See later development of the idea.

but not essential. Clearly man could not have been aware of the full implications of the " fall " or he would not have followed the Serpent and allowed his consciousness to become contracted. Why therefore was he overcome by his " lower nature " ? Because his *higher* faculties were " asleep." The Lord God " caused a deep sleep to fall upon Adam." And here we meet another symbol of the final stage of the " fall," the differentiation of the sexes. For it was while Adam was asleep, i.e. dominated by matter, that Eve was " made," i.e. separated from him. Thus the " fall " was completed when that which had been a spiritual and mystical unity became finally a physical duality (although the unity remained on the higher levels . . . it is *only* on the physical that the sexual duality can exist as such). (cf. Chapter X.)

And here lies perhaps the most remarkable feature of the whole narrative. The Serpent drags Man out of Eden into incarnate life. The *descent* comes to an end with the emergence of the sexes. Man " wakes," and *the desire which was responsible for the " fall " becomes the love which inspires the ascent.*

" It was God himself, who at the end of his great work, coiled himself up in the form of a serpent at the foot of the tree of knowledge." (NIETZSCHE : *Ecce Homo*, p. 116.)

And the name of the Serpent was ICTHUS : the sign of the Serpent was the sign of the prophet Jonas, as of all other heroes who triumph over the Destroyer.

What then is Man ? Humanity in our own times is already highly evolved, having derived by *descent* through at least three cycles of creative evolution. Potentially, that is to say " in the unconscious," Man is also the Son of Man, and the Son of God, and One with the FATHER. As consciousness expands he is destined to become these things successively, by a process of *ascent* which is also spiritual evolution. The driving force behind evolution is the Word, but the symbol of its action varies. Thus it can be shown to manifest as lust, love, gravitation, cohesion, potential (the relationship between the electrical opposites). It is the *integrating* force, the force of mutual attraction. Just as sunlight is the sum of all the constituent wavelengths of the spectrum, so love is the sum of every form of " libidinous " energy, using that word in its widest possible sense. In proportion as a man's aspiration or desire concentrates on a single object, so all subsidiary interests are brought into relation to it. Such a man is combining the various psychic forces in relation to a particular object just as a prism integrates the spectrum colours.

It is of no consequence from this viewpoint whether a man concentrates upon God or the Devil or any inter-mediate objective, but in proportion as his energies are concentrated he will become the vehicle of increased energy. Normally our energies are so dispersed among the multifarious activities of living that no dangerous concentration is likely to be set up. Concentration, however, is dangerous for just that reason. Irrespective of the object, an individual may easily become the storm centre of forces quite beyond his control, and which often seem to come from outside himself altogether. Put in another way, any and every effort brings " libido " into play. Libido is the sum-total of energy for the individual, which may be dispersed or concentrated, degraded or sublimated, but which always obeys the old law of the conservation of energy. Thus in such practices as Yoga, the aspirant, by the very fact that he is aspiring, seems to call into being a force which he may easily fail to control and is quite capable of killing him. The same risk attends self-analysis, though probably to a lesser degree. Even so, however, at least one prominent psychologist, Dr. Stekel, has had reason to deplore the many suicides among his colleagues.

But I do not think that this conception takes us far enough unless we include the notion that every force liberated must encounter equal and opposite resistance. This is implicit in the very concept of the opposites whether in psychology or physics. The bullet is propelled by a force which equally tends to drive the gun backward. The man who tries to project his concentrated thought on any object whatever will experience the same recoil. Finally we must leave the orthodox for the mystical. It seems to me that there can be no property in psychic energy. One cannot say "*my* libido," but only " the libido available to me." Energy is common to the universe, and local concentrations of energy are limited only by the means of concentration. In normal people, as I have already pointed out, there is very little chance of provoking a dangerous concentration because their libidinous outlets are so diverse . . . will to power, finance, romance, and so on. But with the concentration of these energies into a single path there will follow a proportionate extension of the quantity of energy which may be liberated. The perfect man would be able to command all the energy in the universe !

It may seem that we have strayed a long way from Genesis, but the return to it is imminent. We showed that the Word is the symbol of universal energy and also that the human equivalent is " love," the " electrical force." The narrative is concerned largely with the embodiment of this force in man and our latest digression indicates that man, the Individual, still has the full potentiality of the Word. " The Word was made flesh and dwelt among us," says St. John. The Christ is that perfect man whose power is virtually unlimited, the power of the "libido" which moves mountains and raises the dead. But, as usual, the most significant interpretation is not particular but general. The incarnation of the Word is the potentiality of omnipotence in *all* individuals. The energy of the universe is locked up in love : no wonder Krishna is represented with sixteen thousand mistresses !

Only one other primary consideration arises from this analysis of Genesis. It is clear that space/time as we understand it (i.e. in relation to Matter) appeared quite a long way down the *descent*, at the beginning of the third cycle. Yet there must be a beginning and end of the process as a whole. Alpha showed the first movement of the Word : Omega means the final integration . . . which is as near the Oriental conception of Nirvana, "both being and not being," as it is possible to get.

We acknowledge Omega as the limit of our field of vision, but we cannot say that evolution ends. Perhaps perfection remains to be perfected in further schemes, according to the ancient Egyptian tradition of the "gods of the gods." One thing at least is certain, individuality, that is self-consciousness, cannot be destroyed . . . except perhaps by its own choice. It is unimportant whether we consider the first and last stages of the plan as existing in a conceivable set of dimensions. Just as it is impossible to imagine the consciousness which animates an ant-hill, so the conception of time beyond time is impossible. Yet even here we are provided with a certain amount of firm ground, for, as a matter of experience, we know physical time to be existent only in relation to Matter. As consciousness rises above Matter so do we shake ourselves free of time.

Physical time gives place to what Dr. Alexis Carrel calls "inward" time, and that, in turn, gives place to eternity, where we are altogether "timeless."[1]

There is nothing astonishing in all this; every day the clock measures Matter, but our consciousness is very largely unconnected with Matter. We do not notice the passage of time *unless some change is desired*. With the conquest of desire, for "the presence of the loved and the absence of the unloved," comes the conquest of time. And with that, we may suggest, comes the opening up of intuition, which alone finds reality in such statements as the following:

> "I am the God Atum, I who alone was.
> I am the God Re at his first splendour.
> I am the great God, self-created, God of Gods,
> To whom no other God compares."

"I was yesterday and know to-morrow; the battle-ground of Gods was made when I spoke. I know the name of the great God who tarries therein.

I am that great Phœnix who is in Heliopolis who there keeps account of all there is, of all that exists.

I am the God Min, at his coming forth, who placed the feathers upon my head.

I am in my country, I come into my city. Daily I am together with my Father Atum.

My impurity is driven away, and the sin which was in me is overcome. I washed myself in those two great pools of water which are in Heracleopolis, in which is purified the sacrifice of mankind for that great God who abideth there.

I go my way to where I wash my head in the sea of righteousness. I arrive at this land of the glorified, and enter through the splendid portal.

Thou, who standest before me, stretch out to me thy hands. It is I, I am become one of thee. Daily I am together with my Father Atum."[2]

[1] Cf. Dunne's theory of "serial" time.

[2] See *Psychology of the Unconscious*, p. 53, quoting the above, "Rising at Day out of the Underworld."

But though the full meaning of the above is beyond the ordinary processes of intellect, it is by no means beyond analysis. The worshipper, projecting himself to the day "Omega," when he is become "one with the Father," recognises the inner mystery of the Word in a way which admits of no misconception.

"I am the God Min, at his coming forth, who placed the feathers upon my head."

Now Min was the virility principle, called for that reason the "shameless." The feathers represent "spiritual truth" (as already suggested), and in particular the truth *of the two worlds*, i.e. of Spirit and Matter. This truth is evidently obtained through sex, for Min "placed the feathers upon my head."

Again we are recognising an expression of *sublimation* as the key of immortality. Truly Behemoth is "the beginning of the ways of God" (Job xl, 15 ff.)! And what is Behemoth but Libido, the source of energy, the very well of that "indeterminable and variable 'x.'" Part of our argument may at least be regarded as having reached a conclusion. We have placed a series of values upon "x."

The Freudian, brave champion of irrefutable logic in the face of decency, would find no difficulty in giving a meaning to the following utterance ; and would regard the qualification as superfluous.

"He that believeth on me, as the scripture hath said, out of his belly shall flow rivers of living water."
". . . But he spake this of the Spirit."

(John vii, 38.)

We have recognised the River of Life in the mutations of energy, whether physical or psychic. More strictly the river consists in the sublimation of energy according to a definite route and a definite plan. And even on the physical *level* sex occupies only a very small part of the field. Psychology recognises the " will to power," desire for wealth, success, social position, and so on, as channels for libidinous energy . . . but such energy is not gross sex, already it has been subject to a certain amount of sublimation. Yet *all* energy is ultimately derived from (or referable to) Libido, which does not stand for sex as the world understands that word, not the sex of the cinema, but the relationship between " maleness " and " femaleness," positive and negative.

And now let us look a little more closely at Adam and Eve, whose story, besides being of great importance in itself, contains valuable clues for the interpretation of the classical myths which are to be dealt with later on.

In the first place the " fall " has been shown to consist in *materialisation* in the widest sense of that word which is at the same time literal. I mean that the continued descent of consciousness eventually resulted in the formation of physical bodies :

" And the Lord God made for Adam and for his wife coats of skins."
(Gen. iii, 21.)

But that is a minor point ; what really concerns us is the use of the basic symbols upon which a very large proportion of myths are based. Typical arrangements show Adam, the hero, the Christ, the Dragon-slayer, as the Sun ; while his sister, wife, and mother (the Dual Mother) is the Moon. The crux of the question, therefore, is the link between the Sun myths and the Genesis story, and such a link is by no means hard to find.

" And he placed at the east of the garden of Eden Cherubims, and the flame of a sword which turned every way to keep the way of the tree of life."
(iii, 24.)

Thus the return to Eden is from the East, with the Rising Sun which is expanding consciousness. Consequently the " fall " is *westward* with the Setting Sun of the Father (*descent*) and the rising Moon of materialism. Adam, like Osiris, goes on a journey in the Underworld (under-heaven world), to reappear as the Son Horus. Jesus " rises from the dead " having " overcome the world."

Now the symbol of Spirit is fire, and the symbol of *activity* (especially of the male) is the sword, so the " Sword of Fire " is the power (activity) of Spirit. When Adam " fell " his nature became that of Earth, and he could no longer live in an environment of fire (Spirit). Therefore the Garden is " guarded by Spirit " which Adam cannot pass until he has transmuted his own Earth into Gold, water into fire (wine). Then, being once again of the same nature as fire, he crosses the threshold (firmament) of the garden to the Tree of Life.

In order to make this concept of the Sword quite clear, we should bear in mind its more conventional associations as the weapon of war and strife. For there is no other weapon so potent in creating strife in the mind of man. The moment the spiritual fire awakens in him (when the sublimation *consciously* begins) he is at war with himself and with the Moon. But as the war proceeds and the fire *burns up* his " lower nature " the individual approaches the " birth of fire," when his nature, hitherto " watery," becomes " fiery " (cf. transmutation).

As to the Tree, we have seen that the Tree of Know-ledge stands for *incarnation* and incarnate experience generally.[1] Similarly the other Tree is Death. Yet it is

[1] " My saull and Lyfe stand up and see
Quha lies in ane Cribe of Tree
Quhat Babe is that so gude and faire ?
It is Christ, God's Sonne and Aire."

(Old Scots Carol.)

quite obvious that a man may die without having reached
the state of " re-birth," the " awakening " which alone
provides the passport to Eden.  On the other hand his
consciousness might have reached that level before
death took place.  Can we reconcile these two points of
view ?  I think we can, for the Death Tree has nothing
to do with physical death, but refers to the " overcoming
of the world."  To reach the Tree of Life is to become
" dead to the world."  Yet symbolically the two Trees
are *birth* and *death*, whatever the details of their interpretation ; in other words they are special signs of the Dual
Mother, who gives spiritual birth as well as physical
birth, death as well as life.  For consciousness confined
to the physical is spiritual death.  Hence the apparent
paradox.

These few correspondences have cleared up a number
of loose ends, and can now be reduced to tabular form.

| Tree of Knowledge | Tree of Life |
|---|---|
| Birth | Death |
| Creating Mother | Destroying Mother |
| Birth of Water | Birth of Fire |

But we can take the argument a little further.  There
is an eleventh-century psalter in the British Museum
(No. 5 Bible Room) in which Christ is crucified, not
between *thieves*, but between *trees*.  In other words the
crucifixion is represented as standing between birth and
death, the symbol of both ; without the understanding
of which birth and death are alike meaningless.  Christ
has been shown to represent self-consciousness, and the
Cross has appeared as the " marriage " of the opposites
upon which the extension of consciousness depends.
Moreover, the opposites find their physical expression
in *male* and *female*, so that the full symbol just cited

shows consciousness " crucified " against Adam and Eve, between birth and death. We are reminded of the ancient tradition that Adam was buried at Golgotha. In more abstract terms the extension of consciousness depends upon the attainment of the " mystic consummation " to which there is but one road. This road goes by various names, but all of them are founded upon the same idea, the integration of the opposites. It is of small consequence whether we speak of the " Way of the Cross," " Tao," " The Holy Eightfold Path," " The Path of the Arrow," or the " Quest."

Of Jesus of Nazareth it is said :

" He is our peace who hath made both one . . . having abolished in his flesh the enmity ; for to make in himself one new man, so making peace."

(Eph. ii, 14.)

The teaching of Gautama Buddha may be summarised as follows :

" The presence of the unloved is suffering and the absence of the loved is suffering. Suffering springs from desire (for the presence of the loved, etc.). To be free, alike of the loved and the unloved through the conquest of desire, is to enter into Nirvana."

The Book of Manu declares :

" Whoso holdeth himself free from the opposites, that one is redeemed."

But the most perfect expression of the idea which I have been able to trace comes from Tao Tê Ching, No. XXVIII,[1] which I venture to quote in full :

" He who knows the male, yet cleaves to what is female
Becomes like a ravine, receiving all things under heaven,
And being such a ravine

[1] See WALEY : *The Way and its Power.*

He knows all the time a power he never calls upon in vain.
This is returning to the state of infancy.
He who knows the white, yet cleaves to what is black
Becomes the standard by which all things are tested ;
And being such a standard
He has all the time a power that never errs,
He returns to the limitless.
He who knows glory, yet cleaves to ignominy
Becomes like a valley that receives into it all things under
    heaven,
And being such a valley
He has all the time a power that suffices ;
He returns to the state of the Uncarved Block."

In this quotation three points stand out as of particular interest, being expressions of the mystic consummation and its consequences. They are all symbols which we have already identified, though perhaps the last may seem to be disguised.

(i) " *This is returning to the state of infancy.*" . . . Clearly the Chinese author recognises the principle of re-birth.

(ii) " *He knows all the time a power* . . ."

    (*a*) that he never calls upon in vain,
    (*b*) that never errs,
    (*c*) that suffices.

We have seen that in proportion as the opposites are united, the integrating force is progressively active, becoming less and less limited as consciousness expands. This force is that of the Word which, ultimately, i.e. as the power of Unity, is omnipotent . . . the omnipotence of " God," FATHER/MOTHER.

" My Word shall not return unto me void, but shall accomplish that which I please and prosper in the thing whereto I sent it."
(Isa. lv, 11.)

But it is this same force which is "locked up" in Love, the liberation and sublimation of which is the Way itself.

(iii) " *He returns to the state of the Uncarved Block.*"

It is necessary to examine this notion with some care because a monumental error has been built upon it. I mean the common Western attitude to Nirvana as a state of negation. It goes without saying that Nirvana is the " Uncarved Block," and the fact of " return " is clear enough from the foregoing analysis of Genesis. But the idea of returning to a prior state of existence does not arise. The " Uncarved Block " and " Nirvana " alike refer to the *level* of FATHER/MOTHER into which all things reintegrate. We should have said perhaps, *to* which all things return, rather than, *into* which all things reintegrate. For though the Son regains the infinite altitude, he is not what he was before. . . . For between the past and the present, between Alpha and Omega, lies the whole field of experience, that very experience which makes his " generation " (humanity) " wiser than the angels." Nirvana, in fact, is not consciousness destroyed, but consciousness *expanded to infinity*. . . . Hence the simile of the " Uncarved Block " and the state which is " both being and not being."

But we have not yet finished with Adam and Eve, who were prevented from returning to Eden, not only by the Sword, but also by the Cherubim. We have seen that humanity is able to pass the first when the consummation has been reached which transmutes his own nature into that of Fire. When he is " born of fire " he is free of the Sword. Yet nothing has been said of the Cherubim who also must be overcome.

We have indicated that there is a symbolic correspondence between Macrocosm and Microcosm, in each of which play *four* great forces (dual Father and dual Mother) which are connected with the four traditional *elements*. So far it has only been shown that Water stands for the *female* and Fire for the *male*; Air and Earth have hardly been touched upon; yet it must be obvious that such a symbolic correspondence does exist and might be expressed as under:

| *Dual Father* | | *Dual Mother* | |
|---|---|---|---|
| Air | Fire | Water | Earth |
| (Descent) | (Ascent) | (Birth) | (Death) |
| | Son | | Daughter |
| | | Creator | Destroyer |

Treated as the representatives of *forces*, these four elements will be represented in the Individual, presumably with a suitable vehicle for each.

The third term is, of course, in each case a form of consciousness, but I cannot in the present context find words in which to distinguish it respectively on the different levels. It may appear as though I have taken the plunge into that miasma of mysticism which I so carefully set out to avoid. But please remember that the foregoing arrangement is only an approximation. It is designed to illustrate a method so that we shall be able to pursue the general enquiry. Such things are primarily for use as tools.

At all events the Cherubim are gradually taking shape as personifications of the four elements, from the fusion of which comes the consummation. The *four* must become *two* and the *two* must become *one*. The " consummation " or " re-birth " about which so much has been said, is thus dependent upon *the fusion of the diverse elements of consciousness.* The Cherubim must be " overcome " before the Sword can be faced, for Adam remains " of the earth earthy " until he has transmuted these elements into the unity of Fire.

For what it is worth, let us now apply this concept of the Cherubim to the famous vision of Ezekiel, in which the following points are of outstanding importance :

The Cherubim are collectively a *Man* (Ez. i, 5) ;
They are *four* in number (verse 4) ;
They are ruled by Spirit (love) (verse 20) ;
They are joined together (verse 11).

These correspondences certainly fit in with what we should expect to find if, in fact, the vision of Ezekiel is based upon the unconscious recognition of those abstractions which appear under such symbols. But the prophet introduces many complications, some of which go beyond our present scope. However, it seems to me evident that the appearance of each of the Elements (Cherubim) symbolises a characteristic of the Individual. Thus a further set of correspondences emerge :

Man has the feet of a beast (verse 7) ;
And the face of a beast (in the dual aspect of *dominance* (Lion on the right) and *compliance* (Ox on the left) ) ;
And the wings of a bird ;
And the face of a bird (verse 11.

Thus man includes the Brute (body), Human (soul), and Divine (spirit). He is at once a beast, a man, and a bird.

" Man is a God and a brute, with his head he aspires to the stars, but his feet are contented in the grasses of the field ; and when he forsakes the brute upon which he stands, then there will be no more men and no more women, and the immortal gods will blow this world away like smoke."

(JAMES STEPHENS : *The Crock of Gold.*)

This is " Homo Sapiens " as represented by the figure under that title in the Tate Gallery. The incarnate Individual stands upon a Fish, and from his heart rises an Eagle.

Apart from general considerations, there is, of course, the familiar one of the " cloven hoof," especially that belonging to Antichrist (the Destroyer or Daughter) . . . Satan. The association is obvious in so much that the foot is in contact with the Earth which is the element of the Destroyer.

But also we should not forget the word " cloven," for that which is *cleft* is disunited, incapable of union (consummation), hence peculiarly appropriate to the personification of the disintegrating force.

The symbolism of the Cherubim is not yet exhausted even in so far as we are capable of reading, for there remain the Lion and the Ox. Now it has been suggested that the first two terms stand in the same relation to one another as the Mystic and Physical *levels.* Body and Soul in fact are " opposites " from the union of which the Spirit is liberated (born). Such opposites are given the abstract names of " male/female " or " dominance/ compliance," the latter being psychological terms derived from the known significance of " male " and " female."

Now a conspicuous thermiomorphic symbol of *dominance* is the King of Beasts—Lion, and that of *compliance* is the Ox, for obvious reasons. So the " inferior " nature of the Individual is represented by the vision as consisting of these two opposites in detail relationship with a whole series of abstract symbols. The Individual is Eagle, Lion, and Ox (the first being

liberated by the union of the other two). He stands
upon the Destroyer (cloven hoof), but his ultimate
nature is Fire (verse 13). Though he *exists* on three
levels (feet, hands, face), he *consists* of four Elements
(Cherubim).

We are now in a position to sum up the whole argument, for the relationship between the Elements and the
Terms provides the full pattern of the essentials, a
septenary pattern. True, we know nothing about the
actual nature of the elemental forces ; Air, Earth, Fire,
and Water mean little more than " a, b, c, d," in an
algebraic formula, yet these symbols do convey a
meaning in respect of relationship.

Thus we have already discovered that the Elements are
represented on all three levels. It has also been noticed
that the " dual Father " who differentiates into *descent/
ascent* is countered by the " dual Mother " of *metabolism*.
These four are clearly related to the Elements. For
instance, the physical Mother requires the attribute of
Water, and incarnation becomes the " birth of Water,"
just as freedom from the physical (i.e. death) is referred
to as the " birth of Fire." Again, Fire is so obviously
the *ascending*, in the common sense, that it compels the
recognition of Air as associated with *descent*. . . . And
was it not the *descent* of Spirit which " breathed into
man's nostrils the breath of life " ?

But the most important consideration which arises is
that of the Christ and Antichrist as respectively Son and
Daughter, the one a totality of spiritual force expressed
*as an individual*, the latter a totality of *material force* equally
personified.

A great deal hinges upon this relationship, which will
be dealt with more fully in the chapter on the Golden
Apples, and, later, under the heading of Œdipus.

But it is essential to understand now that both these concentrations of power are represented in the ordinary man and woman. They are, if you like, our arch-opposites. Only self-consciousness, which includes *will*, stands between them to control their interaction.

Thus at one end of the scale there is a cosmic triunity of absolute consciousness, while at the other is the trinity of individual consciousness, whose opposites are as Christ/Antichrist. According to what may be regarded as a law of opposites, the two forces must be recognised as of necessity equal. It is only the action of self-consciousness which can determine the degree of sublimation or otherwise, the degree of identification with one or the other . . to use the more common expression. Yet this statement should be qualified to the extent that, by definition, the material powers are finite, mortal, temporal, while the Christ-powers are in no way limited. At its simplest the former stand for *desire*, the latter for *love*.

The strange thing is that all these complex abstractions are implicit in the comparatively simple narrative of Genesis, which, however incorrect our interpretations may be, is revealed as a unique concentration of " unconscious " symbolism. Yet . . .

" The account given in the first chapter of Genesis, which has been so much praised for its simple grandeur and sublimity of thought, is merely a rationalised version of the fight with the dragon, a myth which for crudity of thought deserves to be ranked with the quaint fancies of the lowest savages."

(FRAZER : *The Dying God*, p. 108.)

Of course Genesis is founded on the Dragon myth, for that is the " typical myth," the essential ingredient of all myths. Wherever there is aspiration, sublimation, effort, there is the fight with the Dragon. Whoever destroys what is base to build what is noble, fights the Dragon. Genesis is based upon the Dragon ; so is the Golden Bough !¹

Said Groddeck : " God and the world are in the symbol." Even the " lowest savages " seem somehow to understand that truth. . . . " Thou hast hid these things from the wise and prudent, and hast revealed them unto babes." (Luke x, 21.)

¹ Frazer's Dragon is superstition and ignorance, upon whose head the Golden Bough weighs heavily.

# CHAPTER FIVE

## THE GOLDEN FLEECE

" Bring me my bow of burning gold ! "

(BLAKE.)

AT least one broad distinction may be recognised between different classes of myth, the essential difference consisting in the fact that while one type places the emphasis on the *attainment* of the treasure, bride, or prize, the other is concerned more with the adventure itself. It stands to reason, I think, that the latter class will include the more abstract and mystical stories such as the Holy Grail and the Chemical Nuptials, while the former includes every type of tale from simple dragon slaying (St. George) to the intricate web of circumstance which surrounds the Argonauts.

If, after our analysis of the psychological basis of myth, we may assume that certain abstract ideas will be thrown up into consciousness in symbolic terms, and that these naturally become organized into traditional stories of heroes, it follows that the attainments of these heroes can be brought into relation with the abstract terms themselves . . . particularly with the mystic consummation. Thus we may even lay down certain conditions at least some of which each and every " Consummator " must fulfil. First, he must prove his identity as the spiritual Son, with which is entailed his opposition to Mother Matter. Secondly, he must adopt the " Way of the Cross," which means to say he must go on a difficult journey, fight a series of battles, endure hardship, and so on, in the course of which certain enemies must be overcome. And the enemies can also be identified, for, collectively, they represent his " lower nature," " mortality," represented by the animal-nature (Fish/Man), or, in more detail by the four " mystical " Elements. In fact he must *sublimate* his animal nature and conquer the Elements before the consummation is attained. Earth, Water, and Air must be transmuted into Fire . . . only then, when the hero is himself " fire," can he overcome the last obstacle and receive the treasure, virgin, or liberation from mortality.

Very naturally it is unusual to find more than a few of these ideas included in any one myth, and yet, in spite of the inevitable confusion, alteration, and addition consequent upon travels both in space and time, some of the great myths retain a degree of fundamental meaning which is not unworthy to compare with Genesis. The first which we shall consider is that of the Golden Fleece, not so much because of its mystical pre-eminence, but because it introduces a consideration which so far has only been touched upon, pending an opportunity to deal suitably with it. For the myth of the Fleece, unlike the vast majority of classical myths, may be said to hinge from a ritual sacrifice upon which the magical qualities of the relic depend. I think the full story may be divided into three "chapters," each of which is in itself a complete myth in the sense that it is sufficient to convey the essential inner meaning of the relationship between the opposites and the nature of the consummation.

The first of these chapters describes the Ram in its rôle as saviour of Phryxus and Helle, and culminates with the sacrifice of the animal, whose fleece is hung in the

grove of Ares and guarded by a sleepless dragon. . . .
In other words the immortal treasure is hung on the
*tree of blood*, for Ares is essentially the god of blood.
And the tree of blood is the Calvary Cross, otherwise the
Tree of Life.

The next " chapter " describes the identity of Jason,
while the third deals with the " voyage " itself, the perils
and hardships of the Argonauts, and the *attainment*.
Quite obviously we have here a wealth of material, some
of which is still new to us. It will be necessary therefore
to clear up those two important ideas represented by the
Tree of Blood and the Sacrifice, especially the sacrificial
skin or fleece.

The connection between blood and the consummation
has already been established, and so has the identity of
the Tree of Sacrifice, so that the fleece hung up in the
grove of Ares appears as a composite symbol which
only needs the addition of *gold* to confirm it as an
expression of the treasure of immortality. For gold is
the attribute of divinity, and especially of the Christ as
King, i.e. he who has transmuted the base elements into
gold. Gold, in fact, is closely connected with *fire* as a
spiritual emblem, and was no doubt used in this sense
by the Alchemists, whose famous Magnum Opus was
not concerned with material transmutation, but mystical
transubstantiation.

" Behold he knoweth the way that I take : when he hath
tried me I shall come forth as gold."
(Job xxiii, 10.)

". . . the fire shall try every man's work of what sort it is."
(1 Cor. iii, 13.)

" For gold is tried in the fire, and acceptable men in the
furnace of adversity."
(Ecclus. ii, 5.)

And the place of the " trial " is clearly the place of sacrifice. Thus the Golden Fleece in the Grove of Ares becomes the symbol of the successful trial, the victory of immortality.

But it is probably advisable to reinforce our own conclusions with a quotation :

" It is not astonishing that the Christian legend transformed the tree of death, the cross, into the tree of life, so that Christ was often represented on a living and fruit-bearing tree. This reversion of the cross symbol to the tree of life, which even in Babylon was an authentic and important religious symbol, is also considered entirely probable by Zöckler, an authority on the history of the cross. The pre-Christian meaning of the symbol does not contradict this interpretation ; on the contrary, its meaning is life. . . .

The student of medieval history is familiar with the representation of the cross growing above the grave of Adam. The legend was that Adam was buried at Golgotha.  Seth had planted on his grave a branch of the ' paradise tree ' which became the cross and tree of death of Christ."

(JUNG : *Psychology of the Unconscious*, p. 153.)

And now what is the significance of the Fleece ?

There are abundant records of religions, both lofty and degraded, where the skin of the sacrifice was held in the greatest veneration. On the face of it there is an obvious link with the mystical " body and blood " as interpreted by Christianity, that is to say the skin or fleece is the symbol of the hero's sacrifice, the vehicle of the " gospel " of immortality. For where the hero triumphed so shall his followers. Moreover, such a relic would have considerable magical power, recognised in its most abstract symbolism by the Christian Eucharist, which, like every other sacrifice ceremony, aims at the identification of the worshipper with the sacrifice. Such an interpretation may seem to fit only the higher form of sacrifice, but we can see that the same ideas can be easily degraded until the body of the sacrifice is recognised as the fertility—or virility—principle while the spiritual aspect is hidden from view. Thus the " Corn Spirits " give their virility (fertility) to the soil, to beasts, and humans. The sacrifice of the warrior gives courage to those mystically associated with him, either by eating the flesh or by contact with the blood ; and similar ideas must lie behind every form of sacrifice, which serves always as the link between the worshipper and those forces with which he wishes to come into contact.

Thus it is only natural that the skin of the sacrifice should be held in the greatest veneration, and at the same time be associated as closely as possible with the devotee.

In some cases, as in Greece, it was sufficient that the skin be touched or stood upon, but more often the worshipper clothed himself in it, thus assimilating himself into the body of the sacrifice. Where the victim was an animal in default of a man or woman, it was usually one of those symbolic beasts connected with the " magic force," i.e. a virility principle such as the Bull, Boar, Goat, Ram, or a fertility principle such as the Cow, Cat, Dove, Sheep (by association with the Great Mother), and so on. It is rather curious to find that even in cults, such as that of Mithra, where the bull-sacrifice was revoltingly crude, there was nevertheless a definite mystical conception of re-birth.

Thus when the Mithraic bull was slain, the blood flowed down through a grating under which the neophyte waited in white robes. The great quantity of blood drenched him to the skin and he came up out of the pit dripping with it, to be hailed immediately as *re-born*. So much so, in fact, that for some time afterwards he was fed on milk

on the assumption that it was fit diet for an infant. Thus
contact with the blood or skin is clearly an expression
of the psychological event which has been variously
recognised as the following : birth of fire, return to
Eden, entry into the mystic level, crucifixion (past),
hanging on the tree of life (or death), identity with the
spirit (God, body of God, Sacrifice, Hero), identity
with the " magic " force (of the ascending spirit).

All these ideas may be conveniently summed up in
the one word " Eucharist," though I admit that the
lower forms of the sacrifice very thoroughly conceal
the higher meanings. Such, for instance, are those
harmless spring festivities quoted by Sir James Frazer
where young men dress themselves up with the horns
of a stag or bull ; while the more primitive spring
sacrifices such as that of the virgin of fecundity have
scarcely more claim to respect. It is interesting to notice
how the emotional attitude of such rites is captured in
Stravinsky's ballet-music " Le Sacre du Printemps,"
while the action amply bears out the symbolic significance
of the climax.

But it is not our present task to analyse sacrifice in
detail ; such a task really requires a book to itself. We
are concerned solely with the magical quality of the
Golden Fleece, and hence with the skin of the sacrifice
generally. Thus these brief excursions may be summed
up with, perhaps, the most thorough example of the
practice which is conceivable.

" Xipe was widely worshipped throughout Mexico, and is
usually depicted in the *pinturas* as being attired in a flayed
human skin. At his special festival, the ' Man-flaying,' the
skins were removed from the victims and worn by the devotees
of the god for the succeeding twenty days."

(LEWIS SPENCE : *Myths of Mexico and Peru.*)

We are now in a position to consider the myth of the Fleece more generally, first of all in relation to the hero who attained it. Already it is clear that this attainment is equivalent to the regaining of a kingdom . . . Eden, and it is therefore not surprising to find that Jason's quest of the Fleece is dictated by the desire to *restore the kingdom* to his " people " (parents) who had *fallen* from their kingly estate.

Before he can set out to fulfil his destiny the young hero has to acquire the necessary qualities, beginning with the discipline of his animal nature as the first stage in the process of sublimation which is the psychological equivalent of his life's adventure.

We are not surprised, therefore, to find that the educator of Jason is a *Centaur* (Chiron), and that many of the trials in the long voyage of the Argo represent further stages of the same process. In the analysis of the vision of Ezekiel and the deductions that followed therefrom, it was recognised that before the consummation is attained the lower Elements must be transmuted into Fire (or Gold), so that the voyage or other journey of the hero should include a battle with each of the three grosser elements, Earth, Water, and Air.

Jason is in perpetual trouble with Water, though the *dual* nature of that Mother is only revealed in Scylla and Charybdis, excellent illustrations of the opposites between which the " way of the cross " must steer. Earth, as two great rocks, the Symplegades, tries to crush him at the entrance to the Black Sea, but by following a *dove* he escapes, and the conquered element thereafter remains immobile, instead of being actively engaged in the destruction of all such voyagers. The Air remains, however, and only yields to him through the conquest of her birds of evil which are *half women* ; the Harpies, whose characteristic is filth. Thus with Earth, Water, and Air conquered . . . and thereby lending him their peculiar powers, Jason approaches the end of his journey.

As might be expected, there await him in the country of the Fleece (Colchis), fire, a serpent, and love. Admittedly the final act in the drama might have been worked out in half a dozen different ways in which none of the traditional incidents took any part. There is an extraordinary flexibility in such symbolism and the interpreter is continually in danger of making " something out of nothing." On the other hand it is strange how frequently quite a straightforward tale which should apparently be firmly set upon a " true " symbolic basis refuses to yield any connected results at all. Not so in this case.

To cross the mystical threshold of Eden the hero must be identified with fire, and in the Jason story this is accomplished most ingeniously by the incident of Vulcan's Bulls. Now Vulcan was a god of *fire* and *gold*. He made equally Cupid's darts and Jove's thunderbolts, and his fiery nature was reflected in these bulls whose incandescent breath no mortal could withstand.

Jason therefore had to become immortal, and this was achieved by the *love* of Medea. Thus, not only were the bulls successfully dominated, but the rest of the quest was most happily facilitated. It will be remembered that having dominated the bulls, Jason yoked them to a plough and sowed into the prepared ground the famous dragon's teeth from which arose a crop of armed giants. The giants, however, when confronted with Jason, became so bewildered that they fell upon one another and conveniently ceased to exist as rapidly as they had sprung up. The conventional tale describes how Jason threw dust in their eyes, and, being thus blinded, they fell upon each other. That a host of armed men, even being possessed of as little intelligence as the classical giant, should suddenly turn on each other because momentarily confused by dust is rather a "tall story"; and while "tall stories" are quite at home among myths, even there common sense must be admitted. And it seems to me that common sense can suggest a better reason for the chaos of the host.

Now the only other sower of dragon's teeth was Cadmus, whose city was the same as that of Jason and Œdipus, the immortal Thebes.[1] And, what is more, Cadmus was himself a Consummator. The significant part of his myth refers to a conflict with a dragon from whom he extracted the teeth and sowed them; with the same result that attended Jason's seeding, except that five of the giants remained alive to be his servants. These five giants (possibly the five senses), helped their master to found the city of Cadmea, afterwards Thebes. As King, law-giver, and craftsman, Cadmus bears the essential symbols of the Hero, but it is after his death that the really interesting links are forged. For Cadmus was worshipped *as a serpent*, and in this respect seems to have been identified with the healing serpent of Æsculapius.[2]

We have already met this symbol in the healing serpent of Moses, otherwise the fire-serpent. Further, the analysis of Genesis showed how the serpent of the Fall is transformed into the Ascending Son, the Christ, that "radiant and perfect serpent"; and it has been shown that the process of sublimation goes through the same sequence. The serpent of desire (water) is sublimated into the serpent of love . . . the fire-serpent;

[1] Thebes in Boetia.
[2] See OLDFIELD HOWEY : *The Encircled Serpent*.

—and this is what had been going on ever since the Argo
set sail.  By the time Jason is confronted with the giants
he has already become *identified with the fire-serpent*.

The next consideration is a purely psychological one.
Where a desire is repressed it is recognised that other
desires come into being, the libidinous energy making
use of any convenient channel which presents itself.
Repression, in fact, leads to disaster, for the more desires
(serpents) are repressed, the faster they breed.  The only
remedy is sublimation, or *controlled* transference.

The mythological way of expressing this is found in
very many dragon stories where, as soon as a head of the
monster is cut off, one or more new heads arise in its
place.  This happened to Hercules in his conflict with a
seven-headed water-serpent, the Hydra, as we shall see
in the next chapter.  To apply the principle to Jason is
easy enough.  Had he not already sublimated his lower
nature, he would have become an easy prey for the
multiplication of the Destroyer, but being of the nature
of fire (twice-born) the serpents of death are powerless
against him.

Nevertheless, we have still not explained how it was
that these serpents or giants (the classical giants are
represented with serpent legs) attacked one another on
confronting Jason.  Well, the hero was of the nature of
fire . . . he may have dazzled them by his brightness.
This idea is put forward as a piece of plausible guesswork based on an interesting parallel, though it should
not be forgotten that our chief concern is not so much
with *how* the event occurred as *why* it is significant.

The parallel is that myth of Horus, the Egyptian
Consummator (q.v.), which recounts how the armies of
the evil gathered to do battle with Ra, representing the
forces of good, or more accurately, those of Light against

Darkness. Now Ra was the Father, Horus the Son, and in the inevitable sequence of the Christ-symbols, the latter acquires the power of his Father, who is represented as the Sun. Horus, in fine, takes upon him the attributes of the Father through the power of the Word (Thoth), and becomes transformed into the disc of the sun.

" And Horus of Behut-t flew up into the horizon in the form of a great Winged Sun-Disc, for which reason he is called Great Lord, Lord of Heaven, to this day. And when he saw the enemies (of Ra his father) in the heights of heaven he set out to chase them. . . . And he attacked with such terrific force those who opposed him that they could neither see with their eyes nor hear with their ears. Each one killed his neighbour in a moment of time, and there was not a single head who was left alive."[1]

(BUDGE : *From Fetish to God in Ancient Egypt*, p. 468.)

This makes it quite a reasonable assumption that Jason equally *dazzled* his enemies, being of the nature of the Sun since he was " born of fire." But the myth of Horus does not account for the *why*. In which respect I would suggest that it has been almost the main theme of the argument that the *ascent* is accomplished by a progressive *integration*. As the hero rises, the lower dualities resolve into unity, and in practice (on the physical level), it must be evident that the aspects or manifestations of the Destroyer are infinite in number. But to the Consummator this vast number of enemies decreases as he ascends, until all the evil forces appear to " cancel out " into that which is neither good nor evil, but

[1] " The hieroglyphic text of this legend and the reliefs which illustrate various portions of the narrative are cut on the walls of the temple of Horus of Edfu in Upper Egypt."

*unity.*[1] Herein lies the most reasonable interpretation of the dragon's teeth, for Jason was *the personification of the integrating force.*

Obviously little remained to be done after the victory of Jason over the Bulls, so that when he came to the grove of the Fleece the "sleepless" Serpent which guarded the treasure was in fact asleep. Whether this sleep was merely the recognition of Jason's immortality and invulnerability or whether it was due to Medea's magic is not a point which need detain us. For Jason could not then have been defeated by any material power, already he had passed the Cherubim and the Sword, and the Tree of Life stood before him as his just reward. And this mention of the Eden myth indicates another interesting excursion, for without the recognition of the Tree of the Fleece and the Tree of Life as one and the same, the myth which accounts for the presence of the Fleece at that remote place remains more or less incomprehensible. Briefly, the tale is this.

A man and a woman, Phrixus and Helle, are driven out of their home by Mother Ino. To save the pair Zeus sends the winged Ram with the Golden Fleece. But Helle is drowned before their destination is reached,[2] and so conveniently frees Phrixus for marriage with Chaliope, a princess. The Ram is sacrificed in honour of Zeus, the "aider of the flight" (Zeus Phyxios), and hung upon an oak tree in the grove of Ares.

Without too much attention to detail, let us hazard an interpretation to link up with Jason on the one hand

---

[1] In the Cadmus myths there were five giants left, but five is the number traditionally associated with integration, being the totality of dual Father (sun) and dual Mother (moon) in the face of Heaven (unity).

[2] Hence the "Hellespont."

and Adam on the other, both, as we have seen, representing with varying success the figure of the Christ.

Adam and Eve quit Eden as Phrixus and Helle leave home; the former are driven out by the Serpent, the latter by a Mother. After leaving Eden the next important piece of symbolism is concerned with the Deluge, by which " material " humanity were drowned while the spiritually-minded were saved in the Ark. Phrixus is faithful to the divine messenger, Helle is not, and Helle is drowned. Phrixus is rewarded with the usual marriage symbol, and no doubt becomes " twice-born " through the sacrifice of the Ram, as the devotee of Mithra became re-born by the sacrifice of the Bull, and Noah by re-emergence from the Mother Ark. In fact Phrixus runs his course as a Consummator at least in the bare essentials, having attained immortality with his Princess. The Ram was hung upon an oak, that mystical tree, which in Druidic rites was treated as a cross by the simple process of stripping the side branches all except two. The oak, indeed, is still so generally regarded as a " magic " tree that the unconscious association with sacrifice almost " goes without saying." One need only mention the thirteen volumes of *The Golden Bough* !

" The hanging of the sacrifice on the tree is a generally widespread custom, Germanic examples being particularly abundant. The ritual consists of the sacrifice being pierced by a spear. Thus it is said of Odin (Edda Havamal) :

" ' I know that I hung on the windswept tree
    Nine nights through,
  Wounded by a spear, dedicated to Odin
  I myself to myself.' "

(*Psychology of the Unconscious*.)

And so it was not only the Fleece that hung upon the Oak of Ares, but Phrixus, the mortal Phrixus sacrificed

to the immortal Phrixus who was then " born."   Here
the two serpents come in again, for the physical body of
man is his serpent, his lower nature (with special reference
to potency);   but the re-born, mystical body, is the
fire-serpent.

" As Moses lifted up the serpent in the wilderness, even so
must the Son of Man be lifted up."
(John iii, 14.)

Just one more point.  It has been frequently implied
that the two trees of Eden are in reality one . . . the
Tree of Life, of which one aspect is physical, the other
mystical.  It is thus understandable that many mythological heroes are born from or in close association with
a tree, as well as dying under the same sign.  They are all
" twice-born," and the sign of their dual mother is the
Tree, especially the tree as a *cross*, in which form the idea
of duality is emphasised.  It is the Tree at all events
which leads men from the cradle to the grave, and it can
hardly be doubted that this is the fundamental significance of the term the " way of the cross," which thus
becomes the way between the trees, between the
opposites, the incarnate road of the knowledge of good
and evil.

Then Jason's journey is his incarnate life ; the journey
represented as a voyage . . . a common metaphor.
What is uncommon is this, that the Argo is furnished
with a magic figurehead of *Oak*, which, being gifted with
speech, effectively leads Jason along the right path.

Thinking now of the phonetic link Ark/Argo, both
of which presumably come from the same root as that
Ark of the Covenant which was the focus of the " magic
force," we can see how closely the mystical language is
interwoven.  I am not suggesting that the sole signifi-

cance of Noah and his Ark is the incarnate journey of the individual at the end of which he is re-born, but I am suggesting that *one* of the meanings which can be read into the Deluge myth is not with reference to generalities, but to the Individual. In other words the Deluge, like Genesis, has a meaning on more than one level, possibly on all three. In fact almost any myth may have *four* separate and distinct meanings. . . . It may describe what actually happened, or the symbolic presentation of such a happening, *and* what the symbolic significance of these events is *in terms of the individual*, as well as *in terms of the evolution of humanity*. Naturally it is not many myths which include all four, but nevertheless the four can exist, and, when the Hero is personified on all four, we have, of course, the Triple Christ as a traditional or even historical person.

Perhaps my methods may be criticised on the ground that from these analyses much is omitted which will not fit in with my scheme . . . in other words, I am guilty, at least negatively, of twisting the evidence to suit the proof required. For this reason I want to state my position with the utmost clarity. It is true that when establishing the significance of a narrative I ignore a great deal, partly because that which is left out may be significant but not essential, and partly because it is definitely *out of harmony*. In fact I am looking for *harmony*, and am therefore entitled to isolate those factors which agree together according to certain principles. To take a specific instance, Jason is said to meet his death in a singular manner, which I cannot fit in with the essentials of a Consummator myth. It is related that he was sitting one day beside the rotting hulk of the Argo, when a beam fell from above and killed him. Now it may be that the incident has a symbolic value, but it certainly does not

have a place in the basic harmony of the myth. Therefore the incident is omitted in the foregoing analysis.

We are rather apt to imagine all things as neatly
divided into classes, the true and the false. But, as
psychology very soon discovered, that which is true in
consciousness is not necessarily true in the " unconscious " and vice versa. We have to move in a realm
where an idea may be both true and false at the same time.
The myth of Jason is not (historically) true. . . . Yet
the myth of Jason is true. Truth depends not so much
upon the data as the perception ; *it is an attribute of
nothing except consciousness*, which is the implication of
that traditional reply to Pilate's question : " It is neither
in heaven nor in earth, nor in the waters under the
earth." As form and colour are alike imperceptible to
a blind man, so are truth and beauty to an Observer
whose consciousness is unable to respond to truth and
beauty. But the verities are revealed in proportion with
the extension of consciousness.

Our duty is to find the meaning of symbols as nearly
as possible in terms of consciousness. It will be recalled,
for instance, that we began this enquiry into myth by
making an arbitrary distinction between two different
types, first those " extroverted " tales, such as this one of
the Golden Fleece, which are concerned primarily with
incidents, battles, and so on (especially the treasure or
prize), and, second, those whose interest centres on the
quest itself. Typical of the last is the legend of the
Holy Grail where the mystical significance of the story
is not concealed but insisted upon. Nevertheless,
symbols cannot be dispensed with, and the story still
requires interpretation. Finally, in frankly religious
teaching, such as that contained in the traditional speech
of Jesus of Nazareth, the spiritual significance is insisted

upon almost to exclusion of the physical . . . the "incidents" are entirely subordinate to the doctrine. But all of them, from Adam to Jason, and Jason to Galahad and Jesus ; all are founded on the same theme of the quest for the mystic union, which is *liberated consciousness*, including immortality. We said earlier that the Triple Christ's ultimate significance is evolving consciousness. Now the essential symbolism of mythology (using the word in a very broad sense) is seen to centre on the same idea. By the time we have finally defined in the next chapter the more important symbols of the Consummator, we shall be in a position to attempt to deal with this evolution on its own ground.

"I am the way, the truth, and the life : no man cometh to the Father but by me."

(John xvi, 6.)

---

## NOTE

*The Ram of Abraham.*

I would suggest that the Ram of the Golden Fleece is essentially that which was sacrificed in place of Jacob. Both were the especial animals of the Creator and both were sacrificed, being comparable in this respect to the *body* of the Hero. (Cf. the Pig of Set.) But particularly the Ram is the embodiment of virility, and as such will become apparent later on as the "beginning of the ways of God," the grossest embodiment of the sex-force, *from which the ascent begins*. (Cf. Behemoth and the Lamb.) Here, then, is another sense of *sacrifice*, not in terms of persons but of forces, the beast standing (*a*) for the *body*, and (*b*) for the *force* (blood), which is sublimated into the "love" that confers immortality. In this connection it is interesting to note the legend of the Ram of Abraham, which, it is said, was created before sunset on the sixth day. . . . In other words, it was the last form to be made, the end of the *fall*. Moreover, it dwelt in Eden under the Tree of

Life and had drunk the waters of the River of Life which we shall find to be the "river" of love. (Chapter X.) In the Jewish tradition the beast is predestined to be sacrificed by Abraham, who is, of course, a Hero, and the circle is thereby completed in relation to the Ram of Phryxus; for both are the embodiment of the magic force of immortality. But the ram which is slain by Abraham is that " which was slain from the foundation of the world," the gross expression of love, which, by the *sacrifice of blood*, is transmuted from the animal into the divine, from the Ram into the Lamb (asexual).[1] There are, in fact, two Rams just as there are two Trees, one of mortality and one of immortality, but both of *love ;* and both for that reason are symbols of the Consummator.

It is recognised that some of these points must appear somewhat obscure at the present juncture, but they will become clear in due course. For the Jewish tradition see *Myth and Legend of Ancient Israel*, Rappoport, 3 vols.

---

[1] Psychology would here emphasise the " castration complex " which is closely bound up with the " inversion " already dealt with. The " Lamb " is the castrated Ram.

# CHAPTER SIX

## GOLDEN APPLES

THE best known of all myths of the magic apple, apart, of course, from the Eden story, is that of the classical hero Hercules, the very complexity of whose tradition testifies to his pre-eminence. This very human personality was, and still is, perhaps the most completely formed figure of all classical myth. Indeed, his very completeness, and the masses of unimportant trimmings which have been accreted round the core of his extraordinary career have done much to obscure the fundamentals upon which his fame really rests.

This man was a son of God by a human mother, and after a long life of hardship and even slavery, in which he followed of his own deliberate choice that hard path, the " way of the cross," he was " taken up to heaven " by his Father, to be worshipped thereafter throughout the classical world. In the examination of his myth we shall find abundant evidence that he was indeed worthy of the title of Consummator, which can already be recognised in the characters under which he was worshipped. He was the Saviour (Soter), and the Protector (Alexikakos). He was all his life a " man of sorrows " and the Wanderer, Hegemonios. He was the *source of inspiration* (Musagetes) and, above all, the Conqueror (Kallinikos). Such is the nature of the hero whose trials ended with the achievement of the Golden Apples of the Hesperides.

And who are the Hesperides ? I think that about the nearest equivalent in one word is " Cherubim," since these four Daughters of Night dwell on the threshold of Eden, at the place of the crucifixion, at the *end of the world*. In classical terms, their garden is set in the boundless river Oceanus near that ultimate place where Atlas stands supporting the vault of heaven. And the garden is in the extreme west, region of the setting sun, for Hesper is the star of the west, the evening star. In solar symbols the Sun is the Father and the Moon the Mother ; but the Star is the sign of their Son whose life is renewed out of death. So the evening star is the Christ star. And now the symbols become rather more complex, for if the Hesperides are themselves the Cherubim who guard the Tree of Life in the " land of the glorified," what is the rôle of the serpent Ladon, that hundred-headed monster who guards the tree ? Up to now we were at liberty to assume that having conquered the Sword and the Cherubim, the hero had no more to do than pluck the golden fruit. But Ladon need not detain us unduly, for, like the dragon which guarded the Fleece, he is easily overcome, and the only reasonable explanation for such a triumph is that the " crucifixion " of the earlier trials has conferred upon the hero the necessary powers, and the Serpent is no longer to be feared. . . . In other words Ladon only *summarises* the enemies of the hero. As to Ladon's identity, it has been established that the two Trees are really one, having a dual aspect, and it follows that there is but one guardian serpent which is that familiar reptile from Eden, whose dual aspects correspond with those of the Tree. The snake represents *love* and *hate*, or *love* and *desire ;* it is at once the power of

Christ and Antichrist, a conclusion to which we have been brought by various gradual stages.

For instance, the Serpent was seen to be the embodiment of the " fall," the disintegrating force. But the Christ is himself the " radiant and perfect serpent," the integrating force. The extraordinary importance of the symbol hinges upon this fact, and it is for this reason that the dual rôle seems at first sight so confusing. We have seen, moreover, that all forces in their totality are resolved into *love* (though the word has little connection with the " love " of ordinary speech). But to every power without exception there is an opposite, while consciousness (including *will*) holds the balance between them. Thus the integrating power is opposed by a complementary disintegrator, personified quite naturally as Antichrist, in whom is summed up the activity of the Destroyer in all its phases.

As Christ is " triple " . . . at once a universal power, a psychological energy and an Individual, so is Antichrist. Moreover, their powers are equal. If it were not so there would be no balance in the unchanging Unity. For the individual that state of balance is only arrived at through the long processes of evolution, so that in practice he is seldom " balanced," having to a greater or less extent failed to become " free of the opposites " ; or in Christian terms, having failed to " overcome the world." (There is an implicit inconsistency in the above statements which will be resolved just a little later on : great accuracy is hardly required at the moment.) Though Christ and Antichrist represent equal and opposite forces, the former is eternal while the latter is temporal. Antichrist is the power of Matter, and, in the Unity, Matter ceases to exist as such. Nor should it be imagined that Antichrist is herself evil, for no power or " thing " can be evil in itself. The ethical question, as we have said before in regard to Truth, only arises *in relation to consciousness*. Antichrist only appears evil to an Observer who is unable to recognise the material forces from the viewpoint of the Father . . . which is of little *practical* importance, for obvious reasons. But it is of some practical interest to know that neither in the recognition nor in the worship of such forces is there anything essentially evil, *if* they are regarded " in the knowledge of the Father," for Father and Mother are One. Yet in practice they are not assessed in terms of Spirit, but on their own level ; and so they have inevitably provided a historical trail of slime . . . the records of degraded nature-cults, sorcery, and Satanism.

But such generalisations are somewhat vague, and to clear them up we must enlist the aid of more symbols, chief of which is the famous " Apple of Discord " which Paris gave to Venus. This, too, was a *golden* apple, so that it is connected *a priori* with the Hesperides myth ; but in opposition to it, as will become apparent. At first sight Paris seems himself to be a true Consummator, for his mother dreamed of him as a *fire-brand*, and he was called the Protector and the Shepherd ; but his myth indicates that he was not strong enough for the " way of the cross," and his weakness was exploited by the power of the Apple. In effect, the famous " Judgment of Paris " directed his aspiration . . . if one may term it that, not to spiritual power and wisdom, but to carnal love. Athene and Juno were both passed over as less desirable than " possession of the fairest," with which bribe Venus persuaded him to award her the prize. In fine, the love of Paris was not spiritual ; it was not really love at all, but *desire*, and his story is therefore a story of *failure*, judged from the standpoint of the mystic consummation. In particular it was a failure to *sublimate desire*, and as such provides a close parallel with the " fall " of Adam.

Tradition says that the apple was golden, but evidently the adjective should be " gilded," for desire and love often seem the same. It is by their effects, however, that they are known. The apple of pure gold, the prize of the Hesperides, is the symbol of the Christ, but the apple of desire does not grow upon the Tree of Immortality, but upon that other Tree which brings only the *knowledge* that comes with incarnate life through the strife of the " way of the cross," the " knowledge of good and evil."

Such consequences are as clearly described in the myth of Paris as they are in Genesis. For Paris, though indeed he does come to possess the fairest of all women, Helen of Troy, is led through deceit, bloodshed, and dishonour. His old love Œnone, the only person who could have saved his life, refused to go near him ; even his corpse was dishonoured (by Menelaus). And he was killed by Hercules, who is himself the true Consummator, and whose enemies must therefore be the " children of desire," the powers of darkness. But we have only gone into this story to point out that the Apple when put to proper use is the passport of immortality. Paris did not put it to proper use. Like Adam, he " fell," and the Apple was to him the symbol of the Serpent of Eden, the sensual desires in their familiar psychological sense (will to power and possession, chiefly of sensual satisfaction). For this reason the Apple must be associated with Antichrist, whose natural territory is just that which we have recognised above . . . sex and its derivatives, especially money. So interest shifts from the " Judgment of Paris " to the origin of the Apple.

The fruit was put down on the table at a *wedding feast* by the sour-faced Eris, who hoped in this way to spread discord in place of harmony ; ostensibly because she had not been invited to the celebrations, actually because it was her nature to make strife.   Her classical description is as follows . . . " sister and companion of Ares, and like him insatiate of blood ; in Hesiod she is daughter of Night and mother of trouble, oblivion, hunger, pain, murder and carnage, brawls, deceit and lawlessness." This means, if it means anything at all, that Eris is the embodiment of the Destroyer, otherwise Antichrist.   It should be specially noted that she is a daughter of Night, and as such might well correspond to the totality of the Cherubim, as Ladon in the Hesperides myth corresponds to much the same principle . . . by summarising the enemies of the Hero.   So the Apple of Eris was of the Serpent for all its golden sheen, not the snake of Fire but of Water, not ICTHUS but the Hydra.

Now Christ is the Son of the Sun, and so, by the same token, is Antichrist Daughter of the Moon.   Such are the primary links from which more detailed relationships can readily be deduced.   The powers of the Sun are Light and Heat, while the Moon presides over Darkness and Cold (cf. Nastrond.)   The Son wields the power of his Father as the " Light of the World," while the Daughter is invested with the powers of Darkness.   Again, the Son is born of a virgin, and the daughter is born of a harlot, though both derive ultimately from the same Father/Mother.   There are, in fact, three " generations " corresponding to the three *levels :* The FATHER/MOTHER represents the great-grandparents, the Dual Father and Dual Mother furnish the grandparents, and the gross (material) aspects of these together provide

Antichrist with parents, who are, of course, personified as humans, just as there are human patents for the Christ.

So much for the main requirements, which are quite detailed enough to make identification easy if we can find a suitable person. But how are we to find such a one ? Well, in the first place it is obvious that " white " religion will not be of much help ; we must go, if not to Satanism as such, at least into the border-land of paganism. And the best place to start our enquiry in such an environment is obviously with the Moon herself the Great Mother of antiquity as of the present day, who is the *dual* Queen of Heaven. On one " side " she is the Virgin, on the other the Harlot. . . . Indeed, she was referred to in ancient Asia Minor as the " virgin harlot," a paradox which effectively united her dual aspects. The " white " Virgin is, of course, the immaculate Mother of the Christ, while her " black " counterpart is the harlot Mother of the Antichrist, the Destroyer, the Huntress who kills her lovers.

With this information we can arrange the parentage of Christ and Antichrist in abstract symbols :

### FATHER/MOTHER

| Dual Father | Dual Mother |
|---|---|
| Father/Creating Mother | Father/Destroying Mother |
| CHRIST | ANTICHRIST |

As in some example of Mendel's law of inheritance, from the union of a " white " and a " black " is produced in three generations an " all white " strain and an " all black " strain. In other words, the parents of Christ are both " white," while the parents of Antichrist are both " black." This is easy enough in the case of the Mothers, whom we distinguished very early in the enquiry as corresponding to " black " and " white," but it is not so easy in the case of the Fathers whom we have not so far separated in the same terms. Yet it must be evident that in fact there is a "destroying Father" and a " creating Father " in the same way that these forms are appropriate to the Mothers. The Spirit *descends* and *ascends*, and clearly the former is a disintegrating process, while the *ascent* is integrative and therefore " creative " ; since that which is new, whether a new individual or a new stage or degree of self-consciousness comes about only by a process of integration.

Perhaps this will appear more evident in symbolic terms. The Sun's Heat can be both creative (germination, etc.) and destructive, just as the Moon's darkness can be either that of the grave or the womb. And, of course, the personification of the Destroying Father is very well known under the form of Satan, or, better, Lucifer. For this is the Disintegrator *par excellence*, whose " fall " is never ending, a *descent* which continues to extinction. Hence that widespread myth of the " fallen angel."

" I beheld Satan as lightning fall from heaven."

(Luke x, 18.)

But the story is more plainly told in classical terms. Phaethon drove the chariot of the Sun (his Father) in such a way that he burnt up part of the earth by coming too close, and froze other parts when he wandered off into space. For this destruction, whether wilful or accidental, Jupiter-Apollo hurled him down with a *thunderbolt* (cf. " lightning " *supra*). With this information we can complete the personification of the family-tree in respect of Antichrist.

FATHER/MOTHER

Light (Jupiter)//Darkness (Latona)
Dual Father      Dual Mother
Destroying Father   ///Destroying Mother
Phæton           Queen of Hell and Sorcery
Lucifer          Diana, Istar, Hecate
(" the light-bringer ")
Satan

ANTICHRIST

Eris

Aradia

Here, then, is the personified Antichrist, as Eris, whom we know something about, and Aradia, the only *complete personification* which I have been able to trace ; one who occupies the same position in the " old religion " as Jesus of Nazareth occupies in Christianity. Until the end of the last century it seems that both lived side by side in Italy, and probably elsewhere under differing names. It would be strange if both were not alive to-day. But the Aradia of Italy is of peculiar interest to us, because the system of which she was " headstone of the corner " was directly connected with the classical divinities, especially Diana. So there is a direct link between her and the myths with which we have been dealing, and we are thus able to use throughout the same set of names, a convenience which makes all the difference . . . or so it is to be hoped, between simplicity and obscurity.

" Aradia ! my Aradia !
  Thou who art daughter unto him who was
  Most evil of all spirits, who of old
  Once reigned in hell when driven away from heaven,
  Who by his sister did thy sire become . . .

And when the priests or the nobility
Shall say to you that you should put your faith
In Father, Son and Mary, then reply :
' Your God, the Father, and Maria are
Three devils. . . .
For the true God the Father is not yours. . . .'

And when a priest shall do you injury
By his benedictions, ye shall do to him
Double the harm, and do it in the name
Of me, *Diana*, Queen of witches all ! "

The above extracts, which must surely be self-explanatory, are taken from C. G. Leland's *Aradia, or the Gospel of the Witches* (London, 18..). This remarkable work is based upon a manuscript which Leland received, after years of patient enquiry, from an authentic peasant practitioner of " *la vecchia religione.*" It does not appear whether or not there exists a complete " scripture" analogous to that of Christianity, though certainly some part of the great mass of traditional lore had found its way into pen and ink if not actually into print. But the point is a minor one, for us interest centres in the fact that through Leland's research we are able to compare the essential " black " symbols with those " white " ones with which we are already familiar. Not that the " old religion " is one of Satanism *primarily ;* its very antiquity makes us assume that both " white " and " black " are represented, though in the long struggle against Christianity it was natural that the " black " should more and more predominate in opposition to the Church.

" Even yet there are old people in Romagna of the North who know the Etruscan names of the Twelve Gods, and invocations to Bacchus, Jupiter, and Venus, Mercury, and the Lares or ancestral spirits."

(Op. cit., vii.)

Such religion can hardly have been witchcraft as the word is understood to-day, especially if some fragments of the fundamental significance of Bacchus and Jupiter had lingered. But the coming of the Church must have left the " old religion " with only witchcraft to call upon, since allegiance hitherto owned to Bacchus and his father Zeus, had been claimed . . . and enforced, in the new religion of Jesus and His Father. Thus, by the end of the nineteenth century it was natural to find the " black " predominating even to such an extent as to be synonymous with the " old religion " itself.

"I may say that witchcraft is known to its votaries as *la vecchia religione*, or the old religion, of which Diana is the Goddess, her daughter *Aradia* (or Herodias) the female Messiah, and that this little work sets forth how the latter was born, came down to earth, established witches and witchcraft, and then returned to heaven." (Op. cit., viii.)

It is interesting to note that Antichrist is here represented as returning to heaven, which involves modification of the conventional view of heaven as " the place of the good." Aradia was certainly not " good." But if, on the other hand, " heaven " in this context refers first to the mystic as opposed to the physical *level* and finally to the ultimate Unity, then there is no difficulty. After all, each of the three Terms must be present on all levels, together with the derived forces. Supposing for the sake of argument that Aradia became the incarnation of *desire* just as Jesus became the incarnation of *love ;* it must not be forgotten that, whatever the personal effect of their lives, in each case the power is equally abstract. During their incarnate life the appropriate force would act through their *personality* (the miracles of Christ are paralleled by the miracles of Diana), but this power is derived from the universal forces which have already been recognised, so that the power of Aradia is as alive to-day as ever, just as the power of Jesus is alive. But neither the one nor the other can operate upon the physical level except through individuals "tuned" to transmit it. At which point we should leave this slight digression which tends to raise a whole crop of new problems as yet hardly within the scope of the argument.

" Aradia is evidently enough *Herodias*, who was regarded in the beginning as associated with Diana as chief of the witches. This was not, as I opine, derived from the Herodias of the New Testament, but from an earlier replica of Lilith bearing the same name."
(Op. cit., p. 102.)

Now Lilith was the demon wife of Adam . . . according to " Rabbinical literature " (*Encyc. Brit.*) and is connected with the Lilit of Asia Minor. (Cf. Tanit the Moon Goddess.) In fact we find Aradia to be typical of those Moon-goddesses whose attributes were predominantly destructive, that is to say, who represented the Destroying Mother which is the *dark side of the Moon*. We have seen that Diana, personification-in-chief of the Moon, is the mother of Aradia, and the " Queen of witches all." Now in Egypt the goddess Bubastis or Bast, who was identified with Mut, the Great Mother, headed at one time a very flourishing cult of *cats*. Indeed, the city of Bubastis seems to have been famous as much for cat-cemeteries as for its civic amenities. . . . " All cats that die are carried to certain sacred houses, where, being first embalmed, they are buried in the city of Bubastis " (Herodotus).

Now the symbolism both of Bast and the cat is complex and I have no wish to examine it in detail; but this one point, that the cat is very closely associated with the Destroyer, even as far back as the cult of Bast, is of peculiar interest. For Aradia's conception came about through a cat. It is related in the " Gospel of the Witches " how Diana became desirous of her brother Lucifer, but the latter apparently still kept certain principles. He refused to have anything to do with her. Diana, however, being aware that there was a pet cat which slept in his room, took upon herself the form of the animal, and so found the object of her desire. For in the darkness of the night she again took her own form, overcame Lucifer by blandishments, and conceived Aradia. And from that distant time, even to the present day, the cat has been recognised as the typical companion of witches. It is easy to see how the association has developed from the immemorial cult of the Mother generally, and perhaps from that of Bast in particular. For though Bast was identified with the Sun, which is quite inconsistent with her rôle as Mother, there is so much which confirms her position in the " equation " that there can be no doubt of her true significance. Bast included the attributes of Mut, consort of Amen, and Sekmet, the fierce crocodile goddess. Now Mut, or, better, Isis, clearly stands for the Virgin, Sekmet for the Harlot; to use a distinction already drawn between the two. And it is therefore confirmatory to find that the latter is regarded as " the female counterpart of Min," the " shameless." Moreover, Sekmet had a lioness-head as well as the more usual crocodile, thus linking her with the Sphinx of Œdipus (q.v.).

Regarded from a different angle, the witch is identified with Aradia as the Christian is identified with Jesus. In a sense, therefore, the witch *is* Antichrist, just as the Christian is a " member " of Christ. This identification extends naturally to such attributes as the cat on one side and the lamb on the other. Now the Cat, and especially the cat of Diana, was associated with the Moon. Thus the " Gospel of the Witches " preserves a strange account of the making of the stars :

" Diana went into the street ; she took the bladder of an ox and a piece of witch-money which has an edge like a knife . . . and she cut the earth, and with it and many mice she filled the bladder, and blew into the bladder till it burst.

" And there came a great marvel, for the earth which was in the bladder became the round heaven above, and for three days there was a great rain. And having made the heaven and the stars and the rain, Diana became Queen of the witches ; she was the cat (moon) that ruled the star-mice, the heaven, and the rain."

(Op. cit., p. 20.)

But the cat must be regarded as a side-issue ; obviously the centre of interest resides in the fact that the union which produced the Antichrist is represented as *incestuous*. Early in the enquiry we intimated how that this was the symbol of the highest of all unions, that of the divine Son with Father/Mother ; now it appears equally as an expression of the grossest of all intercourse. This can lead to only one conclusion. Just as *love* has ceased to have the meaning of " affection " as in ordinary speech, and appears instead as a sovereign abstract power, permeating the universe both visible and invisible, so also does *incest* take its place as the *perfect expression of union*, i.e. love. For love brings about the integration of the opposites, and obviously the most absolute integration is symbolised as incest. So we have to agree with the psychologists that it is upon the Œdipus myth that the mysteries of the mind depend, as though from a central seat of power. But we have to go further than the psychologists since we are dealing not with one *level* but with three. Incest is the clue to symbolic relationships at all levels, and Œdipus stands forth as a vital clue towards the understanding of the Triple Christ.

In fact, having established the nature of the " indeterminable and variable ' x ' " . . . at least sufficiently for the present purpose, we have now learned to recognise the symbols of the *action* of this energy. The symbols are those of *family relationship*. Integrating energy is the sovereign power, and " love " its symbolic expression. The absence of love means the presence of its opposite . . . desire or hate—Aradia. In fact, whether for Jesus of Nazareth or for Aradia, the mysteries are equally concerned with love, and the method of their expression is family relationship.

*Relationship between the Terms and their derivatives at all levels is represented in family relationships of love and hate, of which the most perfect (intimate) is incest.*

" Think not that I am come to send peace on earth : I am not come to send peace but a sword. For I come to set a man at variance against his father, and the daughter against her mother, and the daughter in law against her mother in law. *And a man's foes shall be they of his own household.*"

(Matt. x, 34 ff.)

" If any man come to me, and hate not his father and mother, and wife and children, and brethren and sisters, yea and his own life also, he cannot be my disciple."

(Luke xiv, 26.)

Without wishing to begin an analysis of either of these quotations, I would draw attention to the fact that both are primarily concerned with the *mystic level*. Physical love and mystical love are opposites, for one derives from desire (Aradia), the other from Spirit (Jesus) ;

therefore physical love can seem as hate from a spiritual standpoint. Yet a man may love the members of his family spiritually; that, however, is a state of affairs not implicit in the quotation. Before it can happen all the *false* affection, which is really *desire*, must be sublimated. (Cf. Chapter XI.)

We now have to apply this *key of the family* to the field of myth, which appears as little more than the expression of such relationships in an infinity of differing ways. . . . Between gods and men, and men and women, kings and commoners, beasts and humans, brothers and sisters, and mothers and sons. And this fact suggests a possible explanation for the psychological importance of myths, religions, and arts which make use of such symbols; and which do not?

The psychologist would readily concede that the resolution of " unconscious " conflicts would be assisted by their projection into art. The very process of exteriorisation is beneficial, and so is the complementary process. I mean that not only the originator of a work of art, but all who experience it, receive at need an " unconscious " benefit; hence the tremendous power of the great myths and the universality of symbolical religion, a term which may even be held to include all theology using the concept of a divine Family, whether directly or indirectly.

Perhaps the most thorough example of family relationship run riot in myth is to be found in the classical pantheons, where there was indeed so much promiscuity that many of the relationships have to be given up as hopelessly entangled. Yet, as we have already seen in connection with the Fleece, certain basic relationships remain true to the requirements of the equations. There is thus a classical family headed by Zeus and Juno, dual Father and Mother, whose various derivatives include the Saviour Son and the Destroyer. The Egyptian system is almost equally complex, but perhaps not quite so obscure as that of Greece and Rome. In fact we shall endeavour to make quite an elaborate reconstruction of the essential Egyptian symbols when considering the Solar allegory. This reconstruction will be found to concern itself largely with the family strife of Horus and Set, Horus and Isis. (Cf. Ormaz and Ahriman in the Zoroastrian faith.) It will be remembered that the sign of Horus is the Winged Disc of the Rising Sun . . . and that his birth was miraculous. He waged perpetual warfare with his uncle Set, whose connection with the Serpent comes by way of the Greek Typhon, son of Gaea (Earth) and father of the Hydra and the dog Orthos, both slain by Hercules.

Now Set was symbolised as the Pig, especially the Black Pig; and swine in general were for that reason regarded as most thoroughly unclean. In fact it was the business of a special class of " untouchable " to look after them. The pig has, of course, been quite generally regarded as " unclean," especially as representing the animal nature of man, in which respect its name is used even to-day as a term of abuse. In this connection a triple bronze head in the Victoria and Albert Museum (No. 321 West Central Court) is of particular interest, for it presents three faces, a Pig, a Woman, and a God, respectively; and these, of course, correspond with the three *levels* which we have already seen to be represented in the individual as body, soul, and spirit. The Pig, in fact, stands for the body, especially (boar) for virility, and as such was a fit emblem of the Evil One whose chief business is sex. Thus Set is Antichrist, and it follows, even if it were not already patent, that Horus is Christ. But there was a strange Egyptian custom which is at first sight rather puzzling on this understanding. For on one day of the year, about the time of the spring equinox, the detested Pig was elevated to an honourable place and was actually worshipped. Now the equinox is the time of the solar " crucifixion " and the date at which the death and resurrection of all the Corn Spirits, Vegetation Gods, and so on, are celebrated. Again, some of these Consummators were killed by a pig (boar) (e.g. Attis and Diamid). It is therefore more than surprising to find the Antichrist, the power which is responsible for the death of his divine opposite, elevated to public worship at the very time when the death of the God is being lamented. It seems to me that in *physical* terms the problem is insoluble, but the moment it is regarded from a mystic standpoint, we see light. The Consummator is certainly killed by Set (katabolism), but it has been abundantly demonstrated that such death is the very gate of immortality, a *necessary* prologue to the resurrection or " re-birth." So it appears that the Pig and the battle *which he inspires* is the " way of the cross," the *means* of the ultimate triumph of the liberated spirit. Without the " knowledge of good and evil," that is to say without Set (for the opposites are inconceivable apart from one another) there would be no " way " and no immortality. Therefore the Pig comes into his own as representing the *body of the Hero* (cf. *The Bread of the Eucharist*, q.v.), and as such he is honoured as well as dishonoured. The " family strife " of Christ and Antichrist are in the same sense both good *and* evil, or is it easier to say " *beyond* good and evil " ? For we have shown that love alone is the sovereign power and all others can be resolved into it or into its negative (desire/hate), into the power of Light or the power of

Darkness. Thus Nietzsche's dictum becomes understandable when he says :

" What is done out of love always takes place beyond good and evil."

Let us put this boldly into our own terms. . . . Consciousness can only expand through conflict . . . " family " conflict. By means of this conflict the individual acquires the knowledge of good and evil, and this knowledge reveals the law of love. Here a further development occurs, for it becomes clear that the power of love is inseparable from an attitude of loving. . . . In other words, the power is an attribute of consciousness, part of the Observer. Thus *it is the Individual himself who calls into being the powers of Christ or Antichrist according as he loves one or desires the other*.

We are now able to state in clear terms the whole relationship of the individual to the opposites.

*Identification with the opposite causes consciousness to adopt a certain attitude, which in turn evokes a corresponding force.* So all the vast complexity of phenomena resolves, in so far as you or I are concerned, into a loving or a hating attitude. . . . Bearing in mind that hate is equivalent to desire,[1] the negation of love and not a separate force, just as cold is the absence of heat and not a separate force. Which reminds me that it is sometimes suggested in traditional mysticism, especially in Swedenborg's works, that *heat* is the cosmic symbol of *love*. There is a great deal of parallel evidence to this effect, especially in the figures of speech which involve such phrases as

---

[1] The best way to recognise that hate is a form of the inclusive term " desire " is to recall how hate is *selfish* and therefore opposed to love which is essentially *unselfish*. Further hate is negative desire —instead of desiring the presence of " x," it is his absence.

" warm affection," " burning love," " warm-hearted," and even " warm welcome." If this is accepted, the analogy between the two, that is between *love* and *heat*, may be taken as accurate, thus opening up a new avenue of enquiry as to the real significance of the Cult of the Sun.

It seems to follow from the italicised statement above that a man's ruling affection will determine *all* subordinate affairs, even his environment on all *levels*, because the ruling force holds him to one particular object and all that appertains thereto. If he desires physical satisfaction *to the exclusion* of higher considerations . . . he desires Aradia and the power of Aradia is with him. If he loves only the Golden Apples of the Hesperides, then quite another power will respond and will arrange, if it is permitted to do so, all lesser things. And here we come to the threshold of another crop of mysteries, of Faith, and Grace and the like, with which we are not concerned since this book can go no further than the broadest basis of the law of love.

" Seek ye first the kingdom of God . . ."

" Thou shalt love the Lord thy God with all thy heart . . ."

" Where thy treasure is, there shall thy heart be also."

And all this arose from the mystical significance of the Pig ! But there is a more general significance wherein the Boar becomes the Guardian of the Tree, the Serpent Ladon. This is the Beast of Revelation (xiii) whose defeat must precede the " Marriage of the Lamb," Paradise Regained ; the beast which comes up out of the Sea, and which is numbered 666. In fine, it can hardly represent anything in the world at large other than the attitude which desires the material to the exclusion of the mystical. It is this *materialism* which has identified recent civilisation, not with integration but with disintegration; and the inevitable response has not been lacking. The Hero always stands for humanity, and so Paris played a part for all the family of nations, which have followed him along the same path of deceit, bloodshed, and dishonour for the sake of the Apple of Desire. Yet I have used the past tense, because the cycle of the Beast may be coming to an end.

Irishmen will remember that the last battle between the massed forces of good and evil takes place in the Valley of the Black Pig. From that fearful strife no mortal is left, and the horses welter in a sea of blood until the girths rot from their bellies for lack of a hand to undo them.

"And the winepress was trodden without the city, and blood came out of the winepress, even unto the horse bridles."

(Rev. xiv, 20.)

The blood of the Eucharist is *spirit*, and the blood of *winepress* and of *battle* is equally *spirit*, because mortality is changed to immortality; and so in truth there is no " mortal " left alive. But we are near to the limit of words in an intellectual sense; only the poet can take them on into the realms of intuition.

### THE VALLEY OF THE BLACK PIG

The dews drop slowly and dreams gather : unknown spears
Suddenly hurtle before my dream-awakened eyes,
And then the clash of fallen horsemen and the cries
Of unknown perishing armies beat about my ears,
We who still labour by the cromlech on the shore,
The grey cairn on the hill, when day sinks drowned in dew,
Being weary of the world's empires, bow down to you,
Master of the still stars and of the flaming door.

(W. B. YEATS.)

All this strife comes from the Judgment of Paris, which was that of Adam and Eve in respect of the same Apple of the Serpent, Libido, Antichrist. The gilded fruit which Eris left upon the table is that same one which was the origin of the " fall." And it is equally clearly the attribute of sensuality, for which reason it could not be other than the reward of Venus, who, in the myth, underlines her rôle by bribing Paris with " possession of the fairest." Paris, in fact, had little choice in the matter, since he was too weak to sublimate desire into that love which would have brought him not Helen of Troy, but the Golden Apples of the Hesperides.

These are they which grew upon the Tree of Life, the fruit of the mystical attainment, which is not only of gold but of *burning* gold, fit reward for Heroes, and among them for one Alcaeus or Alcides, afterwards Hercules, whose symbols shall speak for themselves.

1. He was born of Jupiter and Alcmene and was thus a Son of God having a human mother, destined to overcome the Destroyer by reason of his potential divinity.

2. Because of this same divinity he was hated by the material powers personified in Hera, who sent her *serpents* to destroy the child in his cradle.

3. Again by reason of his parentage, the babe was possessed of super-physical (i.e. spiritual) strength, and he strangled the serpents, one in each hand.

4. The first stage of his education was naturally concerned with the discipline of his lower nature . . . the brute that is in all men ; and so he is represented as learning from the Centaur Chiron, a personage who is frequently represented in the rôle of tutor, presumably for the reason just given.

5. Having reached the time of " going out into the world " which is adolescence, the young Hero is confronted by the personifications of Virtue and Vice, who offer him the inevitable alternatives of sorrow and suffering or ease and riches. Nevertheless the choice is rightly made, and the Hero adopts the " way of the cross " otherwise that hard road sponsored by Arete (the virgin) as opposed to the easy way of Kakia (the harlot).

> " Young Hercules with firm disdain
> Braved the soft smiles of pleasure's harlot train ;
> To valiant toils his forceful limbs assigned,
> And gave to virtue all his mighty mind."
>
> (DARWIN.)

6. Throughout his life he was either a slave or a wanderer, being one of the Argonauts, and also the servant *of his brother* and a certain Queen Omphale.

7. Among the almost incessant struggles and "labours" he overcomes one after another the three lower elements of Earth, Water, and Air, finally becoming identified with Fire before undertaking the last " labour," that of the Golden Apples themselves. The first of the labours, on the other hand, was concerned with the Nemean Lion, *whose skin the Hero afterwards wore*. Then came the famous Hydra. As soon as one head was cut off two more appeared, so that the monster, and all others of a similar nature . . . they are legion, is worthy to rank as the representative of *desire*. For it is recognised that where one desire has been *repressed*, the libidinous energy

finds other channels more or less indirect. The only remedy is transference or sublimation. . . . Presumably killing the monster refers to the latter. It is also interesting to note that (*a*) the Hydra is represented with several female breasts,[1] and (*b*) she is only overcome through the agency of Fire, the Hero using fire-arrows and cauterising the stumps of the heads to prevent others appearing.

So much for Water. Earth was overcome in the person of a certain Giant, a son of Gaea (Earth), who was able to renew his strength each time he touched the ground. Hercules only triumphed by holding him aloft until he weakened, thus indicating that the Hero's strength was *not earthly* (physical). I indicate this particular labour as typical of Earth symbolism although several other battles could be referred to the same idea, including those various animals which, in one way or another, represent *virility* (Lion, Stag, Bull) and even fertility, the Mares (?) and the Cattle of the Sun. Air was represented by the metallic Birds of Stymphalus, whose beaks, claws, and wings were of brass (i.e. *false* gold. Cf. the *gilded* as opposed to the *golden* apple). Moreover they were man-eaters, so that by no stretch of imagination can they be reckoned as symbols of the Spirit like the Dove or Eagle.

At all events, between Serpents, Beasts, and Birds, the Hero effectively subjugates the Cherubim or Elemental powers, and so prepares himself for the final effort, it being understood

[1] See H. A. GUERBER : *Myths of Greece and Rome*, p. 132.

that in such conquests the power of the vanquished force is integrated with the Hero, so that he becomes stronger for each adversary overcome. This, too, strikes me as an apt psychological analogy.

8. Hercules is identified with Prometheus (Fire) by rescuing him from captivity in the same way as he is identified with the other Elements, but the Prometheus episode is represented as occurring later than the others, which is what we should expect, namely, that all the subordinate powers are fused into the one integrating force of *love*.

9. Nor should it be forgotten that Hercules deserved to be ranked as a great lover, having five women very closely associated with him (Megara, Iole, Omphale, Deinara, Hebe), but it is of more interest to find that before setting out on the final quest he went through the symbolic *inversion* which we recognised as derived from the ritual of sexual taboo. In short, he became " androgyne," being represented as the slave of a woman (Queen Omphale) who herself adopted the Lion Skin and Club (another inversion), while he was clothed and employed as a woman . . . an occupation which he in no way seemed to dislike, on the ground, or so it is believed, that he was in love with Omphale. This, however, is an assumption which we can leave out ; the point is that he did go through a period of inversion.

10. Finally the Hero conquers Death and Hell, even bringing the powers of Hell to the upper air, albeit securely bound, and returning them in due course to their proper place. This narrative of

the capture of the Dog Cerberus deserves to rank with the simple dragon-slaying tales, such as St. George and St. Michael, but may well contain a more complex significance.

11. Finally Hercules is killed by the conjunction of Woman and Beast (Deinara and the blood of the Centaur Nessus), or rather he is not killed, for the divine Father Zeus himself takes up the immortal soul from the funeral pyre, whereon Hercules had placed himself of his own free will. So, having "descended into hell," he may be said to "ascend into heaven" even "at the right hand of God."

12. But there is one more clue. He is given a *new name* comparable to the new name of the Christ cited in Revelation. But Hercules, unlike his Archetype, has a new name which—at least ostensibly—is known. . . . Acides became Heracles, on the ground that he was "renowned through Hera," much as Osiris might be said to become Ra through Set (so far as I know this relationship is not traditionally expressed), or Jesus to become "Alpha and Omega" through the Cross. For, in the case of Hercules, all his trials and tribulations were directly attributed to Hera, so that his way was that typical one of opposition to Mother Matter, battle against Antichrist, and a lifelong quest, which we have recognised as the "middle way" or "way of the cross."

No doubt it would be possible to work out the foregoing correspondences much more elaborately, but there seems little point in so doing since the essentials are few and clear. Besides, it is to be borne in mind that most of the great myths contain so much material that it is easy to get lost if the fundamentals are not rigidly adhered to, and some myths are so tangled that the symbols prove mutually contradictory. But this is not the case with Hercules, whom we can definitely claim as corresponding to those symbolic requirements which were arrived at by general, that is to say, *abstract* terms, and were then translated into physical symbols. Hercules, in fact, presents a typical divine Hero, Man/God.

All who follow that " way " must pass through the same phases as did Hercules and Jesus. The Lion and the Hydra must be overcome (sublimated), Fire must become the essence of the individual, having all base things transmuted. But before such freedom and power can be won their opposites must be experienced.

---

*Note* 1. *Atlas.*

There is, of course, an alternative version as to how the Hero finally obtained the Apples . . . by trickery. Hercules induces Atlas to get the prize for him, and so presumably never enters the Garden himself, or faces Ladon. Now, as it seems to me of the utmost importance that the Hero should complete his quest, I have no choice but to ignore this incident in favour of the lesser-known " direct " climax where the Hero, like any other " dragon-slayer," passes Ladon and himself plucks the fruit. It is clearly inconsistent for the Consummator to conform to all the important symbolic requirements throughout his career, and then suddenly become so changed as to have his final reward brought to him. On the other hand it is certainly possible that Atlas himself has an " unconscious " significance which I have missed. The whole question illustrates at once the advantages and disadvantages of the present method.

*Note 2.  The Eucharist.*

Frazer proved conclusively that all the principal Heroes were " Corn Spirits " or " vegetation gods " ; such, for instance, as Osiris, Tammuz, Adonis, Attis, and their more primitive types.  The essence of such cults is the recognition of the *body* of the God as the *means* whereby the regeneration is accomplished, and further, that the symbol of this vehicle is the Corn of Bread by which the mortal body is nourished.  Bread, in fact, stands for the mortality which precedes immortality, the *way* to immortality, and hence for incarnate life itself.  Bread is the " staff of life " in this sense, and the *incarnate* individual is the " way."

Let me summarise these ideas :

*Bread* . . . Body . . . vehicle of incarnate experience (of good and evil), hence the *means* whereby the rebirth is achieved, Mother, the " way of the cross."

In the same way the Blood of the Eucharist is seen to represent the *immortal* principle, otherwise the Father, and, from the " taboo " associations, especially the magical *power* of the spirit, otherwise the Holy Ghost. In fact, though to *eat the body* is to enter the *way*, to *drink the blood* is to become a medium of the " magic " force, to experience an " immaculate conception." No doubt the Wine is denied to the laity by the Roman Church for just that reason . . . indeed, even the Knights of the Grail on the course of their Quest never received the Wine but only the Bread.  Obviously for such power as resides in the *blood* to be manifest through one who is " unclean " would be to risk disaster, for this is the same power which killed Uzzah from the Ark of the Covenant.  At the same time it must be recognised that in order to bring the power into manifestation at all it would be a necessity for both priest and worshipper to know exactly what they were doing . . . and to be in a special state of sensitivity. Therefore the risk in practice is negligible. But into questions of practice we cannot enter, it is sufficient to indicate that the Body (Bread) is the vehicle of the Spirit (Wine); it is the way towards the sacrifice of blood, which is the door of immortality.

We should not leave this subject of the Eucharist without reference to the wine-cults as such, of which the best known is that of Dionysus or Bacchus. Clearly, if what we have been saying about the Sacraments is correct, we should be ready to find an echo of the truth in the symbolism of such cults, and we need not expect disappointment.

Bacchus was a true Consummator. He was born of the Sun and the Moon (Jupiter/Semele), and miraculously came forth out of the thigh of the Father himself. He was educated, like Jason and Hercules, by a beast-man, in this case the goat-man Silenus. Like them also he was hated by Hera, but interest centres upon his more mysterious attributes. His mystical title was ICTHUS, and his symbolical " wine " was a compound of Fire and Water (sunlight and water). He possessed—according to the legend of Midas—the Philosophers' Stone (q.v.); that is to say he could transmute the *material* into the *spiritual* (cf. *water* into *wine*). His bride Ariadne is made immortal, even as the Bride of Christ is held by the Church to become immortal.

However degraded the cult may have become through the traditional weakness of the flesh, according to that almost inevitable tendency which we indicated very early in the enquiry, there can be little doubt that in its essence the cult of Wine held no mean portion of the truth : " I am the vine, ye are the branches."

# CHAPTER SEVEN

## MYTHS OF THE QUEST

" There is a great spiritual symbolism which has come down
to us through several houses of tradition; it is not, I think,
communicated in a plenary sense by any one school: it is
rather the harmony of all. As if with Pentecostal tongues, it
speaks to those who can hear, but according to the laws of
symbolism."
(A. E. WAITE : *The Holy Grail*, p. vi.)

IN setting out the fundamentals of the second category
of myths according to the arbitrary distinction
previously drawn, our task is considerably lightened
because by now both the method and the tools should
be familiar. Accordingly there will be less explanation
of fundamental symbols.

But if this point represents the beginning of the
*application* of the present method, it presents also an
opportunity for taking stock, so that we are in no doubt
as to where we are, or whither we are going.

The quotation at the head of the chapter speaks of the
" laws of symbolism," which is a phrase conventionally
devoid of accurate meaning. But what we have already
reviewed must, if it has any meaning at all, have remedied
that defect. We showed that Freud's discovery of the
symbolism of the unconscious, as set forth in the
*Interpretation of Dreams* (1909), was not only the beginning
of a new science of healing. Freud and his followers,
chief of whom were Jung and Adler, discovered the
" laws " of symbolism in their restricted (sexual) form,

and so recognised the importance and power of the force of the unconscious. Among these powers was that, or those, represented by the famous " Œdipus Complex " upon which it is no exaggeration to say that the whole of such symbolism depends. For *Œdipus is the human statement of the Christ relationships*, he is at once the Individual and his potentiality.

But this is a theme which is dealt with fully at a more appropriate place (Chapter IX) ; for the time being we need only remember that all we have tried to do is to extend the existing psychological theory a little further. We have found that symbolism is really a language, the key to which is the framework of three Terms and three *levels*, thus providing nine basic symbols. From these nine quite a large " vocabulary " can be built up, especially when the Terms are differentiated—as for instance where the duality of the Parents is separately treated.[1] Nor should it be forgotten that this " framework " is not entirely ignored even in orthodox psychology, where both the " opposites " and differing " levels " have been recognised, together with the " redeeming symbol," the child. Perhaps the most thorough development of this orthodoxy is to be found in Jung's theory of Psychological Types.

But that is a by-way which we need not follow ; it is sufficient, having made our own key, to try the lock and abide by the results.

*The Four Treasures.*

" Once upon a time " the Tuatha da Danaan, who are the Children of the Gods, left their home in Paradise and

---

[1] Thus, when the Third Term is regarded as *triple* (child, sacrifice, king) we have *seven* Terms on each *level* or twenty-one key symbols in all.

came to Ireland, bringing with them four magical
" signs," one from each city, from Finias, Falias, Gorias,
and Murias. There was a Stone called " Lia Fail," the
Stone of Destiny, a Cauldron of Immortality, a Spear
and a Sword of magic power; but of these the Stone
and the Cauldron take pride of place.

The latter came from Eden with the other treasures,
but is primarily associated with the Goddess Keridwen
of Cymry, finding a place in many and various myths
by no means confined to the Celtic world. Clearly the
symbol is a " Mother," so much is evident from the
usual association of such vessels in psychology. And
this " Mother " has three distinct rôles, for she provides
an inexhaustible supply of food, magical power, and,
finally, immortality ; in fact, the symbol has its significance on all three *levels*. Needless to say the greatest
emphasis in the myths is laid upon the physical attributes
of the Cauldron, though the more abstract significance
is usually quite easy to recognise. For instance, the food
would only be supplied to those who were " clean,"
being specifically denied to such obviously " unclean "
persons as those who were " coward or forsworn." But
the nourishment of the body is completed by the food of
the soul, in this case appearing as three magical drops
which were distilled from the Cauldron to convey to
their possessor all manner of wisdom and understanding.
Finally, those dead men who were allowed to rest in
the Cauldron, regained in a short time all their former
vigour—with the exception of the power of speech.

Here then is summarised the rôle of the Mother-
symbol which gives physical food (mother's milk) and
even physical life (birth); thence mystical food (the
experience of incarnate life, love), and finally the spiritual
food. Combining all these ideas, the Cauldron becomes

the passport to immortality, the *means* whereby the hero attains the consummation. It is in this sense that the Second Term (Mother) seems to become confused with the Third Term, but there is no difficulty if it is remembered that the confusion only arises with the *abstract* Third Term, the Consummation rather than the Consummator, for the Consummation can only be arrived at *through the Mother*. (Cf. Œdipus.) According to the sexual analogy, the Father enters the Mother, who gives birth to the Son, who in turn plays the part of Father, a character who is thus " re-born."

But let us return to the traditional Treasure of the Tuatha da Danaan and see how these symbols are used.

When Bran the Blessed, King of the Isle of the Mighty, which is Britain, fought with the Milesian Irish for the sake of his sister Branwen, the men of England were nearly all slain, but the Irish put their dead in the Cauldron and so kept their host at full strength.

In spite of almost certain defeat Bran did not lose courage. Presumably he recognised himself as the Hero who, by virtue of his spiritual power, could never be defeated. As though to emphasise this, he is represented as having for his chief ally Pryderi, son of Pwyll, Lord of Annwn, which is another name for Paradise. In fact Bran must overcome the Cauldron, and so must all such heroes in order to attain their immortality. Strangely enough the myth does not represent Bran as overcoming the magic of the Cauldron in person, but another hero took it upon himself to deputise. This he managed by feigning dead among a heap of Irish slain. He was duly thrown into the Cauldron with the rest, and, once there, he braced arms and feet against it and so with great strength burst the iron into pieces. Psychologists will recognise here the usual birth symbol of " breaking out " or " tearing," such as is incorporated in the "typical myth " already mentioned.

And so Bran triumphed, obtaining not only his sister (sister-wife ?), but also the Cauldron ; for being a *magic* vessel it was able to be taken back to Britain[1] in spite of having broken in pieces.  This is exactly what we should expect, for such symbols are of necessity eternal—the unconscious seems to have no idea of time and is no more " reasonable " than dream.  It may seem strange that I should insist upon the triumph of Bran when we are told that at his own request he was beheaded.  True, the head retained the gift of speech, but it was not the whole Bran which returned to England, and finally the head was buried upon the White Mount where now stands the Tower of London.  How, then, did he triumph ?  Well, we already know that re-birth from the Mother is only obtained through the sacrifice of blood, in other words through mystical, and perhaps physical, death.  So, just as the man who broke the Cauldron is said to have burst his own heart in the process, so is the great Bran doomed to the same fate.  " Nought but suffering raises thee beyond thyself."

So much for the rôle of the Cauldron as giver of immortality ; it remains to cite its other attributes as giver of food and inspiration, the physical and mystical gifts respectively.  We need hardly be precise about the first, for all the magic cauldrons of myth and fairy tale have the provision of unlimited food as their first and sometimes their only claim to fame, while on the other hand even the Holy Grail is not above such physical functions.  As regards inspiration, however, the best tradition is the Welsh one where the Cauldron distills a magic brew, all of which is poisonous except three drops, these, however,

[1] The Cauldron of Keridwen is presumably the same vessel.

give great magical power. It is also worth noting that the drops do not go to the obvious candidate, but to a very humble individual, Gwion Bach, the son of Gwreang of Llanfair. . . . Heroes are not to be judged by the richness of their clothes.

As for the Stone, it is so closely connected with the Cauldron that I propose to treat them both under one head, that of the Holy Grail, representing the most complete development of the idea and the most fertile source of all such symbolism. The Grail, in fact, was not necessarily a vessel at all, and is actually described in more than one instance as a Stone. In regard to the actual Lia Fail, however, . . . if the word " actual " is not out of place. It is said that this, the second of the treasures of fairyland, was primarily a coronation stone. When a candidate for kingship was one of the spiritual " heirs of the kingdom " the Stone would voice its approval, but if the candidate were a mere Milesian (materialist) the Stone would remain obstinately silent. At all events it was connected with a magical succession of kings destined, of course, to bring about the ultimate overthrow of the powers of darkness, for the Stone and Cauldron have as their common *raison d'être* the victory over matter of the Spirit of Man. It is therefore rather curious to find such a strong and widely recognised tradition in regard to the present coronation stone in Westminster Abbey, which is popularly connected with Lia Fail, just as the Kingdom of Britain is sometimes regarded (for quite other reasons) as the Stone Kingdom. But such speculations are outside our province. Let us return to the Grail.

One way or another this, the greatest of all Christian treasures, combines the attributes of both Stone and Cauldron, so becoming entitled to a unique position

among symbols even when the semi-historical traditions
are ignored.  The Grail is at once the means of the Hero's
quest and the reward of its fulfilment, it is the combina-
tion of " bread " and " wine," and as such it was anciently
called by very high names indeed, . . . " The Crown
of all Earthly Riches, Pure and Precious, Lapis Exilis."
Such titles remind one of the Philosophers' Stone so long
ridiculed as a piece of alchemical hocus-pocus, but which,
like the Elixir of Life, is found to bear a very different
heritage when the traditions are carefully examined.

" If there is one thing which appears more clearly than
another in some books of the Philosophers it is that the
Stone of Alchemy is not a stone at all and that the Elixir of
Alchemy is not a brew or an essence which can be poured
out from ewers or basins."

(A. E. WAITE: The Holy Grail, p. 456.)

Reverting to our own terminology, it appears that the
Grail *includes* the subsidiary symbols of Cauldron, Cup,
Stone, Ark, and so on, under their various forms and in
their differing traditions, all of which are there summarised in the consummation symbol, *par excellence*.
The Grail is the apotheosis of the Golden Apples as
Jesus is the apotheosis of the Christ.  Now we begin
to appreciate the arrangement of our "framework,"
without which it would be next to impossible to describe
the Grail except in terms of its derivatives, a method
which could cause only confusion.  As a *consummation
symbol*, however, its rôle is clear enough, it only remains
to confirm this attribution from the legends.

The essential Christian myth is that the Grail was used
to contain the blood of the Crucified, and that thereafter
the magical treasure was perpetuated, so that men went in
search of it, hero-Knights who followed the " Quest,"

the " Way of the Cross." To all who were on that road the Grail stood as their inspiration and their goal, summarising in one word the whole significance of the Mystic Christ.

So long as there was no means of description save in physical terms, such matters as shape and appearance are of importance, but when there is no longer only a physical " language," then we are at liberty to discard the limitations which that *level* entails. In this sense it is of small consequence whether the Grail is regarded as a Cup, Dish, Stone, or Cauldron.

" I have said that the sacred vessel is sacramental in a high degree, at least in the later developments : it is connected intimately with the Eucharist ; it is the most precious of all relics in the eyes of all Christendom indifferently. . . . And if at the same time the roots of it lie deep in folklore of the pre-Christian period, in this sense it is a Dish of Plenty, with abundance for an eternal festival, like that which the Blessed Bran provided for his heroic followers. So also, from another point of view, it is not a Cup but a Stone ; and it comes to this earth owing to the fall of the Angels. . . .[1]

" It is like the Cup of the Elixir and the Stone of Transmutation in Alchemy . . . described in numberless ways and seldom after the same manner ; yet it seems to be one thing only under its various veils ; and blessed are those who find it." (Op. cit., p. 21.)

But it is proper to cite more detailed correspondences between the Grail and its derived Stone and Cauldron (or Cup).

[1] The " fall of the Angels " is a variant of the Irish tradition which regards the Tuatha da Danaan as having their origin in Paradise. At all events the Treasure derives from the mystic *level*. This idea is quite consistent with the Genesis myth, the Tuatha da Danaan representing humanity prior to their expulsion from Eden.

The place of the Grail, otherwise the place of Attainment, is a Castle called the Castle of Souls or the Castle of Eden. By almost universal consent it is no building made with hands, but itself belongs to the *Mystic Level*, the land of the Ever-Living. Those who are engaged upon the Quest have therefore to conquer the threshold of another world, and it is thus that Arthur Pendragon seeks the " Spoils of Annwn," and Pryderi, son of the Lord of Annwn, finds a *golden bowl* in a magic castle, whither he had gone in chase of a *boar*. Let Taliesin the Bard speak from the " Spoils of Annwn " as translated by Thomas Stephens :

" Am I not a candidate for fame to be heard in song,
In Caer Pedryvan four times revolving !
It will be my first word from the cauldron when it expresses ;
By the breath of nine damsels it is gently warmed.
Is not the cauldron the chief of Annwn in its fashion ?
With a ridge round its edge of pearls !

It will not boil the food of a coward not sworn,
A sword bright flashing to him will be brought,
And left in the hand of Llemynawg,
And before the portals of hell, the horns of light shall be burning.
*And when we went with Arthur in his splendid labours,*
*Except seven, none returned from Caer Voriwid* (the enclosure of the perfect ones)."

(Taken from Lewis Spence : *Mysteries of Britain*.)

It should be noted that " hell " here means the *mystic level* which is the home of the Grail, and as such refers to Eden. Later on, in a different context, it will be possible to disentangle the various names for the *levels* in mythological tradition, assigning Hades, Hell, Sheol, and synonyms to that world which appears shadowy from the incarnate standpoint, in fact the *mystic level*, otherwise Eden. On the other hand, Gehenna, the place of fire, seems to refer to the *spiritual level* wherein the *gross* man, the worm that dieth not, must suffer. Only they who are " fiery " can live in fire. Finally, there is that place of punishment and obliteration which occurs as the *cold* hell, Niflheim, Nastrond, the lowest hell of Dante. Here there is no spirit (fire), and therefore nothing but Matter with its destiny of ultimate obliteration. In fact none of the popular ideas about " hell " are reasonably correct ; for instance, it is " hell " that the hero visits in the hour of his mystical triumph, just as Arthur's quest of the Cauldron is called " The Harrying of Hell " (Annwn). Again let me quote Waite :

" When Perceval visited the Castle a second time he found it encompassed by a river, which came from the Earthly Paradise and proceeded through the forest beyond. . . ."

(Ibid., 77.)

" We know that behind the Grail Castle, according to the Perlesvaus, there was the Earthly Paradise, and that the House of the Holy Vessel was also a Castle of Souls. We know that, according to the Zohar, the Garden of Eden is placed in a position which corresponds with that of the Grail itself. We know that both were removed, the Grail into heavenly regions and the Garden of Eden into that which is no longer manifest." (Ibid., 446.)

If we may now regard the place of the Grail as established, there are other equally important considerations which await attention. In the first place it is obvious that the Grail is a source of great magical *power*. Now the only magical power we have so far identified clearly is that " electrical " force which proceeded from the bi-sexual Ark of the Covenant and slew Uzzah and others who came into contact with it. Further, it was discovered that the power of the Ark was the power of the Word, and we are immediately reminded of the miraculous speech of the Stone of Destiny (and of the head of Bran). The Grail also spoke occasionally and even produced words on the rim of the vessel, while the Cauldron was "full of melodious song." But without going into details it is sufficient to identify the Grail with the Ark, for once that link is admitted, the nature of the power follows automatically by the argument from *taboo* as much as it derives, in the opposite " sense," from the power of the Christ : both are Love.

Now tradition asserts that the Grail was transported in an Ark :

" Those who bore the Ark of the Grail on their shoulders walked over the intervening waters as though on dry land : of the others, those who were in a state of grace crossed on the shirt of the second Joseph as if on a raft ; but the evil livers were left to fare as best they might until ships could be found to carry them."

(Ibid., 182.)

This Sanctuary of the Grail then appears as charged with the same force as was that other sanctuary of the Androgyne Divinity, the Ark of the Covenant. For it is described how one Evalach, a Knight of the Quest, entered the " Ark of the New Covenant " although warned by a voice from a burning cloud. Enter he did, and though paralysis and blindness overtook him he counted the loss as slight in comparison with the joy which he had from the vision of the Grail. For he retained only the use of his tongue, and with it praised God unceasingly for two centuries, during which time he lay in a chapel in the presence of the Host, waiting for the healing which would only come from the accomplishment of the quest of Galahad.

Here we are in the presence of one of the most difficult points of the whole theme of the Grail . . . the sickness or wounding of the Fisher King until the completion of the quest by some other person, usually a nephew. (Cf. the Set/Horus relationship.) In passing it may also be noted that the title of the Fisher is brought into relation with the Mass of Fish which is associated with the Grail in the course of its journey westward. I do not claim to make the " office of wounding " clear in particulars, though I think that its general significance can be appreciated in the light of what we have learned of the symbolic castration which has been shown to overtake the Hero as the sign that he has triumphed over the flesh. Before he becomes King the Hero must become " in the image of God," i.e. androgyne, and to symbolise this we have the stories of sexual inversion, castration, and so on ; but we have not yet considered what this symbol means when applied to the power of the Ark. The " impure " person is wounded by the Ark, and such wounding is through the power of " love " which at its lowest is sex. Now the brute-in-man is summarised as sex, i.e. desire (cf. 1 John ii, 15), and it is this brute which renders him " impure." Therefore he is wounded *sexually*, the magic force invading the impure (gross) parts of his being and from there dominating (wounding) the entire character. In this light it is understandable how the King is the victim of the " office of wounding," the Dolorous Stroke which smites him " in both thighs." Such a character has been brought into contact with the Word before he has overcome the " flesh." And further, he is made whole only through the Hero who has indeed " overcome the world and the flesh " at the end of his quest. Thus the Warden of the Grail awaits the Consummator.

Obviously there is one inconsistency in all this, which may perhaps be accounted for by the exigencies of the narrative. . . . It is difficult to see how the Warden of the Grail is a King. For the King *has* overcome the flesh, while the Warden, since he is wounded, evidently has not. Perhaps it seemed only correct to invest the Keeper of such a Relic with the title of King, perhaps there is another " unconscious " association which I have not seen. At all events such considerations are details.

So now we may return to the Four Treasures, the first two of which as Stone and Cauldron are seen to be related as male/female *and to be combined in the unity of the Grail, which is androgyne.* In other words *the Two Treasures are the Two Terms, and the Grail is the (abstract) Third Term.* As such they are recognisable on all three *levels,* providing equally nourishment for body, soul, and spirit.

The other two Treasures, the Spear and the Sword, are also represented in the Grail literature, the latter taking precedence for our present purpose only, and that in view of a peculiar magical property, namely, that it will break in but one encounter; for the rest it is invincible. It will be rejoined, however, from the broken pieces by a Consummator in person and no one else—unless it be the smith who made it.

Now, leaving out of account those attributes which seem to derive from the conscious rather than the " unconscious " . . . I mean such as the Sword being that which slew the Baptist, or those worn by David and Solomon . . . we are interested first in the fact that it appears *predestined* to the Hero, the weapon which he alone can draw, as Arthur drew Excalibur from the stone in which it was embedded, and thus proved his own kingship. Yet even for the Hero it breaks, although he has the power of mending. I do not mean to go into details : it seems sufficient that we remember the magical sword of Genesis which " keeps the way of the Tree of Life." That weapon was of the spirit, and as such it had power over all that was mortal (Adam and Eve). Such also is the power of the Sword of Quest, which conquers all earthly enemies and yet must in one circumstance break in pieces. Surely the occasion is that upon which the Hero leaves the physical realm and enters the enchanted land of Eden ? In short, the Sword avails nothing against Death ; but after death it is re-born as the Hero is himself re-born. The will and the aspiration which carried him through life, though apparently defeated, " rise again."

Of a similar nature are those invincible weapons of Fairyland of which the Sword of Lugh is typical. This is, in all probability, that same which was a Treasure of the Tuatha da Danaan, otherwise the Sidhe, the Everliving. Now Lugh was a solar-hero and the counterpart of Llew. He was called the Redeemer " of the Long Arm," presumably to emphasise the sweep of the Sword which he held in that hand, or as a phallic symbol with the same significance.

In fact, whichever way one looks at it, there is only one broad conclusion possible ; the invincible weapon is the sign of the spirit-in-man, more particularly it is the spirit of the Quest. As such it belongs of right to all true heroes, all Consummators, among whom is numbered Lugh, the son of Kian, who is a " Father " according to the attributes of Apollo ; and hence the Sun, and the Heir of the Sun, who is the Christ, who is the Knight of the Quest (or *in* the Knight). The Sword, in fact, stands, as nearly as words can find a meaning, for the Mystic Christ, by definition just that spirit-in-man which we have already deduced. The Grail, in fine, is the means and the end of the Quest, while the Sword is the strength which enables the Knight to succeed. One represents the *process*, the other the *power*. To find the Grail is the purpose of life and the power of the sword is the life-force, *élan vital*, which fails only at death, the moment of the breaking of the Sword.

True, Excalibur did not break, but it failed ; and, as though to emphasise the discrepancy, Arthur did not die. He went to Avallon, which is the " place of the golden apples " (etym. the " place of apples " . . . I am thinking of the Burne-Jones painting in the Victoria and Albert Museum when I say *golden* apples). And in that connection it is interesting to find that one of the resting-places of the Grail is supposed to have been the Isle of Man, which is also called the " Magic Isle " and the " Isle of Apples." Waite in this connection relies on Hall Caine and Nutt (*vide* op. cit., 316), where the following note is appended :

Cf. . . . " concerning the Shining Land and the Tree of the Shining Land. Its leaf is breath of life, its bloom is youth, and its fruit is fulfilment of desire. The boughs of the Tree seem to be of silver, its blossoms are white, and the fruits are golden apples. The Shining Land is the Land of the Living Heart, the Land of Manannan, whose Magical Stone recalls the Cauldron of the Dagda : it was a Stone of Everlasting Store."

Here is the Eden symbolism completed, for the fruit of the first Tree is Silver and the fruit of the second is Gold. Now Alchemy associated the Moon with the former, and the Sun with the latter, representing, of course, Matter and Spirit. Thus :

" It (Gold) is the Child of the Sun, while silver is the Daughter of the Moon, the light of which is borrowed from the solar orb. The Hermetic Arcanum is this : Communicate the Sperma Solis to the female matrix of the Moon. . . . The artist who does so kindles an independent fire or light and transmutes ·☽ into ☉, i.e. Silver into Gold."

(WAITE : *The Brotherhood of the Rosy Cross*, p. 463 (reporting).

Compare the following Taoist expression of the same idea :

" The sign K'an ═══ water, the abysmal, is the opposite of Li ══ . . . It represents the region of *eros* while Li stands for *logos*. Li is the sun, K'an the moon. The marriage of K'an and Li is the secret magical process which produces the child, the new man." *(The Secret of the Golden Flower.)*

Surely these short quotations summarise our whole field ? The " artist " is the Consummator whose destiny is that " transmutation " of what is mortal into immortality, whether in terms of silver and gold, sun and moon, or under the semblance of a quest achieved and a treasure attained.

So the Sword takes its place with the other Treasures as something more than the wand of a wizard. It is the spirit and the will toward the goal, the power and inspiration of the " Knight " through all his mortal life, apparently broken on the Cross, but again made perfect in the fulfilment of the Consummation.

> " I will not cease from mental fight,
> Nor shall my sword[1] sleep in my hand,
> Till we have built Jerusalem. . . ."
>
> (BLAKE.)

As the last of the Four Treasures, there is still the Spear to be dealt with, and this obviously partakes to

---

[1] Being *divine*, i.e. spirit, the weapon is that of the Father, and I would therefore regard " *thy* sword in my hand " as a more accurate symbolic expression.

some extent of the nature of the Sword, just as the Stone partakes of the nature of the Grail. Indeed, as far as Celtic lore is concerned, there is little more to be said, though in the traditions of the Grail the Spear has a peculiar interest.

It will be remembered in the first place that in considering the Sacrifice generally, we discovered that the " hanging on the tree " and the " piercing " were both widespread customs as attested by Frazer and Jung in their respective fields, the latter making it clear that the rite is intimately connected with those " unconscious " fundamentals which we are dealing with in the equations. I think it follows reasonably that the instrument of the rite is the Spear and no other weapon, since the Spear alone is specially adapted for piercing. At all events, in the Christian legend there was a traditional spear having this function, that of the Roman soldier Longinus. It is related further that the weapon was brought westward with the Grail and that it continues to distil at the point drops, or even streams, of the sacred and symbolic *blood*. From a psychological point of view we should also remember that the Spear is a phallic sign and hence may be assigned as the weapon of the Destroyer ; not so much of the Mother as of the " fallen " Father, Lucifer, as revealed in the analysis of Aradia. And so it must be concluded that the essence of the sign is Death, *physical* death. This is the power which *apparently* defeats the Hero, while at the same time it is (like the Pig of Set) the means whereby immortality is attained.

Let us beware now of over-generalisation, for it is tempting, though not perhaps entirely justifiable, to conclude the significance of the Spear as follows.

It is phallic, destroying, death-dealing. On the other

hand it is the " gate of immortality," the symbol of the Sacrifice.

We have seen earlier in the enquiry that the sacrifice is comparable to castration, since transmutation is effected by the sublimation of desire . . . sex. To conquer desire was recognised as " to become androgyne," hence to be castrated. The Fisher King was castrated and we have already noted the correspondences ; can we not complete them with the help of the Spear ? For it was (according to one account at least) the Spear rather than the Sword which maimed the King, and we are at liberty to adopt this reading.

It has been shown that *on the lowest level* the Grail is a " battery " (Ark) of the sex-force, and that as such it destroys. Since the Spear embodies this destroying force as its special attribute, its rôle is that which may be assumed from the manner of its appearance. For the Spear appears in procession, dripping blood . . . an object of awe and terror, above all an *object of warning*. And the warning would be in this form. Beware of impurity, for the impure are destroyed by the same spirit which opens the Gate of Life. The Rich King Fisher was not clean, and the power of the Spear maimed him until such time as the Quest should be completed.

And let me add one final word. The Fisher is the *uncle* of the Consummator (Perceval), and it has been noted that Set was the uncle of Horus, being also the Destroyer.

Suppose that the Fisher King is death ? Death is, then, the Keeper of the Grail just as the Serpent is the Keeper of the Tree. The fruit of the Tree and the Holy Grail are both consummation symbols, and it follows that their guardians are both destroyers.

He who would enter the Castle of Souls for the

eucharist of immortality must perform the same tasks as the classical hero. He must overcome the Dragon, a battle which is now expressible in mystical terms. For the battle with the dragon involves the blood-sacrifice of suffering, and this idea is well expressed in the Grail literature as the long and arduous journey of the Knight of the Quest. Only when the Knight becomes " dead to the world upon the cross " can he attain his victory, for then the Keeper is no longer his enemy. He is shown the Grail : he receives the apples, the eucharist, the crown, the golden fleece, the new name.

Such considerations as these emphasise the significance of the fact that the Sword breaks in the *presence of the Keeper*. Further we are able to understand why the wounded King is only healed at the end of the Quest, for the Destroyer is an integral part of the cosmic scheme, and though each individual must separately fight his battle, yet ultimately a time will come when all humanity attain to the Tree of Life. It is this *cosmic* attainment which is signified by the healing of the Fisher, the return of Aradia " to heaven." The Dragon, the Serpent, the universal forces of destruction are finally absorbed into the Unity when the quest of all humanity has been fulfilled at the " marriage of the Lamb which was slain from the foundation of the world " ; in other words at " Omega," which is described by Isaiah in unmistakable words :

" And he will destroy in this mountain the face of the covering cast over all people, and the veil that is spread over all nations. He will swallow up death in victory ; and the Lord will wipe away the tears from off all faces ; and the rebuke of his people shall he take away from off all the earth."

(xxv, 7.)

It will be remembered that the " rebuke " of the Fisher

King was his wounding in the thighs. . . . Love had become desire[1] and desire held him back from the attainment of perfection. So long as desire rules in the mind of man he is cut off from the mystical reality, he is " wounded in the thighs," he is " veiled." For the veil of Isaiah is the firmament between the physical and the mystical *levels*, that which separates the living from the dead, and which hides from the sight of men that magical " mountain " wherein is the Castle of the Grail, the alchemical " Mons Philosophorum "; closely connected with the Grail on the one side and with the Mount of God, Horeb, on the other. Indeed, the resemblance is so clear that comment is unnecessary, the quotations speak for themselves. . . . And yet perhaps there may be a reminder that the Treasure in either case is in the Mystic Christ, born, sacrificed, and crowned in the ultimate destiny of all men, the sign of whose power is the Word and the Voice of the Word, and the Sword of Flame.

Compare the following précis of a letter by Thomas Vaughan, ostensibly on behalf of the Brothers of the Rosy Cross. It is quoted by A. E. Waite at somewhat greater length (*Brotherhood of the Rosy Cross*, p. 380) :

" The truth is that no one looks for treasures in the place where God has stored them up. It is hidden from most of the world but not from those who are of God. The second part (of the letter) describes an Invisible Mountain of the Wise and the way to arrive thereat.

(1) It is in the midst of the earth or centre, at once far off and near, containing most ample treasures, but such as the world does not value.

(2) It is reached only by man's toil and endeavour.

[1] In the wide sense of the Buddhist " desire for the presence of the loved and the absence of the unloved," whether persons or hings or abstract ideas.

(3) On a certain night, described as most long and dark—Compare the ' Dark Night of the Soul '—the seeker shall set out to find it, prayer being the preparation for his journey.

(4) The Mountain shall be reached at midnight—meaning when the dark night is darkest.

(5) On arrival thereat a great wind shall shake the mountain and shatter its rocks in pieces.

(6) The adventurer will be attacked by ' lions, dragons, and other terrible beasts,' . . .

(7) The tempest will be followed by earthquake, and in the destruction thereafter of the terrene rubbish by fire the treasure will be discovered.

(8) But it will not become manifest till the night and its darkness are over, or otherwise until the Day-star rises.

(9) The treasure includes ' a certain exalted Tincture, with which the world—if it served God and were worthy of such gifts—might be tinged and turned into most pure gold.' ''

A parallel is found in 1 Kings xix, 8 ff. :

" 8. And he (Elijah) arose, and did eat and drink, and went in the strength of that meat forty days and forty nights unto Horeb the mount of God.

9. And he came thither unto a cave and lodged there ; and, behold the word of the Lord came to him, and he said unto him, What dost thou here Elijah ?

10. And he said, I have been very jealous for the Lord God of Hosts : for the children of Israel have forsaken thy Covenant, thrown down thy altars, and slain thy prophets with the sword ; and I, even I only, am left ; and they seek my life to take it away.

11. And he said, Go forth and stand upon the mount before the Lord. And behold the Lord passed by, and a great and strong wind rent the mountains, and brake in pieces the rocks before the Lord ; but the Lord was not in the wind : and after the wind an earthquake ; but the Lord was not in the earthquake :

12. And after the earthquake a fire ; but the Lord was not in the fire : and after the fire a still small voice."

*Arthur Pendragon.*

No doubt our primary consideration is the bearing which the Arthurian romance has upon the Grail, though, as it has previously been indicated, the " Blameless King " stands upon his own merits . . . or, rather, symbols, as a person of peculiar interest. Therefore it is proposed to introduce the subject with generalisations, though it is not intended to burden the reader with much explanation, since the links should speak for themselves.

The first part of our task is obviously to identify Arthur with the Consummator, while the second, our particular business, is to reveal him as that Hero whose symbols are interwoven with those of Cauldron and Grail.

The title of Pendragon is our first clue, for the *dragon* is that *serpent* about which so much has been said, a rôle which it held the world over. And, since the serpent or dragon could occupy a position as any of the Three Terms, so, indeed, it appears in mythology. And the Third is the unity of the other two . . . which is to say that the Golden Dragon stands for the " fiery serpent," the " radiant and perfect serpent " of the Christ. As such the Golden Dragon was the sign of the " heaven-born " of Imperial China, and as such it was also the insignia of Arthur, who is described by Tennyson as follows :

> " Since to his crown the golden dragon clung,
> And down his robe the dragon writhed in gold,
> And from the carven-work behind him crept
> Two dragons gilded, sloping down to make
> Arms for his chair, while all the rest of them
> Thro' knots and loops and folds innumerable
> Fled ever thro' the woodwork, till they found
> The new design wherein they lost themselves."
>
> (" Lancelot and Elaine.")

Briefly the Golden Dragon stands for the Spirit, while those other serpents stand for the dual Mother . . . another point which has already been explored.

In the Arthurian myth these dragons *of metabolism* are represented as the Red and the White, whose perpetual warfare continues *in the earth* until Omega, the day of the Second Coming of Arthur. In fine the forces of Matter persist until the Marriage of the Lamb, when the " first heaven and the first earth were passed away ; and there was no more sea " (Rev. xxi, 1).

> " That one dragon was red as fire,
> With eyen bright, as basin clear ;
> His tail was great and nothing small ;
> His body was a rood withal.
> His shaft may no man tell ;
> He looked as a fiend from hell.
> The white dragon lay him by,
> Stern of look and griesly.
> His mouth and throat yawned wide ;
> The fire brast out on ilka side.
> His tail was ragged as a fiend,
> And, upon his tail's end,
> There was y-shaped a griesly head,
> To fight with the dragon red."
>
> (" Merlin " : ELLIS, taken from *Myths of the Middle Ages* : GUERBER.)

Thus at the outset, he who wears the sign of the Golden Dragon holds also the " balance of power " in a mystical sense, for he is no less than the vehicle of the integrating force . . . in other words the Christ. But there are other signs also which must " ring true," and it is of primary importance that the Consummator should have a birth at least out of the ordinary and preferably miraculous. In Arthur we have both, for on one side he was the heir of his father Uther, but educated by Merlin the Wizard and kept in ignorance of his royal birth; while on the other it is affirmed that he was miraculously born *of the sea*.

In either case the sign is " true," for he who is heir of the Quest is brought up in ignorance of his destiny, and he who has the victory over the world (of Matter) is nevertheless born of that *level*, of the Ever-Virgin. And, curiously enough, she is the sign of Arthur in that he goes to battle bearing " the image of St. Mary, the ever-virgin, upon his shoulder " (*Encyc. Brit.*).

And there are yet other signs. He is identified with Gold, but he must also be identified with Fire, and this we find in the miraculous birth, so that he appears to be born not of water only, but of water and fire. The resemblance to the symbolism of the " second birth " is obvious.

" . . . Wave after wave, each mightier than the last,
  Till last, a ninth one, gathering half the deep,
  And full of voices, slowly rose and plunged
  Roaring, and all the wave was in a flame :
  And down the wave and in the flame was borne
  A naked babe, and rose to Merlin's feet,
  Who stooped, and caught the babe, and cried ' The King ! ' "

(TENNYSON.)

Passing now to the career of this Hero, we find its nature witnessed in two ways, a natural one and a magical, as if they derived from the natural and magical birth respectively. On the former side it is the mission of the King to found an ideal chivalry and to wage life-long warfare against the pagans, clearly the rôle of the Christ ; while on the mystical side he is concerned with two quests, one primitive and the other truly high, yet both deriving from the same root. The first of the quests is that of the Cauldron and the second is of the Grail, the former chronicled by Taliesin in the *Spoils of Annwn*, wherein, as indicated in our quotation, it is related how Arthur and his company cross the frontiers of the *mystic level* and seek there the magic Cauldron, as in the other legends they seek the Castle of the Grail. Indeed, in this " golden age," " the voice of the Quest passed through all Britain, in part by common report—because all or nearly all the Arthurian Knighthood bound itself to assume the task—but in part also by the miracle of unknown voices and of holy foreknowledge." (Waite.) It is of little consequence that the Quest appears in more than one cipher, more than one unlikely legend. Examples have been already quoted, and among them the tale which is of perhaps primary interest concerns Pwyll, Lord of Annwn, whose son Pryderi was stolen by magic and by magic returned to his mortal mother. This same Pryderi, grown to manhood, was in chase of that *boar* which led him to the magic Castle of great richness wherein was a Golden Bowl. But when he touched the bowl he was held fast by a spell which took away from him also his speech, and there he remained.

With this should be compared the description of that Castle wherein was the Cauldron :

" The principle treasure which he (Arthur) and his men carried away thence was the Cauldron of the Head of Hades, that is to say, of Pwyll. In that poem, xxx, Pwyll and Pryderi are associated together, and the Cauldron is found at a place called Caer Pedryvan, the Four-throned, or Four-cornered Castle in Ynys Pybyrdor or the Isle of the Active Door, the dwellers in which are represented quaffing sparkling wine in a clime that blends the grey twilight of the evening with the jet-black darkness of night ; so lamps burn in front of the gates of Uffern or Hell. Besides the names of Caer Pedryvan and Uffern it has these others : Caer Vedwit, meaning probably

the Castle of Revelry, in reference to the wine-drinking there ;
Caer Golud, or the Castle of Riches, Caer Ochren, Caer Rigor,
and Caer Vandwy, all three of unknown interpretation."

(RHYS : The Arthurian Legend.
Taken from SPENCE : *Mysteries of Britain*.)

And now comes the higher expression in which may
be found more indeed than confirmation of the spiritual
identity of Arthur and his Knights of the Quest. For
the final act in the drama of the Grail contains as high
an expression of the fundamental, i.e. " unconscious "
truth, as can well find form in words. In the quotations
which follow I rely upon Waite's account of the German
Cycle, but before plunging into the tale itself there are
two points which I should like to suggest . . . not as
necessary assumptions but as indications towards depths
which the present argument has not reached. The first
is that the Maimed King is also the Knight of the Quest,
the latter representing his higher, the former, his lower
nature. The second, that the whole of the practical
significance of the Grail, as of truth in whatever form it
may find expression, is contained in the Question. For
the Consummation depends upon the Question as upon
no other factor under the control of the Knight. There
can be no receiving in the absence of asking, and no door
opened upon which there has been no knock.

As the end of the long search draws near, the Knight
is confronted with a Sword of Flame which seems to
him a very terrible thing ; yet he goes on—for his own
weapon is of the same stuff. And he enters a land of
" milk and honey," a " bountiful and smiling land, as if
it were the precincts of an Earthly Paradise." He comes
thereafter to a certain town of the Dead-alive, where
there is eating and drinking, laughter and song ; but
their eyes are blind and there is no life in them. This

state of affairs obtains even in the Castle of the Hall of Roses, to which he finds his way and in which he is welcomed as one predestined.[1] There followed a banquet and a draught of wine which puts the Knight into a deep sleep, though the same beverage has no effect upon the living-dead, the Company of the Castle. "Though dead, yet they spoke—and that, it would seem, volubly."

Then came a procession of the Four Treasures under the form following. A Sword is laid at the feet of the Lord of the Castle, who is maimed and weary and old. A Lance exudes three drops of blood, even as the Cauldron of old distilled three drops of Elixir, and the blood is caught in a Salver. A Holy Vessel appears which " contained the semblance of a Host."

" The Master of the Castle received therefore the Bread ; but of the Bread he took only a third part, as if it were the efficient oblation at a sacrifice of the Mass. He drank also the Blood from the Salver, no one but himself sharing in these Elements of a substituted Eucharist. . . .

" Therefore Gawain arrived at a happy season, to see and to speak ; and on contemplating these things he overflowed in himself with the wonder and the mystery of it all, so that, acting on the spur of the moment, importunately he asked that which was vital to those who were suffering from death in life, namely, the Mystic Question, the most conventional of all formulæ : What does it mean ? "

Then the dead do come to life, not suddenly but gradually, and the King with them, so that they " were alive in the flesh and they would go forth in the morning."

It is not for me to set out the significance of the Grail in my own words, for we have indeed come once again

[1] Cf. " The Golden Flower which blooms in the Purple Hall of the City of Jade," a parallel Chinese conception.

near to the limits of expression. Yet I will not close this section without referring to the "Rabbi ben Ezra" of Robert Browning, in which, as I see it, the mystery of the Cup which is not a cup is set forth in no uncertain sense. There have been so many recent quotations that I will add only this one :

> "Look not thou down but up !
> To uses of a cup,
> The festal board, lamp's flash and trumpet's peal,
> The new mine's foaming flow,
> The Master's lips aglow !
> Thou, heaven's consummate cup, what need'st thou with earth's wheel ?

---

*Note.*

There are two subsidiary points of interest connected with the Knight of the Grail, which should not be passed over completely, though they are, in that particular tradition, of a subsidiary character. The first of these is concerned with Perceval's Mother, whom he leaves in order to undertake the Quest. For this and subsequent neglect he suffers—or is made to suffer indirectly— although it is made clear that by any ordinary standards he is not culpable, there being no choice in the matter if the Quest were to be served.

The key to this is, I think, quite clear, namely, the " unconscious " relationship between the symbols Mother and Son. The Hero is compelled to say in effect : " Woman, what have I to do with thee ? " even though he does not, in fact, refer to the woman who bore him, but rather to the material life and standards which he must set aside in the interests of his Father's business (cf. Marriage at Cana). As expressed in the New

Testament this point is dealt with later, but only to extend and exemplify the psychological conclusion which may be expressed as follows. In the individual unconscious as in myth, religion, and art, the Mother is often divorced from her human personality and made to play the part of an abstract symbol. Nevertheless the patient who is psychoanalysed is not in a position to make this distinction any more than the uninstructed reader of myths or dreamer of dreams. Groddeck says somewhere in *The Unknown Self* that he never met a man who did not, to some extent, hold himself responsible for the death of his Mother. But it was the symbol of which he was thinking, not the woman. For life is the Quest, and the condition of that journey is that the "world and the flesh" give place to the spiritual standards. We may say quite simply that the Mother must be abandoned (killed) before we are free to do the will of the Father. The symbols may even find expression in dream or in unconscious fantasy as the *murder of the Mother*, hence the anxiety neurosis noted by Groddeck.

"And there about my bed stand the lovely forms of a better future. Stiff they are, but of radiant beauty, still sleeping . . . but he who shall awaken them would make for the world a fairer face. A hero would he be who could do it.

"*Mother :* An heroic life in misery and dire need!

"*Kule :* But perchance there might be one!

"*Mother : He first must bury his Mother !*"

The quotation is one made by Jung in his *Psychological Types*, though there would be no difficulty in finding parallels from the work of other experts. The particular example, however, is peculiarly applicable to the idea of Quest.

From the psychological point of view, and in reference to the Mother of the Quest, the conventional progress of the Hero corresponds to various steps in the transference or sublimation of libido, of which the most important is that which frees the child from the Mother.

The second point is also concerned with Perceval, whose sword is reconstructed, not in the palace of the Fisher King, but in the place of the Forge. Now this Forge (of Vulcan) is guarded by serpents, which, presumably, are slain by the Hero before the sword can be re-fashioned. The parallel with more primitive myths of the Dragon-slayer is obvious. The Dragon (monster, sphinx, serpent) is slain by the Hero that he may overcome (incest) the Mother for the purpose of a new birth. We have previously found that the Monster represents *death* so that the condition of this " incest " is, in effect, the death of the Hero (cf. the death of Œdipus). The place of the serpent in the present instance is thus the place of death-rebirth, the womb of the dual Mother. This then is the significance of the Forge of Vulcan, for the Hero must attain his immortality *sword in hand*. Not only the body (vehicle), but also his " magic force " must be renewed.

# CHAPTER EIGHT

## THE CULT OF THE SUN

" Out of Egypt have I called my Son."

(Matt. ii, 17.)

### SECTION I

## THE GODS OF EGYPT

IT is hardly to be disputed that the most elaborate of all solar cults was that of Egypt, indeed, the very complexity of the material may seem to be a good reason for avoiding it. Yet I am persuaded that in spite of the chaos and corruption which are the most striking features of the Egyptian religion as it is known to-day, we should still be able to find the traditional equivalents for our abstract terms. The symbolism of the unconscious rides roughshod over all logical arrangements, and so provides a novel viewpoint such as that implied in the following quotation :

" We are apt to stigmatise as ' contradictory ' the apparently confused ideas which run through these books, as through many Egyptian texts, when perhaps it is ourselves who are interpreting them too literally."

(SHORTER : *The Egyptian Gods*, p. 86.)

The method to be followed is clearly the general one which has led the argument to its present position, for, since every phase of civilisation is represented in Egyptian cults, we should expect to find there evidence to confirm many of the conclusions already arrived at. At the same time the wealth of material is embarrassing—especially in regard to the Tuat—and we have to pick and choose only those few symbols which definitely *harmonise*. It is only too easy to recognise the contradictory aspects of the gods of Egypt, arrived at by millennia of varied development and retrogression ; but the existence of contradictions does not preclude the discovery of fundamental harmony, even if it renders the search more difficult.

It will be remembered that our first concern was with the magical force whose symbol-in-chief was *menstrual blood*, and this same blood may well mark the beginning of our excursion into Egyptology. For instance, the *blood of Isis* seems to represent a talisman with just such a force, albeit considerably spiritualised when compared with the grosser forms of taboo. Instead of being maleficent, or at best " canalised " and vaguely beneficent, the power was specifically connected with immortality. We have the identity of the talisman clearly enough displayed in the following particulars :

" The *Tjet*. . . . An amulet which was commonly made of some *red* substance, e.g. red jasper, red glass, red wood, red porphyry, red porcelain, and carnelian, or sand, or reddish agate ; examples in solid gold are known and in gilded stone.

" The *Tjet* is a conventional form of the genital organs of the goddess Isis, and it was supposed to give to the wearer, living or dead, the virtue of the blood of Isis."

(BUDGE : *Amulets and Superstitions*, p. 137.)

" The rubric says that if the *Tjet* be dipped in water wherein *ankham* plants have been steeped, and tied to the neck of the deceased on the day of his burial, it will be the fluid of life to him, and he shall have power of traversing all heaven and earth. . . .

" The real value of the object to the Egyptian was that it possessed the power of the blood of Isis, probably the menstrual blood. . . .

" In a drawing reproduced by Lazone a goddess is seen rising out of the *Tjet* in exactly the same way as we see Osiris rising out of the *Tet*."

(BUDGE : *From Fetish to God*, p. 66.)

Now let us be quite clear about this symbol of the blood. Father and Mother alike rise out of the sign of sexual union which has already been recognised as that of unity, the sign of the beginning and ending of every process at every level. But hitherto we have regarded the blood as associated particularly with the Father in its higher meanings ; only among primitives was the significance of the " female " blood particularly noted. It is therefore desirable to try and clear up the whole position as far as possible at this stage, though the full exposition of the various connecting links must await analysis of the Œdipus relationships.

In the first place it has become clear that Father and Son may be regarded as successive aspects of one person, while the Mother is the essential condition of all living, whether mortal or immortal. *All three Terms derive their power from the sign of wine and their form from the sign of bread.* Body and blood, spirit and matter are the keys of their interaction.

In order to approach the mystical truth we have to make use of the physical symbols, whose relationship is found to be as follows. The Father enters the Mother and " dies " (the " life " is gone out of him), but he is born again as the Son through the sacrifice of the Mother. Thus the blood of the Father is more properly the fluid of life, that of the Mother its renewed form. The Mother is the Gate of Life. To her in due course the Son returns (incest), and here is the third and " key " sacrifice, that of the crucifixion; for when the Son is re-born *from the blood of Isis*, the Gate of Immortality, he is the re-created Father. " I and my Father are one."

Nor must it be forgotten that these symbols are true for every individual. We are all born of the Ever-virgin and the eternal Father (i.e. of love), but we are also born of the harlot and the temporal father (i.e. of desire). Every individual has within him the potentiality of both Christ and Antichrist.

At all events it should now be understandable why both Isis and Osiris rise from the sign of sexual union and why both have their power derived from " blood." . . . At least we speak of the blood of Isis, though Osiris is better known as the medium of the " fluid of Ra," which in physical terms is the semen. And we can see too why the god of sex, Min the " Shameless," plays such an important part in the Egyptian pantheon. He is even regarded as " another form of Amen " . . . what we should read perhaps as the " physical medium of Amen's power." It is Min who, in the Book of the Dead (Spell. 17, Sec. 9), is represented as the power by which immortality is won :

" I am Min at his coming forth. I have placed my two plumes upon my head."

The Commentary then says :

" As for Min, it is Horus, Champion of his Father. As for his coming forth, it is his birth."

Thus the cycle is completed. Amen projects his power into Matter where it is expressed as the *integrating force* in general, and love (in all its forms) in particular. This power becomes incarnate in the blood of Isis

(*Tjet*), and is ultimately sublimated to divinity . . . the Child of Isis becomes the Divine King.

As in the case of Christianity, those who follow the Hero are members of his mystical body and follow his " way." In this connection I put forward a suggestion —it is little more—for the interpretation of a certain class of mystical art. There is among the Gulberkian Collection in the British Museum the figure of a kneeling priest (" Kneeling man with shrine : black stone. No. XV "). It is clear, even from a photograph " full-face," that this priest has one female breast. Moreover the " shrine " rises from the thighs and represents Osiris the King, standing, and wearing the " double feather " already mentioned, which is to say " resurrected."

Now, in the earlier part of this book it became clear that in mystical terms the sexual symbolism of the re-birth requires : (1) That the Hero become androgyne and (2) that the power of sex be sublimated. It was further recognised that the sign of the sublimation was that of " re-birth " (Jonas) whereby the Warrior became (immortal) King. It seems to me at least probable that this symbolism was at one time known in Egypt and that it was incorporated *consciously* in this particular statuette . . . the ideas are probably too complex to have been reproduced " unconsciously " in a single figure. But it is understood that I do not claim this example as justifying these contentions . . . it is mentioned more in the hope that other examples may be brought to light.

The next stage in our general enquiry revealed that the " power of the blood " was incorporated in the *secret name* of God, and here the Egyptian legend provides a lengthy story, most of which is obviously corrupt. In essence, however, it is clear enough. Isis persuades Ra to tell her his secret name, and it is evident that this

name *confers the power* of the god. At first sight this
seems all wrong. . . . How should the sovereign power
of the Spirit be given to the *material* principle ? For the
power of the Name was, of course, that of IHOH, which
was the Word, personified in Egypt as Thoth the
Magician, i.e. one who changes one form into another.
It is for this very reason, however, that we may infer an
" unconscious " meaning. After all, the whole essence
of the divine plan which begins at Alpha and ends with
Omega. . . . Ra's Plan is, if the previous analogies are
accepted, no less than the *incarnation of the Word*. We
have seen that the impregnation of Matter by Spirit
is symbolised in the rôle of Min, as well as in
the parentage of the Consummator (human Mother,
divine Father) and his destiny of *equality* with the
Father.

Now the impregnation of the Mother, in general as
opposed to physical terms, is clearly the passing into
her of the *secret name*, from which the Son is born. In
respect of Isis we find the interpretation confirmed in
the *family relationships*, for Osiris, Isis, and Horus are
beyond dispute the Father, Mother, Son, represented
by Holy Ghost, Mary, Jesus. Isis gives birth to a
miraculous Child who ascends to the throne of his father
Ra, having triumphed over his opposite (Set) and over
the Mother. In practice it is easier to consider Horus/
Osiris as a composite being, the former being primarily
the Child and Warrior, while the latter is primarily the
King. . . . In fine, the pair represent successive phases of
the mystical journey.

To gain a clearer understanding of this Trinity it will
probably be easier to begin with Isis. In her highest
aspect she is co-equal partner with Ra himself, so that
these two form the great FATHER/MOTHER. Thence

are derived the two pairs of terms, Dual Father and Dual Mother, Osiris/Set and Isis/Nepthys, whose characteristics need no further explanation since they run broadly true to type. All four are brothers and sisters as well as husbands and wives, and all are derived from the *abstract* duality of " heaven " and " earth " in the sense in which those terms are used at the beginning of Genesis. Beyond these again is the mysterious, secret Unity, and " triunity," which I dare not particularise too neatly, but will illustrate by means of titles.

It may be said to consist of the overlapping entities called variously Ptah, Amen, Horus-the-Elder, or Ra, and for purposes of convenience we shall use the last inclusive title, which stands for " God " in the sense in which that word is used in Christianity. Incidentally it may be remarked that in using so many " personifications " of " God " the Egyptians hardly differ from the Christians, who are quite content to allow " God " to include such subsidiary *aspects* as " Lord God," " Alpha and Omega," " Jehovah," " Lord of Hosts," " Iнoн," " Ancient of Days," " Our Father," and so on, without troubling very much as to whether they have any relative significance. It is an attitude of mind very difficult to understand, for to common sense it seems unlikely, to say the least of it, that the various biblical authors could have used all these terms at random to mean just the same thing. That they *derive* from the all-inclusive Unity of " God " is quite a different idea, and one which the Ancient Egyptians well knew, at least at their highest development :

"1. GOD is One and Alone and no other existeth with him.
  God is the One, the One who hath made everything.

2. God is a spirit, a hidden spirit, the Spirit of spirits, the great Spirit of Egypt, the divine Spirit.

3. God is from the beginning, he hath been from the beginning, he is the primeval one and existed when nothing else was. He is the Father of Beginnings.

4. God is the Eternal One, he is everlasting and is without end, and he will exist into all eternity.

5. God is hidden, no man knoweth his form. No man hath searched out his similitude. He is hidden to gods and men.

6. No man knoweth a name by which to call him. His name remains hidden (in the Mother). His name is a secret to his children. His names are without number.

7. God is Truth. He liveth through Truth, he feedeth himself thereon. He is the King of Truth.

8. God is Life, and only through him doth one live. He poureth out life on men, he breatheth the breath of life into the nostrils.

9. God is Father and Mother. The Father of fathers and the Mother of mothers. God begetteth and is not begotten. He is the Creator of his own form and the sculptor of his own body.

10. God himself is existence (consciousness?). He subsisteth in all things and remaineth in all things. He is the subsistent Element which increaseth without perishing.

15. God is compassionate towards his worshippers. He heareth the man who appealeth to him. He protecteth the weak against the strong. God heareth the cry of him who is in dire distress, he is compassionate towards the man who appealeth to him. God recogniseth the man who acknowledgeth him; and rewardeth him that serveth him, and protecteth him that followeth in his way." (BUDGE : ibid., p. 380.)

This then is he who is called God and Ra, the ultimate abstraction whose nature is projected into the "family relationship," the human trinity; while between

Him and us are the great cosmic dualities which we recognised in Genesis, the forces which govern the universe and at the same time rule the " unconscious " of mankind.

In Christianity the Holy Ghost (Love) conceives the Word incarnate, Jesus Christ ; in Egypt the Word of Ptah, his *thought*, becomes embodied as Osiris/Horus. So the vital theme is stated and restated in various terms and on various *levels*, perhaps its most homely expression being incorporated in the idea that since Pharaoh is a personification of Osiris, his sister/wife is therefore the personification of Isis, who is visited by the immaculate conception to bring the Heir of Pharaoh/Osiris to birth.

" More exalted of nature than any other god, at whose beauty the gods rejoice. He to whom praise is given in the Great House, who is crowned in the House of Fire. . . . He found her as she rested in the beauty of her palace. She awoke at the perfume of the god and laughed in the presence of his Majesty. . . . He gave his heart to her. . . . The palace overflowed with the perfume of the god, and all his savour was that of Punt."      (SHORTER : op. cit., p. 15.)

So much for the incarnation of Light, the Divine Fire, the Word. . . . Let us now consider the attributes of the Enemy, who is Set, the Serpent, the Black Pig, Stealer of the Eye (of Osiris/Horus), i.e. Destroyer of Light, the Betrayer. Clearly he stands for Death, as indeed does his consort Nepthys . . . the pair are *katabolism*, as opposed to the complementary forces personified in Isis. It should be remembered also that in addition to the human symbol there is often an animal one . . . one stage " lower." For Isis the thermiomorphic sign is Bast, with whom we have already had some dealings—

though with special reference to her *destructive* aspect —while in the case of Set it is Sekmet, the crocodile, arch-enemy of Ra :

" The Fire of the Eye of Horus is on you, burning you, grilling you, frizzling you, stabbing you, spearing you, eating into you, roasting you, setting you on fire, burning you to ashes, destroying every trace of you. Unemi, the Devouring Fire, consumeth you, Sekmet, the blasting fire of the desert maketh an end of you, and Ups-ur adjudgeth you to destruction. Flame, Fire, Spark pulverise you."

(BUDGE : ibid., p. 520.)

This quotation makes two things very clear : (1) Fire as the Element of Ra, and (2) Sekmet as the opposite of Fire . . . the other *three* elements in all probability, but especially Water. But again this is relatively unimportant; it assists us, however, in making a tabulation of the chief characters on a series of *levels*. Though it is no longer possible to separate " cosmic, mystic, and physical "— arbitrary terms in any case—the arrangement is still one of progressive abstraction.

### EGYPTIAN PAIRS OF OPPOSITES
#### (cf. Gen. 1.)

| | | | |
|---|---|---|---|
| 1. | RA Androgyne | | |
| 2. | *Shu* Heat | *Tefnut* Moisture | |
| 3. | *Nut* Heaven | *Gebb* Earth | |
| 4. | *Osiris-Isis* Light-Growth | *Set-Nepthys* Darkness-Decay | cf. Genealogy of *Aradia* |
| 5. | *Horus* Christ | *Mesu Betshet* Sons of Rebellion Antichrist | |

*Note.*—The primal triunity may be symbolised as "two eyes in the face of heaven," i.e. Sun and Moon in Horus-the-Elder.

Though this tabulation may seem rather complex at first sight, it will be seen to fit in with the usual "framework," especially in regard to the Genesis narrative and the relationship between the parents of Aradia and her opposite. It also corresponds with the "canonical," Great Nine of Heliopolis (if we omit Horus and the Sons of Rebellion who are included in their respective Fathers). I am aware that there are several extant versions of the Great Nine, though this one, being given pre-eminence by so great an authority as Sir Wallis Budge, deserves special respect. It should be noted, however, that the original gives Tem instead of Ra, and this is interesting, for the former is Ra *in his creative aspect*, author of the universe, including all the rest of the Nine. He is the Origin which is Alpha, and his symbol is the Setting Sun.

Indeed, the point may be considered further to clarify various aspects of the solar cycle. Obviously there are two great divisions which apply equally to the diurnal and annual cycles, those of manifestation and removal, day and night, summer and winter. Let us call these the *phases* of the cycle whose symbols are Rising and Setting, Khepera and Tem respectively. The former clearly corresponds with the ascent of Spirit, the latter with the *descent* . . . and remember that *the descent comes first*. It is the Father who initiates the cycle which is completed by the Son. Tem, in fact, is peculiarly the Creator, and as such he has another symbol . . . that of the Beetle (*scarabæus sacer*), humble roller of a little ball of dung, which is the World. That, however, is a

symbol we are able to dispense with; the main thing
is to recognise that the two aspects of the Unity which
make up the Cosmic Trinity are (i) Khepri and (ii) Tem
. . . who is really Khepri-in-Ra while remaining distinct
in his own attributes . . . another example of triunity.
Tem is indeed the " Alpha " of the Divine Plan, and as
such he says :

> " I was the Creator in Khepri.
> I created the Creator of creations,
> the Creator of all creations.
> Subsequently I created multitudes of creations
> which came forth from my mouth."

(BUDGE : ibid., p. 141.)

But if Tem is the Creator *in toto* why differentiate
him from Ra ? Because Ra is *more* than the Creator, he
is also, for instance, the Preserver, and as such has
many aspects which are not included in Tem. Ra, again,
has one symbol which is *inclusive*, the Disc of the Sun ;
but this may be " borrowed " by any other god in his
capacity as an *aspect* of the One One. Thus, in practice,
all those gods of Egypt which have a direct connection
with the forces of Light have also a solar symbol.
Such symbols are clearly in the nature of totem signs, and
should not be confused with those others which are
carefully differentiated from the Disc even as their
" owners " are differentiated from Ra. We can follow
these ideas in the form of one of the usual tables of
Terms and *levels*. Needless to say, the arrangement
is not, and could never be, an accurate summary of
the " framework " in Egypt. It does, however, clarify
the situation considerably, and indicates a fuller statement
of the equations of which the Appendix provides only
abbreviated examples.

## TERMS AND LEVELS OF EGYPTIAN GODS

### PRĒ'-HARAKHTI
"Master of the Universe, Lord to the Boundary."
### RA-PTAH-AMON-AMEN-ATEN

| | | | |
|---|---|---|---|
| 1. | *Horus-the-Elder* The Face of the Heavens | *Sun/Moon* The Eyes in the Face of Horus | *Thoth* The Word |
| 2. | R*a*, The Sun | *Khepri/Tem* Rising    Setting | ,, |
| 3. | (Eye of Ra) | *Shu/Tefnut//Gebb/Nutt* Heat Moisture   Earth Sky | Horus The Son Light |
| | | *Mut* | |
| 4. | *Osiris-Ra* | *Isis///Nepthys* Growth   Decay | *Horus-Osiris* Child-King |
| 5. | *Set* Virility | *Bast////Sekmet* Fecundity   Mortality | *Min-Bes* Sensuality |
| 6. | *Apep* Serpent Black Pig "Set Animal" Goat (of Mendes) | Crocodile Cat Lioness | Phallus Serpent |

I think that is about as far as we dare go, though additional correspondences certainly present specious credentials. But we have all the essentials and can afford to ignore the rest, even including Anubis, the "Opener of the Way," whose nature completely eludes me. Actually we only require the *human* equation, No. 4 on the Table ; and so we can leave generalities in favour of the familiar territory of the Hero. The road is plain enough, indeed the composite Osiris/Horus bears nearly all the symbols of the Christ. As in the case of Hercules, it is as well to use a tabulation, chiefly so as to preserve the sense of distinct attributes.

### The Symbols of Osiris/Horus.

1. Horus is conceived of the Spirit (Ra) as well as by human Father (Osiris) and a marvellous Mother (Isis). The Father is a King.

2. The birth of the Child is miraculous. According to Plutarch the event took place *out of time*. His version describes Nut as giving birth to Osiris (who is here the Hero-child) on a day made beyond the year. To make this day, light had been " won " from Ra by Silene (Moon). At the time of the birth a voice was heard proclaiming : " The Lord of all the earth is born."

   In a less abstract account the Child (now Horus) is conceived from the dead body of Osiris, which had been reintegrated by Isis and vivified by Thoth.

3. The Child (Horus) becomes a Warrior. He seizes the diadem from his Mother's head (overcoming the Mother . . . gaining power over matter). He is in constant battle with the enemy of his Divine Father, though destined to ultimate victory.

4. The Warrior-King (Osiris) is betrayed by Set, whose followers nail him down in a wonderful chest of wood which thus becomes his coffin. The chest is set adrift and is eventually washed ashore in a foreign land. There a tree grew round the chest, completely enclosing it. The tree, which was evidently of peculiar merit (Tree of Life) was taken to the palace of the queen of

the land, Atenais, who may be Istar . . . that
Asiatic Mother whose most popular attribute
was the annual slaughter of her lover. Indeed,
it might well have been the womb (or palace) of
the Destroyer which enclosed the Hero (incest),
for the Destroyer is an aspect of Isis[1] in her
capacity of Dual Mother. It is not surprising,
therefore, that Isis found the magical tree and
brought it back to Byblos in Egypt where it
was at one time worshipped. It was there,
presumably, that the Tree of Death became the
Tree of Birth and Osiris rose from the dead to
become co-equal with Ra.

5. The very important myth of the dismemberment of
Osiris should be considered apart from the points
just dealt with, since it represents a cosmic
rather than a mystical allegory. As I see it, the
scattering of the Father's members over the
Earth is equivalent to the diffusion of consciousness, which has been recognised as the descent
of Spirit into Matter. The time when the
diffusion is greatest is clearly at the bottom of
the *descent* (" fall "). Thereafter the *ascent*
proceeds through Matter until the Triple Christ
is born of a human mother ; so that it might be
said that the Mother *reintegrated* the Father so
that from him she might bear the Son. The
point is the most difficult one which we have yet
had to consider, and I have not attempted to
treat it fully, partly on that account, and partly
because it is not essential to the argument. The
implications of the myth in our own terms will

[1] Nepthys.

be found a few pages hence under the symbols of *Midsummer* (q.v.).

From the career of the Hero as it has just been outlined, it is obvious that the peak of the whole system is that of the resurrection, necessarily an abstract and therefore difficult concept. Perhaps for that reason there is a great deal of confusion in the rituals, though beneath trivialities and inconsistencies there is a certain amount of truth which cannot be hidden. After all, it is really of no consequence if whole mountains of falsehood are found in the course of the search for truth. All falsehood together cannot stand in the way of a very little truth. That the Mysteries of Osiris, which formed in their entirety a most elaborate drama, should have included much that is primitive and gross is only to be expected, as Budge himself says :

" . . . There was not the smallest action on the part of any member of the men and women who acted the Osiris Drama, and not a sentence in the liturgy which did not refer to some historical happening of vital significance to the follower of Osiris. Many of these happenings dated from the dawn of the cult of Osiris, and the Egyptians of the Dynastic period, not knowing exactly what they were, followed tradition blindly.

(Op. cit., 515.)

With that qualification, I can confidently refer the reader to the standard sources, and for the sake of encouragement will give two quotations the like of which for sheer power in the terms of their faith are scarcely to be matched even in Christianity. . . . Yet, in a real sense, this *is* Christianity. The first citation is from the Papyrus of Nekht (Brit. Mus. 10471) and is taken from Shorter (op. cit., p. 65).

## "ADORATION OF RA by the Scribe and Royal Commander NEKHT

"He saith, Homage to thee who art brilliant and mighty! When thou hast dawned in the horizon of the sky there is praise of thee in the mouth of all people. Thou art become beautiful and young as a Disc in the hand of thy Mother. Dawn thou in every place, thy heart being enlarged forever!

"The divinities of the Two Lands come to thee bowing down, they give praise at thy shining forth. Thou dawnest in the horizon of the sky, thou brightenest the Two Lands with Malachite.

"Thou art the Divine Youth, the Heir of Eternity, who begat himself and brought himself forth, King of this land, ruler of the Tuat, Chief of the Districts of the Other World who came forth from the Water, who emerged from Nun, who reared himself and made splendid his children!

"Living God, Lord of Love! All folk live when thou shinest, dawning as King of the Gods. O Lord of the Sky, Lord of the Earth, King of Truth, Lord of Eternity, Ruler of Everlasting, Sovereign of all the Gods, Living God who made Eternity, who created the sky and established himself therein!

"The Nine are in jubilation at thy shining forth, the earth is in joy at beholding thy beams, the people come forth rejoicing to behold thy beauty every day."

And the next quotation is "relayed" from Budge (op. cit., p. 521), having come from Papyrus No. 10188 (Brit. Mus.). There have been some omissions in order to reinforce as much as possible the particular aspect of it which is our immediate concern. To this end also notes have been added to certain passages of particular importance.

## "THE LAMENT OF THE SISTERS
### (Isis and Nepthys over the dead Osiris)

"Beautiful Youth, come to thy exalted house at once; we see thee not.

" Hail, Beautiful Boy, come to thy house, draw nigh after thy separation from us.

" Hail, Beautiful Youth, Pilot of Time, who groweth except at this hour.[i]

" Holy image of his Father, mysterious essence proceeding from Tem.

" The Lord! How much more wonderful is he than his Father,[ii] the first-born son of the womb of his Mother.

" Come back to us in thy actual form; we will embrace thee. Depart not from us, thou Beautiful Face, dearly beloved one, the Image of Tem, Master of Love.[iii]

" Come thou in peace, our Lord, we would see thee.

" Great Mighty One among the Gods, the road which thou travellest cannot be described.[iv]

" The Babe, the Child at morn and at eve,[v] except when thou encirclest the heavens and the earth with thy bodily form.[vi]

" Come, thou Babe, growing young when setting,[v] our Lord, we would see thee.

" Come in peace, Great Babe of His Father, thou art established in thy house.

" Whilst thou travellest thou art hymned by us,[vii] and life springeth up for us out of thy nothingness. O our Lord, come in peace, let us see thee.

" Hail, Beautiful Boy, come to thy exalted house; let thy back be to thy house. The Gods are upon their thrones. Hail! Come in peace, King.

" Babe! How lovely it is to see thee! Come, come to us, O Great One, glorify our love.

" O ye gods who are in Heaven.
O ye gods who are in Earth.
O ye gods who are in the Tuat.
O ye gods who are in the Abyss.
O ye gods who are in the service of the Deep.[viii]
We follow the Lord, the Lord of Love!"

## NOTES

*The Sisters.*

Isis and Nepthys clearly represent the great duality, positive and negative, male and female, life and death, who are made one by the sovereign force of love. "The rubric orders that these verses be sung in the temple of Osiris Khenti Amentui, the Great God, the Lord of Abydos, on the 22nd to the 26th days of the fourth month of the season of Akhet by two priestesses. These women were virgins, and they were ceremonially pure."

i *" who groweth except at this hour."*
    The destiny of the Hero is infinite, and there is one occasion only when it appears otherwise, at death.

ii *" How much more beautiful is he than his Father."*
    The Son, unlike the Father, is a product of space/time, the result of a *process of becoming*.

iii *" Master of Love "*—*" God is Love."*

iv *" the road which thou travellest cannot be described."*
    The " road " is the growth of self-consciousness, subjective, abstract. Description in terms of symbols is second-hand.

v *" Child at morn and at eve "*
    i.e. " Twice-born " ; in the Morning born of Matter (Water), in the evening of Spirit (Fire). When he " sets " the Sun re-enters the Mother for the second birth (underworld journey). Thus he is " growing young when setting."

vi *" when thou encirclest the heavens in bodily form."*
    This must refer to the *cosmic* allegory . . . the Child is destined to re-integrate with the Father who *includes* the universe. It may also refer to the mystical crucifixion of Man against the forces of nature. Osiris is sometimes represented crucified against the vault of heaven.

vii *" Whilst thou travellest "* . . .
    The Journey in the Underworld—in the restricted sense of the Egyptian tradition. To be distinguished from the general " unconscious " significance of the phrase. (See later.)

viii *" Abyss "* . . . *" service of the Deep."*
    Even the " powers of darkness " are ultimately vassals of the Lord of Light.

---

We must now shift the emphasis away from personifications to the solar cycles upon which they depend ; for it cannot be over-emphasised that if the " Cult of the

Sun " means anything, it is that the system is built upon the solar symbols *per se*. The characteristics of the various gods are secondary, and the attributes of the Sun the only primaries. Of these we have already recognised the two " phases " of rising and setting, the light and the dark. These now come up for expansion. Reasons have been put forward for starting the cycle at Midsummer instead of Midwinter when the Christ-child is born. It will be remembered that the cycles of creation began with the descent of Spirit into Matter and this movement is the rôle of Tem. It is only after the descent is complete that the ascent can occur . . . there are no " ups " without the corresponding " downs."

And now let us plunge boldly into the complex interpretation which follows from this simple premise. I make no apology for certain aspects which may appear insufficiently supported by logical evidence. It is necessary to give a complete picture . . . as far as possible, of the whole cycle, and I am not justified in omitting portions merely because the explanation that I can furnish is not in itself adequate.

Our first concern shall be specifically with reference to the *annual* cycle, and the divine plan as a whole, though within that *cosmic* allegory are concealed others, particularly that which we have designated *mystical*, i.e. in terms of the individual. As far as possible we shall use the abstract terms, which by now ought to have acquired fairly precise significance, but Egyptian and Christian personification will be used for illustration. As usual we shall tabulate for the sake of clarity.

## Section II

# THE ANNUAL CYCLE

The reading depends upon the following astronomic dates : Summer and Winter Solstices, Vernal and Autumnal Equinoxes. The symbolic Christian equivalents are Ascension, Incarnation, Crucifixion, and All Saints (Hallow-e'en).

### 1.  Midsummer (Alpha)

We have to regard this date as " Alpha," that from which the *descent* begins. Consciousness elaborates a progressive density of Matter and diffuses into it, reaching the greatest diffusion in the densest Matter at the bottom of the " fall." This means that consciousness must be regarded as implicit in all matter, even the minerals ; but, rising thereafter, it becomes more and more concentrated until a single physical body becomes *self-conscious*. It is this event—which might be referred to as " individualisation " if the word were not so unhandy, which corresponds to the birth of the Triple Christ who was incarnate (in the Mother) by that same process of *descent* or *fall*. The birth of self-consciousness, in fact, is the culmination of the long " six months " process which was initiated at " Alpha." . . . The Christ is old, very, very old, or ever he is born as Man. " Before Abraham was, I am."

In support of this contention I would point out that science has no longer any valid grounds on which to oppose it. Self-consciousness is a peculiar phenomenon . . . probably restricted to humanity, which may very well have evolved from what we may call " group-consciousness," a state in which the single organism is a mere unit, and the flock, hive, herd, species, or what not, is the " individual " . . . if that term may be used somewhat out of place. But self-consciousness is more than a mere unit of consciousness, even if it is confined to one physical unit . . . unlike the lower " kingdoms of nature." Theology asserts that this difference consists in the fact that the Individual contains a divine " spark," a spiritual identity. It might be possible to have an Individual without such a spark. . . .

But the point is beyond our necessity. It is sufficient to consider self-consciousness as a product of evolution, " born " when, for the first time, consciousness is so contracted that a unit of self-consciousness coincides with a physical unit.

Now, since a " true " allegory is applicable to all *levels* it follows that if we can demonstrate the continuity of physical life we may (tentatively) infer the continuity of consciousness, of which physical life is a manifestation. And if we can further discover that physical life is derived and sustained from the Sun as its ultimate source, it is clear that we have indirect evidence for the continuity of that divine plan which is the basis of the " Cult of the Sun." It so happens that a well-known American physiologist, Dr. Crile, has produced a theory which, in so far as a layman can follow his technical arguments, *proves the continuity of life*. He recognises no division between what are commonly called the " living " and the " non-living," finding the former to arise from the latter under the play of solar radiation. And he finds further that this solar life is continuous in its *ascent* through the " kingdoms of nature." But let us go to the source itself . . . *The Phenomena of Life* :

" Oxidation produces radiant energy.
Radiant energy generates electric currents in protoplasm,
Electricity is the energy which governs the activity of protoplasm.
Therefore the phenomena of life must be due to radiant and electrical energy."

(p. 17.)

" One recognises three phases of the energy mechanism of protoplasm. The first is the nitrogen of the pre-plant phase ; the second, the carbon of the plant phase ; the third and last, the oxygen or disintegration phase . . . the animal phase."

(p. 361.)

" Thus we have sketched the long road which we have travelled to arrive at the conception that not only this or that but every phenomenon of life can be identified in terms of physics and can be explained in the light of the Radio-Electric Theory. The Radio-Electric Theory suggests that plants are generated by radiant and electric energy ; that animals are constructed and operated by the radiant and electric energy stored in the plant ; that the energy of the body is released by oxidation in the radiogens which are patterned after the solar system ; that, as the result of this oxidation, radiations of different wavelengths are released ; that the genesis of radiation is the first step in the genesis of tissues ; that organisms can exist and function only in the presence of mechanisms that maintain differences of potential.

Thus, according to the Radio-Electric Theory, living organisms are bi-polar mechanisms constructed and energised by radiant and electric energy." (p. 368.)

The phrase " patterned after the solar system " may perhaps require comment, though the rest is clear enough. I think that Dr. Crile has in mind those discoveries in the constitution of matter which recognise the ultimate units as no " matter " at all, being, instead of particles, *abstract* (mathematical) terms expressed as opposites, e.g. electron/ proton, whose activities suggest the macrocosmic activities of corresponding astronomical units. We arrive, in fact, at a conception of Matter which is based frankly on *equations*, states of equilibrium resultant upon the interaction of pairs of forces . . . a love-relationship ! There is, as we have so often inferred already, only one force which integrates the entire universe in all the myriad forms of manifestation. *Sex*, if there be no substitute for that word, balances the stars in heaven as surely as the atoms in a molecule . . . or the " stars " in Hollywood for that matter !

At *bottom* it is all referable to the god Min.

Let me quote Sir Oliver Lodge in a passage where he sums up the views of Lloyd Morgan, Smuts, Whitehead, and Haldane :

" It is surely of interest to find, what seems to be indicated now by the higher physics, that this gradual increase of function with organisation can be traced down in regular succession till we reach the simplest units of all, even down to the electron and proton, which acquire properties when combined which they did not possess when separate. Another illustration from the widely prevalent phenomena of sex differentiation is obvious." *(Beyond Physics*, p. 152.)

In the light of the scientific attitude just quoted, we are now able to regard the solar *descent* in terms of energy, and, further, it is seen that this mathematical conception follows the " framework " of relationships both in respect of Terms and *levels*. Regarded from the standpoint of evolution, it even includes our three cycles of creation, albeit from Dr. Crile's viewpoint, in respect of the *ascent* only, through the three " kingdoms of nature," mineral, vegetable, animal. To gain a complete picture, the " human kingdom " should be super-imposed upon these, and thereafter the three superhuman levels with which we have chiefly been dealing. It appears as though the *levels*, like the Terms, differentiate into pairs, so that, just as we recognise " Dual Father " and " Dual Mother " making a fivefold equation, so do we find the *levels* duplicated above and below the intellectual mean of humanity, making a sevenfold system with forty-nine primary symbols. But all this is very much " in the air " . . . we had better leave it there.

Our immediate concern is with the three cycles of the *descent* which have already been in some measure described. This triple phase is symbolised in the three months of autumn and the three days of the traditional " descent into hell." There are, I believe, " heretical " views which regard the descent of the Christ as occurring before birth and not after death ; but be that as it may, I would like to put forward the idea that the unit of consciousness which is to become self-conscious descends with increasing diffusion even into the densest minerals. It follows that when the corresponding contraction has carried the unit into the human kingdom, there takes place that Immaculate Conception whereby self-consciousness is constituted the " Heir of God." Thus the formation of an Individual is purely animal as regards the body, but the impregnation of consciousness by the Spirit is quite another matter.

Again the full implications are beyond the scope of the present argument, and we shall therefore bring this initial explanation of the solar allegory to an end with a note upon " collective intelligence." It has for long been suggested that flocks of birds, hives of bees, and other such " units," must possess a communal consciousness in order to bring about the marvellous co-operation which is evident among them. Each bird, or bee, becomes as it were a " cell " in a single organism, a single consciousness, and the lower the form of life the more " cells " there are to each such unit. A million flies, ten thousand bees, a hundred lions, and nine cats ? We only want to illustrate the idea, which at least is firmly founded on observed facts and challenges a more adequate—or should I say " plausible "—explanation.

And then, at the top of the animal scale, standing on the threshold of another world, stands Man, the self-conscious, the *rational* animal. Thus fresh significance is lent to a quotation already made.

*Midsummer* is also remarkable for the way in which it is recognised in folklore as the beginning of the *dark* phase of the year. It is the occasion of the " Witches' Sabbat," and all kinds of infernal celebration, as is testified by the many strange customs recounted in *The Golden Bough*, most of which, it should be added, are essentially " white " with the object of securing magical protection during the remaining *dangerous* months until Christmas. And mention of Christmas brings the whole question to a sharp focus, for in my view the significance of Midsummer can never be fully appreciated until it is regarded as the opposite of the " white " festival. Its whole symbolic value lies in the fact that Midsummer celebrates *the birth of Antichrist*. The declining power of the Sun from that date witnesses to the growth of the Daughter as surely as the waxing Sun symbolises the growth of the Son.

## 2. THE AUTUMNAL EQUINOX

As with the opposite date, that of the Vernal Equinox, this event symbolises *crucifixion*, since at this time the sun " crosses the equator " and the powers of Light and Darkness hang in the balance. But, unlike the other day, the Autumnal Equinox is the sign of the crucifixion of Antichrist, the Daughter Aradia. And she is as much immortal as her counterpart, so that death has no power over her . . . a paradox! And yet not such a paradox after all, for Antichrist herself is Death and *her* triumph is ultimate negation. But we are not now concerned with ultimates; the real significance of the event is nearer than that. For the Daughter triumphs by the *power of her Mother*, who has been shown to be the personification of the material forces. Matter, in fact, dominates Spirit, and continues to do so until the descent comes to an end. Death appears to defeat life : and this is the meaning of the " Fall."

As the festival of All Souls, this solar date is well known, and, like that of Midsummer, is the subject of many pages of *The Golden Bough*. It is world-wide in its distribution and, allowing for differences of culture, bears striking similarity to the following type. The dead are regarded as being very near to the living, or perhaps it is the other way round. At all events the veil between them is partly drawn aside, and the powers of death and the dead themselves come into direct contact with man. And it is not usually a cheerful festival, as might be expected, for the dead are ghosts, tenuous shapes, redolent of the grave . . . although it must be conceded that they frequently eat and drink. But it is matter, the physical, which is dominant, the living breath of the Spirit is hidden as it is with those Shakespearean shades, the " sheeted dead," who " squeak and gibber in the Roman streets."

Thereafter the powers of darkness gather more and more force until the Light seems to have been completely extinguished. Thus the Collect for the First Sunday in Advent : " Almighty God, give us grace to put away the works of darkness and put upon us the armour of light."

---

" Not only among the Celts but throughout Europe, Hallowe'en, the night which marks the transition from autumn to winter, seems to have been of old the time of year when the souls of the departed were supposed to revisit their old homes in order to warm themselves by the fire and to comfort themselves with the good cheer provided for them in the kitchen or the parlour by their affectionate kinsfolk. It was, perhaps, a natural thought that the approach of winter should

drive the poor shivering, hungry ghosts from the bare fields
and the leafless woodlands to the shelter of the cottage with
its familiar fireside. . . .

" But it is not only the souls of the departed who are supposed
to be hovering unseen on the day when ' autumn to winter
resigns the pale year.' Witches then speed on their errands of
mischief, some sweeping through the air on besoms, others
galloping along the roads on tabby-cats, which for that evening are turned into coal-black steeds. The fairies, too, are
all let loose, and hobgoblins of every sort roam freely about.

(*The Golden Bough*, p. 634.)

This, of course, in preparation of Christmas and the
*ascent*.

### 3. THE WINTER SOLSTICE—Maedrenack, the Mother's Night.[1]

At midnight the Virgin who is always Virgin, and
whose dwelling is a human being—all human beings—
gives birth to a Son who is conceived of the Spirit as
well as " after the flesh." This Son includes all his
ancestors, Father and Mother, and *dual* Father and
Mother.

Now and again there is born on earth a Hero at this
hour, in whose life truth finds symbolic expression,
defying equally both time and translation. From
midnight, Midwinter, that " darkest hour " on Horeb,
the Light waxes until once again there is a " crossing
over," from which it rises in perfection by the power of
the Father. Thereafter, however, it is hidden, and is to
be found only in the course of the Quest : " A little
while, and ye shall not see me : and again a little while
and ye shall see me, because I go to the Father."

---

[1] It appears that in pagan Britain, as in most other countries,
Christmas Eve was sacred to the Virgin, possibly with primary
reference to the apparent emergence of the " new " Sun from the
constellation Virgo.

(John xvi, 16.) The Christ-child, whether Jesus or Tammuz, Quetzalcoatl or Horus, is a physical symbol to be seen and appreciated in physical terms and by the intellect. But the King is not of this world, and is to be found only when this world and the Land of the Ever-Living no longer keep a closed frontier to the aspirant. Only then will he see the Light for the *second* time. Looked at in a slightly different way, the Light persists *behind* or *in* Matter, so that the apparent triumph of Antichrist in the autumn is only an illusion. Light can be born only from darkness, spirit from matter.

### 4. The Vernal Equinox

Having been betrayed, the Christ is sacrificed: hanged, pierced, castrated, coffined; the symbols varying within certain limits to include, among a greater company, Attis, Adonis, Tammuz, Quetzalcoatl, Chen-razee (Kwan Yin), Krishna, Osiris/Horus, Jesus, and Adam. Adam because at Golgotha that "old Adam," the "brute upon which he stands," is buried for ever and the Heir of God rises up from the same place. This time it is the Son who triumphs *by the power of his Father*, and death itself must die . . . the complement of that paradox already mentioned.

Life rises out of Death, which stands revealed as no destruction at all, save perhaps, of that physical vehicle which is "Cæsar's." I say "perhaps" because there seems no reason why even the physical body must always disintegrate since, granting it to be a function of vibration, it should be possible to raise the "wavelength." Since Fire affects the transmutation of one Element into another, it might also transmute the physical water into the mystical equivalent, the gross body into the immortal body. But again we are going beyond our proper reach.

Returning from the particular to the general, the three months succeeding the Vernal Equinox are seen to "balance" those following the autumn date in a progressive ascent of three cycles, not now concerning the sub-human *levels*—those were traversed before Christmas, but with the superhuman, culminating in the final integration whereby the Son becomes "one with the Father." There are, in fine, at least three resurrections : (i) Entry into "Eden" ; (ii) Entry into "Heaven" ; (iii) Entry into "Unity," the last being best characterised in the Oriental conception of Nirvana.

## 5. THE SUMMER SOLSTICE (OMEGA)

So the cycle is completed and we must leave the mystery with a vague sense that even this is not so much an end as a fresh beginning. The destiny of the Christ is infinite, and one is reminded of the Egyptian conception of the " Gods of the Gods " whose evolution proceeds in some vast scheme as far beyond our God as our God is beyond us.[1] But we have at all events seen something of the intricate interrelationship of the solar year, and have even equated it satisfactorily with abstract terms which were arrived at by an analysis having no *a priori* connection with the Sun or even with religion. No doubt it would be possible to go further, but one suddenly remembers Icarus.

## 6. THE LUNAR CYCLE

Although no direct mention has been made of the Moon, it has been understood in reference to the birth

[1] Cf. last paragraph (quotation) where " Alpha and Omega " speaks of *His* God.

of Antichrist, whose Mother is the Moon.  The attributes
of the Mother have been thoroughly sifted on several
occasions, and the most that is now needed is the
recognition of the Moon's observed affinity with physical
growth and decay.  Gestation periods are all in terms of
Lunar months, sick persons are said to die " at the
turning of the tide," and the tide is the effect of Lunar
activity (Moon-Mother-Water).  Even modern horticul-
turists find that the Moon influences growth from seed,
and in that way close the links which bind them to
distant ancestors whose spring sacrifices were the focus
of so many Vegetation Cults, which, as we have seen,
lead from bestiality to the Eucharist.

Now the chief feature of the Vegetation Cults as such
is probably their insistence upon the period of Winter
as a journey or sojourn of the Light (god of Light) in
the Underworld, and as the Egyptian journey of Osiris,
himself a vegetation god, is perhaps the most elaborate
ritual of such a journey (be it daily or yearly), we cannot
close the subject without reference to it.  Comparison
should be made with the Persephone/Demeter and
similar myths.

It should also be remembered that if Horus-the-Elder
is the Unity whose " eyes " are the Sun and Moon, then
both Sun and Moon are themselves triunities, dual
Father/Son and dual Mother/Daughter, the implied
androgynity being expressed by the *male* aspect of the
Moon (Man-in-the-Moon) and the *female* aspect of
the Sun (Holy Ghost).  These are the true " Great
Nine."

SECTION III

## THE UNDERWORLD

Apart from its possible meaning as the " descent into hell," there is a great mass of tradition concerning a journey made during the night or winter. This idea finds, as usual, its fullest expression in the Egyptian system, but the details are so involved that any attempt at direct analysis is hopeless. Fortunately it is also unnecessary. . . . It will be sufficient if we can discover the identity of this " underworld," for I am persuaded that at least it does not represent an " under-the-earth " realm, except in a subsidiary sense.

From the standpoint of those who are natural dwellers in " heaven," the " underworld " would clearly correspond with the Earth itself. It is only when judged from the material standpoint that " underworld " can be referred to a level beneath the physical, and that is not the attitude of the gods who are represented as making the journey. Again, when Adam and Eve left Paradise, they " went out into the night," the symbolic Winter . . . and yet they remained on earth. The Castle of the Grail is to be found by an earthly pilgrimage, yet the Castle is not earthly, but belongs to the *mystic level* as surely as does the Cauldron of Annwn. . . . Annwn being just such an underworld as that of the Tuat or the classical myths. But the most significant argument against the popular concept of " Hell " is that if such a realm exists upon a level lower than the physical, then it must be perceptible to physical senses. For the *levels* represent degrees of abstraction of which the grossest is the physical world with which we are familiar. A *more* material realm is therefore inconceivable by definition.

To this basic argument may be added the evidence afforded by Eden and the Grail, so that we arrive at a tentative conclusion to the effect that the traditional " journey " is none other than the incarnate life on earth, which is the means or vehicle of the mystical quest. Adam and Eve journey through the underworld as do the Knights of the Grail, Arthur, Osiris, and Jesus ; for the Son of Man lives simultaneously on all three levels, though not necessarily self-conscious on them all. In the case of Osiris, for instance, the journey is made in a boat (body, " ark "), which is drawn through the body of a serpent before being " re-born." The title of the God while on this dark journey is Afu—" body." At all events, " let's pretend " that it *is* this earth of ours which is the " under-heaven-world " and through which we make the dark journey. Then we are here and now in that " place of shades," the " vale of tears," called variously Hell, Hades, Sheol, Annwn, Tuat (esp. Amenti), Niflheim. But if it is comforting to reflect that we are already in Hell, we should not forget that we have to distinguish that realm from the " place of torment " which is Gehenna, a concept found in almost all cults. At the same time it should be remembered that we are restricted to the *physical level* only in so far as we are bound therein by our animal nature. Though his body be on earth a man may nevertheless know Heaven . . . or Gehenna. In fact, whatever the symbols under which they appear, the various realms are fundamentally *states of consciousness*. With which qualification we are at liberty to tackle the signs themselves, using the Egyptian terms to begin with.

First, the " Place of Shades," a description of the

passage of Osiris through the region of Urnes, from the book of Ami Tuat. The God incarnate (Afu) sheds his light upon the inhabitants of this world for a short time, and then he passes on as the Hero's destiny requires. The passage is typical of the language in which such scenes are described. (See Budge, op. cit., 359.)

" *The Second Hour.*

" The boat of Afu now became the ' Boat of the Earth,' and in it the Night-Sun passed through the body of Aker, a god with the head of a bull or lion at each end of his body. Afu was preceded by four boats : (1) the ' Boat of the Full Moon ' ; (2) a boat with the fetish Hathor ; (3) a boat containing an ichneumon (?) from the back of which emerge the head of Osiris and a White Crown ; (4) the boat of the Grain-god Neper.

" Multitudes of the dead lived in Urnes, and when Afu shed his light upon them they all sprang to life and accepted the services of the gods their neighbours, who by Afu's command provided for their wants. When Afu departed darkness fell upon them, and they set up a wail and wept bitterly."

And here is a version of the Egyptian Gehenna from the same book. (Ibid., p. 364.)

" *The Eleventh Hour.*

" On the left bank (of the river of the journey) the region is of blazing fire, which is ruled over by Horus in the form of a hawk-headed man wearing the solar disc and a cobra, and holding a boomerang in his hand. This weapon is really a serpent which, when hurled at an enemy, kills him and returns to the god. Before him, standing on its tail, is the serpent ' Set of millions of years.' Here, too, are the awful fire pits in which the souls, shadows, and bodies of the enemies of Ra and Osiris are cremated ; in one pit the damned are immersed head downwards, and in another they are seen standing up to their necks in the consuming fire. The fires are maintained by goddesses who spew it out of their mouths."

So much for the particulars. It is now necessary to discover the essential generalities. To begin with, Gehenna is notoriously a " place of fire and brimstone." Fire is Spirit, and it requires little imagination or experience to realise that a spiritual environment torments one whose normal habitat is Matter. A " fish out of water " would suffer in much the same way as a " man out of matter." And brimstone is the alchemical sulphur, the material or " earth " principle of the Great Work. Consider the famous statement :

" Where their worm dieth not and the fire is not quenched."

(Isaiah lxvi, 24 ; Mark ix, 48.)

Suppose that the worm (serpent) is the materiality (desire) already mentioned, then if such survives in an environment which is spiritual and *not* material, such a place would become for the unfortunate individual exceedingly uncongenial. The worm, in fact, is our old friend the *serpent of Eden* who has failed to be transformed into the " radiant and perfect serpent."

That being so, we should expect to find the serpent playing a considerable rôle in Gehenna. And so he does, whether in Dante's imagination or in those more average psychic projections of mythology. Curiously enough the most serpentine of all such realms . . . even including the Egyptian . . . is associated with a country where the snake plays a very minor part in the affairs of the people. I refer to the Norse " Nastrond," the " strand of corpses."

The Scandinavians, like the Thibetans, Egyptians, and Israelites, recognise a " multiple " underworld, the various divisions of which evidently correspond, at least to some extent, with the misery or happiness of their respective inhabitants. Such a conception is

wellnigh universal. Have not the Christians a tradition
of the " seventh heaven," which is a common phrase in
conversation ? And presumably there is a counterpart
" seventh hell " as in ancient Jewish folklore.

But to return to Nastrond, which is of the same type
as that ultimate icy pit reserved, in, the " Inferno " for
Judas ; where the arch-sinner, surrounded by ice, is
for ever devoured by a monster—who can hardly be
other than the famous Serpent. In Nastrond is a region
of ice caves whose very walls are formed of wattled
serpents, their fangs dripping perpetual venom. In
utter dark doomed souls wade the poisoned streams.
Let us see what this means in terms of symbolism.

Place of ice . . . place of water-without-heat. Hence,
place of disintegration. Similarly darkness, the combina-
tion meaning that " locality " where there is *no* Spirit
(Fire or Light). Thus, whereas Gehenna is a spiritual
realm where the " worm " which remains in man is
purged away in that perpetual " fire," the ultimate
" hell " is a place where there is no longer any spirit
or any love. Thus those who enter are no longer even
potentially immortal and remain bound by the law of
the Destroyer. It is in a particular part of Nastrond
that the " hopeless cases " meet their final fate, in the
great pit of Hvergelmir, where their corpses provide
food for the Destroyer herself in the shape of the serpent
Nidhug, whose chief rôle is the gnawing of the roots of
Yggdrasil, the Tree of Life. Moreover, the corpses are
" washed " into Hvergelmir, the water-symbol again
dominant.

> " A hall standing far from the sun
> In Nastrond ;
> Its doors are northward turned,
> Venom drops fall in through the apertures ;
> Entwined is that hall with serpents' backs.

There she saw wading the sluggish streams
Bloodthirsty men and perjurers,
And him whom the ear beguiles of another's wife.
There Nidhug sucks the corpses of the dead."

(SAEMUND's *Edda*, trans. Thorpe.)

Such ideas as these bring forward the whole scheme of the *levels* in relation to the Cult of the Sun, and we should expect to find that wherever the solar mythos had attained any considerable elaboration there would follow at least the recognition of the triad Heaven, Earth, Hell. . . . All three can represent states of consciousness which we may successively experience in Piccadilly, but we are not now concerned with such speculations. The main thing is that, if Egypt be taken as typical of such cults, there must appear to the followers a different realm " ruled " by the Sun during day and night, winter and summer ; and since the sun at night was certainly not " on earth," we have already a crude conception of the three *levels*. Such a concept might well have formed the basis of a ritual like that which must have inspired the circles of Stonehenge, Carnac, Avebury, and similar places. Indeed the cult may have been considerably advanced, since the Serpent also comes into the picture.

" It (the serpent) stood for them (prehistoric peoples, Iberians in particular) for the mystery of the rebirth of life. . . . In a deeper and more mystical sense it symbolised the progress and processional from the outer material life from degree to degree in spiral motion through the various points of initiation. . . . A true expression of the spiral motion of the serpent would take us into dimensions beyond human speech."

(Foster Forbes in a broadcast. Vide *Listener*,
Vol. XVIII, Nos. 454–6.)

Whether we are prepared to accept Mr. Forbes' ideas in full by no means lessens the cogency of his testimony, for there is a certain common prehistoric symbol which is very widespread in its distribution and seems to derive from the same ideas. It is commonly referred to as the " cup and ring " and shows a series of concentric circles pierced by a serpentine line. Of this type of carving seven variations have been distinguished, all of which, however, conform to the basic idea . . . concentric circles.[1] The most common class (No. 4) reproduces exactly what Foster Forbes regards as the symbolic essentials of the stone and wood circles, i.e. a sinuous avenue, penetrating various belts to reach the centre. Thus, even such primitive peoples as these may have had some understanding of wisdom long since passed out of general knowledge—that of the evolution of consciousness. But whether they had or not, there is even more significant testimony to be found from prehistory in the British Isles. For instance, there is a relic in the British Museum described as follows :

" Gold-plated sun-disc found with a cremated burial in Lansdown Links near Bath . . . conjectural reconstruction from fragments " (which are exhibited).

The disc is about six inches across and consists of a series of patterns arranged upon three concentric circles, with various other details of interest including the " sacred " number seven used seven times. No doubt it would be possible to suggest an analysis, yet it seems that the details are too speculative, and we shall be content if this remarkable relic is accepted as a link between whatever solar faith existed as the *raison d'être* of Stonehenge, and the highly developed symbols of *Bardass*.

[1] SIR J. Y. SIMPSON : *British Archaic Sculpturings*.

That book, purporting to represent the ancient Druidic teaching as it was known in Wales . . . and which is popularly identified with the megalithic culture, has as its central symbol the same three circles. But in *Bardass*, whatever the historical authenticity of the work, the idea has been carried far enough to bring the argument full circle into the highest realms of human speculation.

The key symbol is shown as a single unit . . . the three circles are essentially one, for all are enclosed in the " Sun " formed by rayed projections on the outer circle. The three, in sequence from the centre, are Abred (the *physical level*), Gwynfyd (the *mystic level*), and Ceugant (the *cosmic level*), which is inhabited by God alone and represents infinity.

The following questions and answers are from Vol. I, pp. 224 ff., and will be found with collateral information in *Myths of the Celtic Race* : T. W. Rolleston :

" Q. Whence didst thou proceed ?

A. I came from the Great World, having my beginning in Annwn (the lowest region of Abred).

Q. Where art thou now ? and how camest thou to what thou art ?

A. I am in the Little World, whither I came, having traversed the circle of Abred, and now I am a Man, at its termination and extreme limits (i.e. on the threshold of the *mystic level*).

Q. What wert thou before thou didst become a man, in the circle of Abred ?

A. I was in Annwn the least possible that was capable of life and the nearest possible to absolute death ; and I came in every form and through every form capable of a body and life to the state of man along the circle of Abred, where my condition was severe and grievous during the age of ages, ever since I was parted in Annwn from the dead, by the gift of God, and His great generosity, and his unlimited and endless love.

Q. Through how many different forms didst thou come, and what happened unto thee ?

A. Through every form capable of life, in water, in earth, in air. And there happened unto me every severity every hardship, every evil, and every suffering."

It will be recalled that the Druidic *secret name*, O.I.V., came from this same book, *Bardass*, and so also does the following profound assertion :

"God is the greatest of all, and the immeasurable of intelligence ;
And there can be no existence to any thing but from intelligence."

We should read in all probability " consciousness " rather than intelligence, for the limitations of the rational faculty itself are too narrow for the Druidic tradition. The intellect is a very useful tool, but it is by no means the only tool by which the universe may be explored, and it has very considerable limitations, the chief of which, from such a viewpoint as ours, is that the further the analysis (of matter) is pushed the more nebulous is the result. Modernity has specialised in such intellectual processes until it appears to squat spider-wise in the centre of a vast web of knowledge which becomes more and more tenuous as it leaves the centre, and which seems to be supported by nothing, leading nowhere, and . . . worst of all, derived from nowhere. In case this seems an exaggeration, let us outline a modern intellectual approach to the constitution of matter, especially the matter of this earth.

Thanks to " popular " science, everyone is familiar with the current theory of cosmogenesis by cooling and condensation of nebulæ, as well as with complementary ideas on the structure of matter. We have—though not often do we stop to consider the fact—become accustomed to the notion that matter, for all its solidity, is something of an illusion. Picturesque analogies have tended to convince the " ordinary man " that the chair he sits on consists more of space than of matter. He can, if he takes the trouble to do so, visualise his own tenuous body as supported by a great number of small holes in nothing, held together by forces unspecified; and that these, combining into atoms and molecules and vibrating with colossal rapidity, somehow give him the impression of sitting upon something " real." (As to " holes in nothing " . . . Matter is said to consist of etheric vortices. Æther is not matter, hence a vortex in æther may be considered a " hole " in " nothing.")

In short, it is a commonplace that *matter* and *force* are indistinguishable, and that the universe itself is reducible to *equations* which are certainly not material, and are probably a function of consciousness. Leading scientists admit the universe as a mental design, among them Eddington, Jeans, Myers, and Lodge, of whom the last named has assembled evidence on just this point in a short work under the title of *Beyond Physics* (1930) from which I will again quote :

" To illustrate the extremely abstract treatment of nature by the modern mathematical physicist, even in its simpler forms, I will refer to an article in *Mind*, expounding a modern view about the nature of matter. In the issue of *Mind* for April 1920, Eddington gave a paper on ' The Meaning of Matter.' The highly abstract mode of regarding matter there advocated expresses it in terms of the tensor $G\mu\nu$ and the curvature of space. Eddington's expression for it, at that date, was $G\mu\nu - \frac{1}{2} g\mu\nu G$ ; in other words, he claims that matter is a variety of space-curvature and nothing else. It isn't that matter is something which curves or warps space, but that matter *is* the curvature."

That being the " reality " with which we are familiar, the thing we sit on, so to speak, we should be ready to consider how the elaboration of matter has been achieved in space/time. The anabolic process evidently begins with *radiation in space* from an unknown source. By processes also unknown the nucleus of a nebula is formed, and from that nucleus ultimately emerges, say, this Earth.

The period of time occupied in the production of the nebula is incalculable and we must start with the gaseous vortex itself. Here the best clue to the nature of the " matter " of which it is composed is provided by the density, which has been estimated at about 1/1,000,000,000,000,000,000th that of air . . . in other words an unimaginably perfect vacuum. (Density for " Orion," *Encyc. Brit.*, VII, 835.) Yet this vacuum represents an enormous elaboration over the state of " empty space " from which the nebula began. In the words of the *Britannica*, " in the ages occupied by stellar evolution a million years is but a day." (XVI, 186.) Millions of years elapsed before the nebula took form, and millions passed before it became liquid, again millions to become a red-hot solid, and again . . .

But let us fix another point of reference. How old is the Earth with all its usual elements ? My reference Bible (1830) says it was created in 4004 B.C., but the *Britannica* puts it at " between 1,500,000,000 and 3,000,000,000 years old." The figures are, of course, beyond the limits which can be " grasped " by the intellect without some fresh standard of judgment, yet they serve well enough to indicate the rate at which the great cosmic forces work.

And if we regard the process of world-formation as indicative of the anabolic process, we have a complementary indication of the rate at which katabolism works in the disintegration of radio-active substances, the densest forms of matter. For anabolism proceeds to the elaboration of the densest matter by *descent*, thereafter, side by side (at least, in some cases) with the rising tide of life, the dense matter breaks down in a chain of *ascent* which appears to lead back again to that " empty space " from which originally it was derived.

Thus Uranium, the densest of all elements, having an atomic weight of 238·2 against 195·2 for platinum, provides the following " generations " indicative of cosmic katabolism :

| | | | | |
|---|---|---|---|---|
| URANIUM | "lives" | 50,000,000,000,000,000,000 | years, | becoming |
| Uranium | $X_1$ | which endures | 23·5 days, | „ |
| „ | $X_2$ | „ | 1·7 minutes, | „ |
| „ | 2 | „ | 2,000,000 years, | „ |
| Ionium | | „ | 100,000 „ | „ |
| Radium | | „ | 1730·375 „ | „ |
| Radium | Emanation | „ | 3·85 days, | „ |
| Radium | A | „ | 3·0 minutes, | „ |
| „ | B | „ | 26·8 „ | „ |
| „ | C | „ | 19·5 „ | „ |
| „ | D | „ | 16·5 years, | „ |
| „ | E | „ | 5 „ | „ |
| „ | F | „ | 136 days, | „ |
| „ | G | „ | ........................ | |

The quotation is from MELLOR : *Modern Inorganic Chemistry* (1925), p. 1030, and it illustrates well enough at once the triumph and the limitation of the mechanistic approach.

# CHAPTER NINE

## ŒDIPUS REX

". . . Behold, this is Œdipus,
Who unravelled the great riddle,
and was first in power."

AND so we come to the very focus of the symbols and the testing ground of our conclusions. Freud asserts : " The beginnings of ethics, religion, society, and art meet in the Œdipus complex."[1] Œdipus is not only the beginning, but the middle and the end also : the famous story is not significant only in a sexual sense ; it forms the most perfect expression of the relationship between the terms of our equation at *all* levels. For the equations are fundamentally " family relationships " and Œdipus *embodied* them in the most intimate form which is conceivable. Psychoanalysis appreciated and developed the symbolism until it appeared as the very sovereign key of mentality. But the psychological field is only one-third of that with which we have been dealing, for above it is the Trinity of Godhead, and below it is the territory of symbolic literature and tradition.

But although there are three equations for the sake of our method, they are reducible to one. For we are concerned primarily with Man, and he is not to be confined strictly to one *level* or another, but exists in some

[1] *Totem and Taboo*, p. 260.

degree on them all. Therefore it is the middle (*mystic*) equation which is the real key, and that is identical with the relationship so thoroughly worked out by the school of Freud. Indeed, since any additional interpretation must be made on the firm basis of those physical terms which are the stock-in-trade of every psychoanalyst, my task is considerably lightened.

In the first place Frazer and others have proved the identity of such heroes as Osiris, Attis, Adonis, and Tammuz, while that "person" which stands behind them all has been firmly linked to Œdipus by the psychologists. At most we have gone one step further in regarding all such heroes as personifications of the Christ, and, therefore, if what has gone before has not in itself proved convincing, the reader may still approach this crucial point in the argument with confidence born of better testimony than mine. Thus in the following short quotation Róheim sums up a great part of the mythological field which we have been exploring, and reduces it, as we have done, to this particular relationship:

"Nor can there be any doubt about the relationship between Attis and the Great Mother; the young Phrygian shepherd was both her lover and son. And if we combine this version with the variants that explain the death of Attis like that of Adonis and Tammuz by an accident that befell him on a boar hunt, and with the version representing Attis the son as killing and castrating his father, we have all the actors of the Primal Œdipus Drama."

(*Animism and the Divine King*, p. 220.)

But there is one respect in which we differ sharply from the Freudian interpretation. Where they are content to reduce the whole significance of the relationship to physical (sexual) terms, we have taken it one step further and sought a meaning in terms of consciousness itself with the aid of the mystical symbols of the Christ. In effect, all that we have so far accomplished has been the assembling of the cast and the preparation of the stage. It remains to see the play. If there are no results we have failed, but if there are results we have a case behind which is the authority, not of myself, for I am only the interpreter, but of the whole field of myth and religion on one side and of analytical psychology on the other. This is peculiarly satisfactory, for it seems that there are two main types for whom my conclusions will have little appeal . . . the orthodox theologian or churchman on one side and the materialist on the other.

But neither type can well set aside *both* authorities, and so there is fair prospect of acceptance for the results, to avoid which the materialist must deny his greatest ally, and the orthodox their scripture. . . . But we are anticipating.

The first step is to make sure that Œdipus *is* a personification of the Christ in the psychological sense, though he is obviously not one of the traditional Christs, such as Osiris/Horus. Thereafter we should be able to bring our argument full circle without any other major difficulties.

" Jesus, as these and many other statements indicate, was a severe sufferer from what Freudians call the Œdipus complex. He had an intense affection for his mother : the apocryphal New Testament has the angels announce that Mary will be ' a holy virgin for one husband, Christ,' and calls Christ ' her spouse and bridegroom.' Christ, in the orthodox New Testament, often calls himself ' the bridegroom ' without naming the bride : the censor within himself or the editors of the gospels was at work here. Moreover, his whole anarchic teaching . . . take no thought for the morrow, lay not up treasures upon earth, and all the impossible rest . . . came from the struggle against the ideas of his putative father, the hard-headed, practical-minded and practical-faithed Joseph."

This quotation is given by J. B. Priestley in his book *Midnight on the Desert* (p. 224). It comes from an American work on " popular science " with the title of " Outline of Man's Knowledge," and Mr. Priestley adds the following apt criticism.

" Though I cannot call myself a Christian . . . nevertheless the kind of hostile criticism of the Christian religion represented by the above passage fills me with despair. It is at once so terribly knowing and so terribly silly."

It must be fairly obvious how thoroughly " knowing " this extract is, containing as it does the essence of that symbolism which is the key of the mystical side of Christianity. And " terribly silly " also, because the relationship of Mary is as obviously symbolic as that between Krishna and his sixteen thousand mistresses. It seems to me the very depth of " silliness " to contend that what is true must be physically true and *only* physically. And yet, in less blatant ways, that is a mistake which we all make. It is difficult to realise that truth is always hidden, and that from cradle to coffin we must of necessity use symbols, not only in speech and writing, but in our very thought. And further, that not even the simplest word expresses *exactly* what we mean, let alone conveying to the hearer the same significance. Even in ordinary conversation this disadvantage is obvious enough, but in art and abstract discussion it becomes so great as to be the dominant factor. For this reason the proper valuation of symbolism must lie at the root of understanding in the widest sense, and it is significant that psychology has recognised this fact. But if the poet's sunrise, the lover's mistress, and the scientist's " matter " are *indescribable* . . . these things which are at any rate *physical* . . . how are we to deal with the significance of music, the content of the mind, the relationship between God and Man ?

Not, at all events, by interpreting the physical in terms of the physical, for such can lead only to a vicious circle. Yet even among psychologists the attitude is by no means rare, though it must require as much blind faith, on the part of those who believe it to represent the whole truth, as is required of the most dogmatic of religions.

At all events the reader should now be prepared for the psychoanalytic identification of Christ with Œdipus, and I will accordingly allow the following excerpt from Róheim's *Animism and the Divine King* to speak for itself. It should be noted, however, that, unlike the last quotation, it does indeed include a very valuable analysis.

THE BAPTISM OF JESUS
   (*The Notes are my own interpolations.*)
   " In the New Testament we have an important account of how Jesus was baptised and of the part played by the Holy Ghost in this act. We summarise the versions given by the various sources with all the details that may be of importance. Jesus was baptised by John, according to his desire, and when he emerged from the water, heaven was cleft asunder and the Holy Ghost descended upon him in the shape of a dove. At the same time a voice was heard from heaven saying : ' Thou art my beloved Son : in thee I am well pleased.'

   " It has been definitely shown by Gunkel and Gressmann that the scene refers to the supernatural succession to the throne. By the descent of the dove or the Holy Ghost the Saviour is recognised both in his capacity of Messiah, the Anointed King of Israel, and as the future King of Heaven. . . .

" A new king can only ascend the throne on the death
of his predecessor. The author of *The Golden Bough* has
shown beyond doubt that the death of the king was not
a natural one. The king, when his strength failed,
succumbed to the strength of another who might be
and originally probably was his son. Gressmann shows
that the dove was sacrificed to Jahve and in ancient
Palestine, as in modern folklore, was regarded as the
bird that embodied the soul of the dead."

(Cf. Jason, who *follows the dove*, his " soul," between the
rocks. The dove especially is an immortality symbol, an
attribute extended to almost all birds, especially the Hawk
and the Eagle ; but the dove, unlike the others, is closely
connected with the Great Mother, being one of her most
important symbols. As to its significance in the present context, we have seen that the spiritual destiny of the Christ is
realised only *through the Mother ;* it is proper therefore that his
destiny be revealed through the maternal symbol.)

" Comparative research has made it quite evident that
the episode of the Saviour's baptism and of the descent
of the Holy Ghost is borrowed by the authors of the
New Testament from older sources. Yet even in its
new setting it is not difficult for analysis, after thus
establishing its history, to interpret the unconscious
meaning of the whole scene. The new King of Heaven,
like his colleagues of this world, ascends the throne after
having killed his predecessor, and thus the Holy Ghost
becomes truly a holy ghost, the bird descending with
the soul of the murdered father to the son and heir."

(Cf. " In the Christian myth man's original sin is undoubtedly
an offence against God the Father, and if Christ redeems mankind from the weight of original sin by sacrificing his own
life, he forces us to the conclusion that this sin was murder."

(FREUD : *Totem and Taboo*, p. 260.)

It should be borne in mind that the " unconscious " takes no account of time. It was shown earlier that the Son becomes co-equal with the Father after the crucifixion . . . in solar terms at Midsummer (Omega). This scene of the baptism is *out of time*, and recognises the identity of the Christ as already fulfilled. Obviously the attaining of the Father's power is properly symbolised as murder. It is more accurate, I think, to express the relationship as follows :

The Father (Alpha) disintegrates (in space/time) to give birth to the Son. . . . In other words the Father *dies* to give birth to the Son. Subsequently the Son dies to give re-birth to the Father. We have seen that to be re-born means also to die, hence to give re-birth to the Father . . . to *become* " one with the Father " is symbolised as *killing* the Father.)

" But we have observed that the whole scene is borrowed, and this time it is possible to indicate the source or sources with a greater amount of accuracy than is usual in such cases. The voice from Heaven is really the voice from Egypt. Thus Plutarch tells us how at the festival of Pamylia a certain Pamyles, when fetching water from the Nile, heard a voice proclaiming : ' The good and great king Osiris is born,' or ' The lord of all the earth is born.' The parallel gains in accuracy by observing that drawing water from the Nile is itself a birth ceremony, for Osiris is the Nile and is in the water from the river, just as baptism is ceremonial re-birth."

" Moreover the exact words that proclaim Jesus as King are the official title of Pharaoh, and Osiris, of course, is the divine ruler of Egypt. The Pharaoh is called the ' beloved son of Ra or Amon ' as the case may be. Norden, not satisfied with this, shows that the Greek εὐδόκησα of the New Testament usually translated, following Luther, by an expression meaning something like 'to delight in,' really means 'to decide for some-body,' 'to choose,' and the King of Egypt is called the 'beloved of Re,' or the 'chosen of Re' (Ra). 'Thou King whom Re hath chosen the son of Re, Rameses beloved by Amon.'

"If the myth is derived from Egypt and originally represented the death of the old king and the ascent of the new king to royalty, it is additionally certain that the scene involves the death of the father by the son and the transference of the soul or life-power to the latter. Apart from other features of Egyptian royalty, to be considered in the next chapter, there is abundant proof for this view in the myth of Osiris, who is, as we know, a prototype and condensation of all Egyptian rulers.

"Now, as we have shown above, Osiris was originally killed and castrated by his son and successor. But the feature of the myth which is specially relevant in this connection is that Isis, in the shape of a hawk, descended upon the corpse of the murdered and castrated Osiris and conceived from him her son Horus. . . .

"Comparing the references contained in the early Fathers to this passage, Usener shows that the original text must have been : 'Thou art my beloved Son whom to-day I have procreated.' This again appears to be a quotation from Psalms ii, 7. Jahve speaks to the King of Israel: 'Thou art my son, I have procreated thee to-day.' "

(The Kings of Israel and Egypt, like Jesus, are symbolic Christs . . . though, of course, in a lesser degree. It seems to me that in this capacity all three hear the voice which says, " I have procreated thee to-day," meaning, " I have given thee to-day a *new* birth." In other words, the baptism in these cases represents the " consummation " which we have seen to be characterised by a *new name*, the function of baptism. Thus in each case a new name is, in effect, given, for the Man is constituted by the Voice the Son of God and the Heir of the Kingdom.)

". . . There are two aspects of this picture. One is that the descent of the Holy Ghost to the Kings of Israel proves that they too, in the unconscious setting, have acquired royal honours for the murderous act, and the other that the passage of the divine spirit from the body is the act of procreation."

(Re-birth is the freeing of the spirit from the body, hence —but not necessarily—death of the body.)

" The myth of Osiris is not the only point of contact with Egypt, for it seems to have been an article of Egyptian belief that every god was destined to die after he had begotten a son in his own likeness (?). When the Pharaoh ascends the throne he receives from the god his father a sort of divine fluid. The Pharaoh lives by the fluid of Ra, and the same fluid flows in his veins. This is a fluid like the rays of the sun, like fire, and the apparition of fire in the water heralds the descent of the dove (an excellent consummation symbol.)

" We have mentioned this mystical fluid, the *sa* ; it is the seminal fluid containing the germs of life. When the burning Easter candles, as symbols of the Holy Ghost, are dipped into the water of baptism, the latter is compared to the uterus and the light is regarded as fertilising the water. There can, therefore, be no doubt that the modern version of the scene given in the New Testament has a past going back untold ages when the Brothers fought for the death of the Parental Tyrant.

" Since the Holy Ghost represents the phallus, the successor, the hero who has the ghost in his body was

the man who had taken possession of the paternal organ
of generation. Naturally, the phallic concept of the
Holy Ghost is fully recognised both by Dr. Jones in his
analysis of this idea and by Flügel, who regards the fiery
tongues of the Apostles as phallic symbols. Indeed, it
can hardly be misunderstood. We must only consider
that the Holy Ghost appears in three principal scenes in
the New Testament. One of these is a conception, and
the third the ecstasy of the Apostles. (In all cases a
symbol *of birth*.)

" In the Catholic liturgy of the Mass the *spiritus sanctus*
is called *digitæ dextræ patris*, and the act of imposition
of the hand either for purposes of healing or for that of
initiation, prophetic enthronisation, etc., is regularly
regarded as a means by which the spirit, the Holy Ghost,
passes from the prophet or priest to the new adept."

(Cf. " I am the Way and the Life." In physical terms the
*way* is symbolised as phallus, the *life* as semen, hence the
Egyptian concept to which Róheim has referred. The Pharaoh
or Christ is the vehicle of the Word (Holy Ghost) and is thus
symbolised as the phallus of the Father.)

" . . . Now Eisler has collected very important
evidence to show that the hand in this connection was a
phallic symbol. A tribe was called B'ne Jamin—' the
sons of the right hand.' Phallic gravestones are called
Jad—' the hand.' The hand is the ideogram of the god
Nebo, and Nebo is the fire-drill."

(The mystical birth of fire out of matter (water), together
with its sexual symbolism, is more readily understandable
in terms of the re-birth of the Son from the Mother. See
FRAZER : *Myths of the Origin of Fire*.)

" . . . Jewish authorities protest against lifting the

hand to the sky when praying. They regard it as an exhibition of the genital organs."

(Cf. Taboo . . . discharge of the magic force.)

" Having thus far shown to our full satisfaction that the dove and the Holy Ghost represent the male member in coitus, we shall now proceed to prove the exact opposite—that they represent the female, the mother. The voice from Heaven says : ἐν σοι εὐδόκησα, ' I have chosen thee,' but in the older version restored by Usener : εγω σήμερον γεγεννηκά σε. We have followed Leisegang in translating γεγεννηκά as ' procreated ' and in referring it to the activity of the male in coitus. But Usener and Gressmann translate it as ' I have given birth to thee to-day.' The festival of the Epiphany, the Day of the Descent of the Dove, was originally Christ's birthday." (Commonly known as " Twelfth Night.")

" Now this would point to a goddess, and, indeed, Gressmann clearly shows that everywhere in the Semitic world the idea of the dove is associated with the belief in Istar or similar mother-goddesses representing love both in its tender and in its unbridled incestuous aspect. Istar is the virgin mother and also the prostitute. The ambivalency of the original idea could hardly be expressed more forcibly than by the fact that Langdon uses the word ' virgin-harlot ' in translating the original Baby-lonian adjective of Istar. The inhabitants of the harem, i.e. the virgins consecrated to the Istar cult, are referred to as ' birds ' (hu), a euphemistic expression for prostitutes, or more especially as ' doves ' (hu tu), and their inhabitations as dovecots.

" In the old Syriac version of our text we find the following modification : ' Thou art my son and beloved whom I have chosen,' and Gressmann explains this modification by the Babylonian view of the King as Son and Spouse of the dove-goddess."

(*Animism and the Divine King*, p. 156 ff.)

Before going on to the main theme, there is a last point which requires emphasis. Róheim analyses the Baptism in such a way as to make it clear that *both Father and Son are androgyne.* . . . Such is the only possible conclusion from his statement of the ambivalent relationship, and it accords very well with our own deductions concerning the nature of the consummation upon which the attainment of the Son depends. Obviously he cannot be " one with the Father " unless he is exactly like the Father, i.e. androgyne ; and to this must be added the significance of the Grail legends which show, perhaps more clearly than lower myths, that the mystical attainment depends upon the sublimation of sex in the same terms. Finally, the castration and inversion of the Hero is seen to complete this same symbolism, the *physical* sign as against the *mystical* sublimation and the more abstract idea of the *spiritual* and *cosmic* Unity.

I think perhaps that a warning should precede our statement of the Œdipus drama itself. Owing to the popularity of psychoanalysis it is often believed that the Œdipus Complex derives its significance almost entirely from personal " wish fulfilment fantasies " which find their expression as unconscious desires for the murder of one parent and intercourse with the other. Needless to say such a view is far too narrow, even for orthodox followers of Freud, while in the present case it cannot be too strongly emphasised that we are not in the least concerned with infantile or any other form of sexuality. In the present context the ancient drama is as abstract as though, instead of *dramatis personæ*, there were conventional mathematical abstractions. Indeed, our immediate task may be expressed as follows :

Dr. Jung stated the object of our general enquiry to be " an indeterminable and variable ' x ' which stands for the physiological activity of the glands at one extreme and the highest reaches of the spirit at the other."

We have found that the symbol or vehicle of this force is the Christ.

We have found that the force is expressed as the incestuous family relationship, viz. Father/Mother/Son.

This relationship is personified in the Œdipus legend.

It remains to show that Œdipus is a vehicle of the force ' x ' and a personification of the Christ.

If we succeed in this task . . . and it is already evident that at least partial success will be achieved, we should then be in a position to interpret fundamental, i.e. " unconscious " Christian symbolism, where the word " Christian " is used in the widest sense of " the symbols of the Consummator." Here again, in the course of the argument a certain amount of interpretation has been already made, but it remains to apply the same method direct to the New Testament, which is clearly the apotheosis of such symbolism in the same way that Jesus of Nazareth is the apotheosis of the Christ. The object of such final analysis and synthesis is to express Christianity as far as possible in terms of consciousness itself through the symbols which have been brought into relation with it.

The essentials of the legend are simple enough ; a son unwittingly slays his father and marries his mother. The same son meets with and overcomes a monster (the Sphinx). The latter clearly relates to the " typical " dragon-slaying myth with which we have been almost continually concerned in one form or another, its highest expression being found in the Quest of the Grail and the identity of Osiris/Horus. The former relates, of course, to the basic physical equation which was our starting point and whose highest expression is the integration of the divine SON with FATHER/MOTHER, forming the cosmic Unity at " Omega."

Œdipus was born to the King and Queen of Thebes (Laius and Jocasta), and because his horrible destiny was foretold, was exposed as an infant, so that by his death the Fates might be cheated. The exposure took place on Mount Cithaeron where the child was hung up by the feet, or with a nail through the feet, presumably upon a tree. From this apparently certain death he was rescued by a shepherd, who took him to the Court of Corinth where the boy was brought up in ignorance of his parentage, believing himself to be the heir of Corinth.

Yet his confidence was shaken following chance remarks at a feast, indicating that he was only the *supposed* son of Corinth and casting aspersions upon his real origin. The young man accordingly sought the Oracle at Delphi, which, as usual, gave no definite answer to his questions, but announced that he would kill his father and marry his mother.

He naturally assumed this prophecy to refer to Corinth, and so promptly left the place in an effort to escape.

While travelling, however, he was insulted by an old man's servant. The fight that followed left Œdipus surrounded by dead bodies which included that of the old man himself, who was Laius, his real father. Of this, however, he suspected nothing.

Arrived at Thebes, he heard that the King had been

slain upon the road, but failed to connect the event
with his own fight. True, he had killed an old man
and his retinue, but there had been no means of knowing
that the fellow had been so grand a person as the King.
Œdipus, therefore, was in no way disturbed, but went
on his way inspired by the confidence which sprang from
his successful battle. In this spirit he undertook to
overcome the Sphinx, a monster half woman and half
beast (lion), with the claws and wings of a bird, who
caused great destruction not far from the city. On
meeting the Sphinx, however, Œdipus was obliged to
put up his sword, which was evidently powerless against
her. Instead of steel he had to fight with wits, for it
was the monster's custom to propound a riddle to
all who passed by, and they who failed were devoured.
It was this same test which the hero had to assay, and it
was understood that if the correct answer to the enigma
were given the Sphinx herself would be destroyed.

> " Tell me, what animal is that
> Which has four feet at morning bright,
> Two at noon, and three at night ? "

Œdipus replied that it was Man himself, who in
infancy crawls upon four limbs, walks upright in the
prime of life, and in the evening of his days must needs
go with a stick.

Evidently the answer "Man" was correct . . . though
the naïve reasons just given can be safely ignored. At
all events the monster forthwith threw herself into the
sea and perished.

Œdipus, hailed as a national hero, married the widowed
Queen and by her had children in peaceful wedlock.

That, so far as we are concerned, is the whole tale,
for the horrid climax, although it *may* possess a more

fundamental significance, seems to me to be more the result of a natural, *conscious* censorship, which refused to allow the hero of so immoral a story to escape unscathed. Accordingly the tragedy of Sophocles ends with the discovery by Œdipus of his own true identity. Mad with remorse he blinds himself and no doubt dies miserably. But the " unconscious " from which the rest of the story undoubtedly comes, knows no morality : it is beyond both good and evil. For this, and the additional reason that it is entirely unnecessary, the main narrative being quite complete in itself, I reject the final tragedy. That I am justified in doing so, will, I hope, become duly apparent.[1]

Let us begin the actual analysis with another quotation from Róheim :

" It is significant that the greater part of the mythical material in which we find an open, or nearly open statement of the Œdipus situation should be connected with divine rulers."                              (Op. cit., p. 310.)

This is exactly what we should expect in view of what we learned in the course of the Baptism analysis, wherein, among other things, it was pointed out that on the physical level one of the great symbols of the Christ was the phallus . . . the " way " and the " life " of the Father. To confirm this in respect of Œdipus let the same witness be called :

" Œdipus means ' swollen foot,' a penis in erection, and we find him on a vase standing opposite a naked Sphinx with the mask of a goat and an erect penis."            (Ibid.)

Now, it has been previously shown concerning the

---

[1] It will be remembered, however, that the final triumph of the Hero is only attained through the symbol of his own death.

*goat :* (i) That the animal represents *virility*, and was worshipped as such evidently on the assumption that its phenomenal sexual power was the symbol of the " magic force " of taboo, which at a higher interpretation is the *divine life*, the " fluid of Ra." (ii) That the myth of the Golden Fleece together with the underlying significance of the Pig of Set, designates the vehicle of virility . . . Goat, Boar, Ram, as the *body* of the Christ. The highest expression of this idea is, of course, that of the eucharistic *bread*. For instance, at the temple of Denderah the Image of the " resurrected " Osiris was made of *wheat*, though his body had also been recognised as the Black Pig from which he arose immortal. (*Vide* BUDGE : *From Fetish to God in Ancient Egypt*, p. 514.) Finally it is remarkable that the *goat* was sacred to Dionysos (Bacchus). This god, whom we have shown to be a Christ, was personified as the goat, and had the title of " the one of the Black Goatskin." Like all Christs he died and was resurrected annually.

So much for the identity of Œdipus *a priori*, upon which grounds we should be allowed to give him the title of Consummator pending further developments.

The legend says that Œdipus killed his father *before* the incestuous union took place, but we need not pay too much attention to such chronology, since it is common knowledge that the " unconscious " no more takes account of time than it does of morality. Here again the conscious " censor " seems to have adapted the material, not on this occasion in the interests of ethics, but in the interests of a connected drama. But it has been established on general grounds that before the Hero can attain the consummation which is union with the Father he must overcome the " world and the flesh." He must " overcome " or have intercourse with, or be reborn from, the Mother, before he gains the power of and co-equality with the Father. We came upon the same difficulty in connection with the Baptism, but there is obviously no real obstacle presented. Actually the Œdipus myth has the Mother-symbol duplicated (Jocasta/ Sphinx), and both of them must obviously, for the sake of the drama, come after and not before the killing of the Father. Yet this murder is really the climax of the whole thing, the Attainment, just as it was in the case of the Baptism. To sum up let us interpret the murder as follows :

In the slaying of Laius, the Son *proves his spiritual destiny*—to wield the power of and " share the throne of " the Divine Father. If this is the case, the question of sequence does not arise, except from our own point of view, by which it is clear that the next step after proving the *identity* of the Hero is to indicate his rôle, his career. (Cf. *Marriage at Cana*, Chapter X.) First we discover the *mystical* parentage of Œdipus, and then what that parentage involves.

But there is a subsidiary consideration which somewhat modifies the position. . . . The destiny which has been revealed is that of *overcoming the Mother ;* but we know that the power by which this is accomplished is that of the Father. Thus, some but not all of the Father's power must be available during the career of the hero so that destiny may be fulfilled. In *this* sense it is reasonable enough for Laius to be murdered *before* the incestuous union, for it is his, the Father's, power which enables the Son to triumph. Again, the Christ works always " in the name " of the Father, and the physical significance of the *name* is, as we have seen, the generative fluid which is transmitted by intercourse, or, more properly, incest. In such terms Œdipus possesses

himself of the Father's penis with which to have intercourse with the Mother. . . . They are Róheim's own
words, of course, but they are used only on the understanding that the reader recognises them for what they
are, the symbols of a mystical relationship which may be
expressed as follows : The Christ overcomes Mother
Matter (World and Flesh) through the Word of the
Father, which is the Way (of the Cross), the Truth, and
the Life (immortality). And he in whom the Word is
incarnate is thus himself the Way and the Truth and the
Life . . . in proportion as he is the perfect vehicle.

Thus we have adequate personification for our three
Terms without bringing the Sphinx into consideration,
and the reason is, of course, that Jocasta takes the rôle
of the *dual* Mother. It is she who gives birth to the
Hero and she by whom he is re-born when he re-enters
her womb under the incest-symbol, in which is concealed
the identity of the Destroyer. It has been shown that
the Dual Mother corresponds to physical birth and
physical death, but that the latter, since it is the " gate "
of immortality," may be assigned to the " creator "
rather than the " destroyer." It is only when this
consideration is taken into account that the necessity
for the Sphinx becomes apparent. While it is psychologically true to speak broadly of " overcoming the
mother," we should in effect recognise that such a
mother is divorced from the family relationship to the
extent that the " family " dual mother gives the *two
creative births ;* the real " destroyer " on the other hand
gives no birth at all but annihilation. The real destroyer
. . . the " world and the flesh," the forces of Matter,
have their origin in the womb (pit) of Nastrond, and their
symbol is the Daughter—or the Sphinx.

Thus the myth of Œdipus shows itself singularly

complete, for while it is interesting when considered simply as a *family relationship*, it is very much more so when the Sphinx is introduced. Laius, Jocasta, and their Son have coincided accurately with the abstract terms, Dual Father, Dual Mother, Triple Son, but, just as Hercules does not fight directly with Mother Hera, so Œdipus does not contend directly with Jocasta. Hera sent serpents against Hercules, and, by the same token, it is Jocasta who sends the Sphinx against Œdipus. In either case the re-birth (incest) of the Hero depends upon his overcoming the enemy, and the enemy is the *guardian of the womb*, the serpent keeper of the Tree of Life.

Without stretching analogies unduly, this symbolism may be taken further. The Hero is Spirit, but the *enemy* is matter, who is now for the first time to be differentiated from the Mother. The Mother is the " virgin-harlot," the *mystical* virgin, but the source of unlimited physical fertility.

The Hero is born from and returns to the Virgin, his " dual mother " who gives both the birth " of water " and " of fire," and who is as much an abstract or spiritual entity as himself. But the *enemy* which he has to overcome is not spiritual but material, not the Mother herself but the *guardian* of the Mother. We know that the serpent of Eden was the representative of sexuality and materialism, particularly the former, and we infer also that this same snake is the guardian of the Tree (womb). Now the physical symbol of the Hero is the phallus (" way " and " life "), and the serpent is also primarily a sex-symbol of the same sort, but with this difference, that the Hero is above the physical, but the Enemy is himself the power of the physical. In fine, the paradox is complete, for the Hero's victory over mortality is gained by the very symbol of mortality. Yet, as usual, there is really no paradox at all, for we have shown repeatedly that the power of the Hero is *sublimated* sex, a power obtained through the conquest of the Destroyer. It is thus very striking to find that both the Hero and his Enemy have the same physical symbol . . . the phallus. Both derive their power from the same source, but in one case it is spiritual and in the other material . . . God and the Devil, love and desire, Christ and Antichrist.

And it is significant also to recognise that the age of gross materialism, the nineteenth century, produced the fullest expression of the *physical* symbols which were virtually worshipped as sovereign powers.

We have seen it to be a general rule that *matter* gives birth to *spirit*. We should expect, therefore, that any fresh spiritual impetus would be born from the furthest development of materialistic thought. Is it going too far to connect psychoanalysis with the latter?

But let us return to our " *dramatis personæ* " and bring this preliminary discussion to an end with a tabulation of some of their representative titles.

LAIUS.   Dual Father, Alpha and Omega, who, in the *cosmic* sense, disintegrates (dies) while remaining Unity. The Ancient of Days, God the Father, the Self.

ŒDIPUS.   Triple Son, Heir of the Father, Child, Warrior, Sacrifice, King, " one with the Father." The Christ, . . . especially the Mystic Christ who in all men is destined to be born, sacrificed, and crowned.

JOCASTA.   The Great Mother, the Dual Mother, the Creating Mother, the Virgin-Harlot.

As the Virgin she is the immaculate Mother of Christ, the Triple Son ; while as the " harlot " she is the source of all physical fertility, from the natural birth of human children to the increase of the " fruitful field."

*SPHINX.* The Destroyer, the Daughter, Darkness, Death, Antichrist, Materialism, Keeper of the Womb, Guardian of the Tree, the Dragon, the Water-serpent.

It has been impossible to avoid a certain amount of confusion, but I hope now that at least the various characters are clear. Especially is it important to recognise that the " harlot " is not a term of abuse, but the symbol of fertility. The Virgin gives mystical birth and the Harlot gives physical birth, both are to be distinguished from the Daughter who gives no birth at all but only death. The dual Father and the Son may be regarded as forming one triangle, while the dual Mother and the Daughter form another triangle, six terms in all, and all derived from a seventh which is the Unity.

Finally I would draw attention to some traditional titles of the Mother of Jesus as given in the Roman Missal (Litany of Loretto).[1] They are arranged in three columns, the Latin being followed first by the literal translation and then by what I take to be the symbolic meaning. The whole should be compared to the titles which are assignable to the Sphinx and which will be reviewed in a moment.

| " Vas spirituale | Thou spiritual Vessel | Womb of re-birth / Womb of the Hero |
|---|---|---|
| Rosa mystica | Thou mystical rose | Flower of Immortality |
| Turris Davidica | Thou Tower of David | Womb of David |
| Domus aurea | Thou House of Gold | Mother of Spirit |
| Foederis arca | Thou Ark of the Covenant | Source of power |
| Janua cœli | Thou Gate of Heaven | Gate of Eden " |

[1] These and other titles are quoted on p. 274 of *Psychological Types.*

All of these should be clear enough with the possible exception of " Rosa mystica." In spite of the fact that we had a good deal to say about the Rosicrucians, I was not then prepared to go into the roots of rose-symbolism. Even now the position is hardly well-defined, but the following suggestions are put forward. We have seen that the victory of the Hero is accomplished through the sacrifice of *blood*, and there is a poetic idea that from this blood the red rose blooms. There is also the tradition of the Cross as the Tree of Life which bears a precious blossom, and there can be little doubt that by unconscious association this blossom must be the red rose. It follows that the flower of the Tree and the Blood is the symbol of immortality, and as such would be the natural sign of the Rosicrucians whose alchemical operations were really concerned with the " way of the cross " and " Domus aurea " rather than the common gold of the earth. It is thus in her capacity as the Mother of Immortality that the Virgin takes as her title " Rosa mystica."

And now we can return to the second aspect of the Œdipus myth. The first was concerned with a hero who killed his father and married his mother, the second deals with a hero who set out upon a journey, overcame a monster, and received a prize.

If the first part is peculiarly psychological, the second is clearly the " typical myth " concerning which so much has already been said. The reason for the extraordinary importance of Œdipus lies in the fact that in him are combined both these types, so that his story forms a sort of " Rosetta Stone " to the symbolism of the hero.

Obviously the Sphinx is the Destroyer, the personification of those material forces whose anthropomorphic representation is Aradia, the Daughter. We mentioned just now the serpents which Hera sent against Hercules, and it is reasonable enough to regard the Sphinx also as being sent against the Hero " to keep the way of the Tree of Life." In the enquiry into classical myths the identity of this Destroyer emerged fairly clearly, and so it will not pass unnoticed that the Sphinx summarises in her genealogy the enemies of most of the heroes of classical mythology.

As a matter of tradition the Sphinx was actually sent against Thebes, if not against Œdipus himself, because Hera hated that city *on account of the birth of Bacchus*. But since Œdipus is the destined King of Thebes the Sphinx is as clearly his enemy as that of the city. . . . It is the story of Hercules and the Serpents repeated in a slightly altered form.

Now the Sphinx was the *daughter* of Echnida, half woman and half *serpent*. " Echnida is derived from the All-mother, the mother Earth, Gaia, who, with Tartaros, the personified underworld (the place of horrors), brought her forth. Echnida herself is the mother of all terrors, of the Chimaera, Scylla, Gorgo, of the horrible Cerberus, of the Nemean lion, and of the eagle which devoured the liver of Prometheus. One of her sons is Orthus, the dog of the monstrous Geryon, who was killed by Hercules. With this dog, her son, Echnida, *in incestuous intercourse*, produced the Sphinx." (*Psychology of the Unconscious*, p. 113.)

After this there is very little more to be said, for the reader has only to check the attributes of the Sphinx's relations to get all the symbols required, which (with the exception of the *eagle*) are representatives of material forces, usually connected with the Elements *water* or *earth*. Especially interesting in this respect is the legend of the Gorgon whose power it was to *turn men to stone*.

She was slain by Perseus, who made her power his own, and, like all Destroyers who run true to type, her home was in the sunless, icebound north.

And now we come to the famous Riddle. That the answer is Man, and *in what sense* it refers to Man, is clear enough. For *Man is Œdipus*, both the individual and mankind in general; his whole life is the answer to the riddle, and the purpose of all living also. Moreover, the answer which alone can lead to the " redemption," alike of the individual and of mankind, is contained in the same terms.

Although more speculative than the argument as a whole, we may even attempt a more detailed answer to the riddle as follows. The " four feet at morning bright " are the four Elements (e.g. the Cherubim of Genesis), the material basis of creation of which the corresponding psychic forces constitute the unorganised animal nature of man, the " brute upon which he stands." But intellectually . . . that is to say in the light of the " knowledge of good and evil," these four are resolved into a simple duality upon which mankind base their rule of life and by which in turn they are ruled. These, in the " noon " of evolution, are the traditional *opposites* from which man is only freed when they are " married " and give birth to that son who is the " third direction," thus making a trinity which holds the opposites in balance. This " birth," or spiritual " awakening," only occurs late in the evolutionary scale, in the evening of man's long journey under the domination of the Mother. But being thus " re-born " the night which envelops him has no longer any power, and after it there dawns the light of paradise. Thus the " three at night."

To round off this crucial chapter let me emphasise that the essence of all these allegories is always the *sublimation of consciousness*, that concept and that alone is the one fundamental which is common to every variety of " true " religion, myth, dream, and even psychology :

" The aim is to strengthen the Ego, to make it more and more independent . . . to enlarge its field of view, and to build up its organisation so that it can appropriate new bits of the Id. *Where the Id was shall be Ego*. This is the work of civilisation."

(RÓHEIM : *Riddle of the Sphinx*, p. 279.)

That which was " unconscious " must be brought into the field of " self-consciousness." Man must first overcome the " four " of his primitive nature, transferring his animal energies into more constructive channels. Then begins the gradual transformation of *desire* into *love*, the " freedom from the opposites." In a restricted sense such a process means the conquest of neurosis and the emergence of a thoroughly balanced personality, but such an interpretation is only a very small part of the wide field which has been opened up to us by the analysis of ancient symbols. We cannot help now but recognise the infinite distance of man's beginning, and the sinuous avenues of time down which he has already travelled far. Nor can we fail to see the lines of these avenues produced into an infinite future.

But there is difficulty enough in speaking of things near at hand, and to attempt to grapple with infinity is both conceited and unnecessary. We have plenty of evidence now for the basis of balanced living :

" With the birth of the symbol the regression of the libido into the unconscious ceases. Regression is converted into progression, damming-up gives place to flowing ; whereupon the absorbing power of the primeval is broken."

(*Psychological Types*.)

This particular symbol is, of course, the Mystic Christ, the "keystone" which is the "head of the corner," the "third direction," the Child of the union of the unconscious opposites.

"The nature of the redeeming symbol is that of a child. . . . The symbol is the middle way upon which the opposites unite towards a new movement, a water-course that pours forth fertility after a long drought."

(Ibid.)

The "water-course" is the "river of life" which is love unhindered by desire, the sublimated "fluid of generation" of which we shall have more to say in the next chapter. Ultimately it is the Word which is the omnipotent power of Spirit, as was indicated in the analysis of Genesis, and as such it is the power of all creation, the ultimate basis of the universe :

"Shining yet hidden, Spirit lives in the cavern (Mother). Everything that sways, breathes, opens, closes, lives in Spirit ; beyond learning, beyond everything, better than anything ; living, unliving.

"It is the undying blazing Spirit, that seed of all seeds, wherein lay hidden the world and all its creatures. It is life, speech, mind, reality, immortality. It is there to be struck. Strike it, my son."

(The Ten Principal Upanishads :<br>Shee Purohit Swami and W. B. Yeats.)

So the "seed" is the "river of life" and the "river" is the "word." Do you remember a quotation concerned with "Ôm," "the word by which the worlds were made"? It is held that Ôm represents Spirit in the sense in which the word is used in the above quotation, and the phonetic spelling of "Ôm" is A-um, wherein the syllables are regarded as "sexed." If this is so we may regard it as the emblem of Ihoh, origin of the Word, and thinking in this way we shall not be surprised to recall that the Christian " Amen," like the Egyptian " Amen," may well signify the same thing. The Egyptian Amen was the androgyne god of the beginning and the end (sunrise and sunset). Like " Alpha and Omega " and Amitābha his attribute is boundless light " in which is no darkness at all." He is Unity, the focus of every system of thought since time began, for without the idea of harmony there can be no thought :

" Hail thou, my Father of Light ! I come having my flesh free from decay ; I am whole as my Father, the self-begotten god whose image is in the incorruptible body.

" Do thou establish me. Do thou perfect me as Master of the Grave !

" This is the mystery of the change in the body of the life which comes from the destruction of life."

(Book of the Dead, cliv.)

## NOTE

Light is used as a symbol of the ultimate Unity because it results from the harmony of the seven colours of the spectrum : Violet, Indigo, Blue, Green, Yellow, Orange, Red ; a sense which sets the concept of Light beyond the rôle of an opposite to darkness, which has no conceptual existence in itself but is merely the absence of light. Cf. Bergson on the notion of non-existence.

# CHAPTER TEN

## JESUS OF NAZARETH

WITH the resolution of the " Œdipus " myth and its " complex " our argument has been carried far enough, though no doubt the symbolic " framework " could be further elaborated, especially in the psychological field. So what remains is more in the nature of commentary rather than continued development. But it is not my intention to give elaborate examples of the way in which the symbolic " key " can be applied, because such have been furnished progressively in the course of the general enquiry. Rather I want to take symbolism to its climax, a height from which the whole of the field can be viewed.

Hitherto we have regarded Jesus from a distance, even though the shadow of the Christ has hardly left the page from beginning to end, from " Taboo " to " Œdipus," for the very good reason that, as we have become increasingly aware, the Christ is the very heart of symbolism. Various forms of expression have been shown to find their focus in terms derived from the Christ : now, however, we have to interpret directly from the Christian doctrine. To develop the method of interpretation has been rather a long and complicated business ; yet at least it serves to show the limitations of unaided intellect.

In the first place let us be quite clear as to what is meant by the word " Christ." Obviously it refers first of all to the Third Term of the *equation* in its most inclusive sense, from which in turn various aspects may be distinguished, becoming less and less abstract until the whole is *personified* in the figure of the historical Consummator. Finally, of the many who have played that supreme rôle, there stands out an undisputed Archetype, the most recent of them all, Jesus of Nazareth. Whether consciously or unconsciously, or by a process of accretion following the termination of mortal life, the Christ gathers and assimilates the symbols by which alone the doctrine can be transmitted and interpreted. Yet, except in a very materialistic age, the truth is not dependent upon interpretation, being sensed under even the most confused intellectual expression. Unfortunately the passing age lost both the " key " which can justify religion in terms of intellect, and also the ability to " sense " the underlying truth. Fair-minded, hard-headed moderns realise that on the face of it the Christ story is a mass of contradictions and that some of it is frankly nonsensical. Such people are presented with a clear alternative. Either they must ignore common sense and take refuge in " blind " faith, or else they must reject religion root and branch as unreasonable and therefore untrue.

A striking example of apparent nonsense is afforded by the emphatic statement of Jesus : " If ye shall ask anything in my name, I will do it." (John xiv, 13, 14.) The plain facts are that asking certainly does not result in getting what one wants, and accordingly the materialist is perfectly justified in rejecting the whole gospel. If the Christ says he will do a thing he ought to keep to it. If he doesn't honour his promises, if his system doesn't work, the whole thing is clearly bogus. And the Church, unhappily being itself essentially materialistic, has done nothing to justify her apparently indefensible position. No amount of sentimentality can justify such an obvious inconsistency as this.

But is it inconsistent in the light of symbolism? I think not. First it must be remembered that the standpoint is not material but mystical. Immediately the word "ask" takes on a new significance, for the material is always the effect of the mystical; spirit and matter may be regarded as cause and effect. The mystic does not ask for the material: he knows that it will follow automatically under certain conditions. "Consider the lilies of the field." To "ask" in this context has nothing to do with "getting something" except in relation to a mystical end.

But even so the statement does not seem to work, for people ask for all manner of mystical gifts, even for such spiritual and apparently unselfish benefits as facility to follow the Christ. But it *still* does not work. Now consider "in my name." What is the mystical name of the Christ, the name *of power*? Surely it is *love* and there is no other comparable title. So the statement really reads as follows: "If ye shall ask anything *in the name of love*, I will do it." Better still, bearing in mind that love itself is the sovereign power: "If ye shall ask anything in the name of love, love will do it."

Now I can say that, on the evidence available, I find the statement to be perfectly true. The catch is, of course, that we confuse love and desire, forgetting that the latter destroys the former. That which you love you will receive in proportion to the perfection of your love, both in degree and intensity. But you will not receive what you desire, for love desires nothing at all. Clearly even this example has brought us to the limit of words. It will suffice to point out that the working of the law of love is only to be known in proportion as the attitude of love develops. There are no short cuts, but ultimately the mountains move.

And now to return to more general considerations, with the warning that no symbol and no theory can be of the slightest use in itself. It only becomes useful when employed with conscious purpose.

Hitherto we have been content to regard the cypher of the Consummator as little more than a symbolic summary · but he is more than that. It is only when the symbol is expressed in terms of personality that the power of it is active. The essential condition for the activity of the " redeeming symbol " is its human embodiment.

The Christ as a subject for intellectual exercise may lead to deep understanding, but for active power there must be an identification of the individual with the Hero, not as man to God, for in the presence of God man cannot stand (*vide* Uzzah and the Fisher King), but as a friend. Friends appreciate each other in exactly the degree of which each is capable : as friendship deepens so does appreciation. The personality of the friend will, in fact, be progressively revealed under those conditions.

I have put these views forward because I want to make it absolutely clear, that, far from reducing Christ to an abstraction, I regard the first necessity as His complete humanisation at the level of each individual.

With these qualifications we are free to review certain of the more striking symbols of the Archetype, the " Triple " Christ who is the essence of the solar allegory and whose chief signs have already been reviewed. The rôle of the Christ is that of the Redeemer : mankind is " redeemed " from the thraldom of matter to regain the " Tree of Life." Such is the " way " and the

" quest," and the work of civilisation. Thus whoever works for humanity works for the Christ and partakes to some extent of the nature of the Christ. In fact it can hardly be over-emphasised that by the very fact of their self-consciousness, all individuals are constituted " Christ " in certain essentials, His " co-heirs."

Thus, although born of animals which *mate*, we are also born of an immaculate conception, the fruit of a spiritual fatherhood and an ever-virgin motherhood. Our life also is the " way of the cross," for, consciously or unconsciously, whether we like it or not, we live incarnate between the opposites.[1] And if our birth bears the symbols of the Christ, so does our death . . . though not necessarily our physical death. For the death of the Cross is a psychological event, a necessary pre-liminary to that " Eden " of expanded consciousness. A man may conquer death before he dies, and by the same token another may die having no such victory.

This last point provokes an illustration from the New Testament which exemplifies the first condition of nearly all such interpretation, namely, to recognise that the viewpoint is not material but mystical. In the Gospels the word " dead " seldom refers to *physical* death, and only on this understanding do such statements as the following become intelligible.

" Let the dead bury the dead : follow me."

(Matt. viii, 22.)

" Verily, verily, I say unto you, the hour is coming and now is, when the dead shall hear the voice of the Son of God : and they that hear shall live." (John iii, 25.)

[1] The " opposites " are, of course, symbolised in the two con-stituents of the cross, the coincidence of horizontal/vertical as male/female being borne out by psychology and particularly well exemplified in the traditions associated with the making of fire by friction.

It will be recalled that Elisha goes to the " Mount of God " as to the Mother (cave), and he goes in the " dark night " as did the Alchemist.   The mystical *night* is, among other things, the unawakened state wherein " reality " is not perceived, but only the forces of matter. In fine, it is the materialists who are the " dead," and in a community of materialists it must needs be that the " dead " bury the dead.   Moreover, the reward of Elisha was a *voice*, and the general mystical tradition is in accord with such symbolism, the " awakening " or " re-birth " being characterised by a " voice which was not a voice, and words which were not heard but felt."   The " unconscious " link in this case derives in all probability from the cosmic Word, the vehicle of divine love, which in the person of Christ is the reward of the Knight of the Grail.   In the same way Jesus appeared to great mystics of Christendom as the lover or bridegroom[1] (the Virgin playing a complementary rôle), while the Jews have the tradition of Bathdol, the " Daughter of the Voice," in which the two ideas of *love* and *word* seem to be combined.

There is another interesting point which arises from the biblical quotation and which illustrates quite another aspect of the *mystical* death.   It is known that the unconscious has no respect for time, and that its thoughts . . . dreams, for instance, bear no relation to the hours of the clock, creating an order of succession which accommodates itself to the subject in hand without reference to the material world.   The unconscious, in fact, is *timeless*.   Thus in the regions from which the Voice is born the hour " now is," while to consciousness it is " coming."

Certainly there is a process of development in time

[1] e.g. " unio physica et mystica " of Mme Guyon.

which will in due course reveal the Voice; but the Voice is none the less part of the eternal identity of man, a perpetual but unconscious *present*. It follows also that the moment of revelation cannot be known by processes of reasoning, but, being a product of unconscious development, it arrives " like a thief in the night," " in an hour when ye are not aware."

Parallel with these considerations it should be pointed out that whereas the " second coming " has undoubtedly a cosmic—though not necessarily physical—significance, we have here revealed it only in the mystical sense, in so far as it applies *individually* to eyes which will become " open " and ears which will mysteriously " hear."

And now we must look into some of the more obvious consequences of this event. It has been shown, for instance, that the power of the Christ is love, and that the same force (voice) is the basis of the awakening. To be "awakened" therefore requires love beyond the standards which obtain in the world of the " dead." Briefly, from the moment when the individual becomes the conscious disciple of the Christ (as well as under less direct circumstances) all worldly love is perceived as the *reflection*, and therefore in a sense the *opposite* of the all-embracing divine love. This might seem impractical, yet it is not. Instead of destroying ordinary affection and ordinary love, the new power infinitely expands it; though in practice with a great deal of difficulty, since the old objects of affection and the old ways of showing it both have to undergo considerable modification.

" If any man come to me, and hate not his father and mother, and wife, and children, and brethren, and sisters, yea, and his own life also, he cannot be my disciple."

(Luke xiv, 26.)

Relativity ! Love because of relationship is a mockery ; yet there can be love in spite of relationship. Physical life and physical ties have no weight in the scale against love, for the basis of both relationship and ordinary life is desire and not love. Love, therefore, appears under the symbol of the destroyer, for in its presence the old, material ties break down, and where before there was the peace of inactivity arises the uncomfortable friction of growth *of which the chief symbols are those of the Œdipus relationship.*

"I am come to send fire on the earth. . . . Suppose ye that I am come to send peace ? I tell you, Nay ; but rather division. The father shall be divided against the son, and the son against the father ; the mother against the daughter and the daughter against the mother." 
                                        (Luke xii, 49 ff.)

But perhaps the most perfect example of the way in which mystical expression involves intellectual paradox, only to be understood from the mystical and not the physical standpoint, is the following :

"He that hath, to him shall be given : and he that hath not, from him shall be taken even that he hath."

                                        (Mark iv, 25.)

On the surface this statement is just as much nonsense as those already quoted, but, like them, it is perfectly clear when regarded mystically. Only *material* possessions can be taken away, and it is of no consequence how great they are, for they are *all* taken away. What then is left ? The mystical " treasure which faileth not," of which the possessor loses nothing at death, but rather gains more. The materialist, on the other hand, must lose " even that he hath." I have used the word

" materialist " again because the meaning has by now become reasonably clear. In biblical symbolism, how-ever, I should have used the word " rich." It is of no consequence whether a man is a millionaire or a pauper : whether he is " rich " or not is a question of attitude (consciousness). And this attitude is characterised by selfishness or unselfishness, the former corresponding to desire, the latter to love. The lover is poor,[1] but the desirous man is rich.[1] Just because desire is associated primarily with things physical, it is essentially dis-integrative. On the other hand love finds its highest expression only with the complete abandonment of selfishness in every form. Alone of the great " treasures," love is to be experienced only when it is freely given away ; in proportion as it is mixed with desire, the sense of possession, so its power disintegrates. When freed entirely from desire, however, love is omnipotent :

" His (the Buddha's) love is the supreme marvel of the worlds, or rather it is not, since other and self are for him identical, since creatures are to him as himself."

(Asanaga, 4th century B.C.)

In practice it is impossible to recognise the dividing line between these useful concepts, yet it is important that their relationship should be remembered. Broadly speaking I suppose it is true to say that never for a single moment are we free from desire in some form or other. Do you desire perfection ? Do you want peace ? Are you fond of life ? Do you fear death, pain, dis-honour ? If to any or all these the answer is " yes " then freedom from desire has not been achieved. And

---

[1] " Blessed are the poor *in spirit* " and those " rich toward God."

who then can say that he is free ? It may seem idiotic to push the argument so far, and yet these questions that I have just asked can clearly be a matter of indifference if love is sufficiently perfect. For then the attitude of loving would completely swamp all other considerations whatever. I say it is conceivable, but most certainly it is not practical. In fact the greatest danger which lies in wait for the " aspirant " whether religious, mystic, or the disciple of some purely abstract ideal such as an economic theory, is the failure to keep his feet on the ground. Inevitably he tends to get lost in cloudland, a country made up of his own ideals, creations of his own mind. He has risen too high and can no longer distinguish the real from the illusion, the true from the false. It is painful to fall, but equally painful to climb too high, too soon, or too fast.

Herein lies the importance of the Unjust Steward whose " lord " is Spirit and whose friends are Matter. Failing to comply with the standards of his " lord " he was at least wise enough to conform to the code of his own class. It is fatal to let go of earth before you are firmly established in heaven. Man is both god *and* brute. He forgets the latter at his peril, for the proper use of the brute within him is just as essential to his progress as devotion to the god. The biblical key to this . . . which includes the Unjust Steward, is that cryptic statement in Ecclesiastes (xi, 2) :

" Give a portion to seven and also to eight, for thou knowest not what evil shall be upon the earth."

The numerals represent the " opposites," for *seven* is spiritual and *eight* material. Eight, however, is not devilish, for that number is the famous *six* of the Beast of Revelation.

And to complete this clue we have only to quote the preceding verse :

" Cast thy bread upon the waters, for thou shalt find it after many days."

What is given to *eight* as *bread* will return as *wine*, in the strength of which the Steward can find better employment. It is the familiar notion of sublimation in a slightly altered form. *Bread* is *water* and *eight*. Seven, on the other hand, is *fire* and *wine*. Bread has been previously established as incarnate life, the path of which is as a voyage. The part of life which in the service of Mammon, the daily routine which seems so meaningless, has an extra significance of which we are not yet aware. What we have put into that " common " life will return as strength which we shall appreciate in times that follow the exchange of this employment for a higher post. There is only one condition : even the service of Mammon must be in the name of love.

One could go on almost indefinitely with examples of this sort, but we should confine ourselves as far as possible to those major points which follow after the identity and destiny of the Christ have been established. I think that the next which should come up for review is that of the re-birth itself, especially in so far as it bears upon the perception of the mystical " Eden." It is hardly necessary to give quotations concerning the Water and Blood since their nature and connections have recurred throughout our enquiry, even from its crude beginnings among the taboos of adolescents. It is known that the rôle of the Consummator is to effect the mystical transmutation and to teach the way of that attainment to those who follow after. Thus of the Hero it is said :

" This is he that came by Water and Blood, not by Water only but by Water and Blood."

(1 John v, 6.)

And of his followers :

" Verily, verily, I say unto thee, except a man be born again he cannot see the Kingdom of God. Verily, verily, I say unto thee, except a man be born of Water and of the Spirit he cannot enter the Kingdom of God."

(John iii, 3, 5.)

It may be remembered that there was only one sign given to humanity, that of the prophet Jonas. Upon that basis, by dint of sundry comparisons from myth and psychological theory, we recognised the symbol of the Christ *in* Jonas, otherwise Oannes, the fish-man who became the mystical ICTHUS. In fact, from whichever angle the problem is viewed, re-birth stands out conspicuously as the focal point of the Hero's career and his chief symbol. It has been shown further that the mystical marriage, from which the individual is re-born, corresponds to the re-entry into, or incest with, the Mother. Marriage in fact becomes equivalent to the re-birth, and it is in this way that the crucifixion becomes recognisable as the consummation.

But this ground has already been covered, and all we can now do is to consolidate it with reference to the Marriage at Cana, the " beginning of signs." The first point of interest is that the marriage is linked with the crucifixion by the mystical " three days " ; resurrection and the marriage both taking place " on the third day." (There is no point in separating the dual event of re-entry into the Mother and re-birth out of the Mother, so crucifixion may here be regarded as *equivalent* to resurrection, the two events being treated as one.)

At Cana it is the Mother who says " They have no

wine " and receives the answer " Woman, what have I
to do with thee ? mine hour is not yet come." Quite
apart from the inconsistency of this discourtesy with
the personal character of the Christ, we have already been
led by the mention of " three days " to expect an allegory.
We know also that Matter has no power over the Christ
until her apparent triumph at His death, and the sign of
Matter is the Mother. We know also that those *who
have no wine* are the children of the Mother, the " dead " ;
for wine is spirit.

In the same way we have found that to transmute water
into wine is that same *consummation* which is common to
every field into which we have enquired, usually expressed
in terms of earth/gold, earth/fire, water/fire, or water/
blood. In fine, the Marriage at Cana reveals the destiny
of Jesus, and his identity is confirmed as that revealed
in other terms at the Baptism.[1] But there are other
minor symbols which are also worth mentioning. There
were, for instance, *six* water-pots, and *six* is the number
of the Beast and of Antichrist, cited in Revelation and
in the Kabalistic " number of Sorath, the Demon
(opposite) of the Sun " which is also 666. (The easiest
way to consider this Antichrist is as an a*ttitude*, i.e.
materialism.) If, after serving the miraculous wine, the
water-pots had become seven instead of six there would
have been a further confirmation of the symbolic
sublimation. Further, these vessels were " of stone,"
which is equivalent to the alchemical " earth," so that
the *water* comes out of *stone* as *the wine* comes out of
*water*. And it should not be forgotten that Christ is
himself the Stone which is " lifted up," i.e. transmuted.
Finally the water-pots were there for the purpose

[1] Compare also : " Wist ye not that I must be about my
Father's business." (Luke ii, 49.)

of *purification* which is again to be connected with *sublimation*.

As to how many of these correspondences follow only from the necessity of giving a connected story I have no idea, nor do I regard it as in the least important; the fact remains that here is one of the most completely detailed pieces of symbolism in the most significant of all places . . . the " first sign " of the Christ, and a primary clue to the meaning of his life on earth.

But we have still not exhausted the symbolism of Cana because a whole vista of truth depends upon the significance of marriage as a practical institution, albeit the outward sign of a mystical union. This consideration brings us very close to the problems of the day, for it is perhaps in regard to marriage that the materialistic attitude is most tragic in its results. And because the question is of immediate importance, I should deal with it even at the risk of a reaction which would involve the rejection of the whole thesis.

God is love on all levels and everywhere. Animals mate, but the gods do not; nevertheless man is a god as well as a brute. God is love, and what love has joined together, let no man put asunder. By the same authority let no man bind together what love, or the lack of love, has sundered.

There is a physical union which we will call *mating*, and also a mystical union which is *marriage*. The New Testament is not concerned with the former, except in respect of tolerance for those who are unable to realise the ideal of the marriage.

Thus it is not man and woman who are " one flesh," but the unconscious " male " and " female." Man has always remained mystically androgyne in spite of the physical separation of the sexes (cf. Genesis), and appears to have an unconscious " sex " which is the opposite to that of the body. Such an idea is by no means strange to psychology :

" Theoretical speculation leads to the suspicion that there are two fundamental instincts which lie concealed behind the manifest ego-instincts and object-instincts : namely (*a*) Eros, the instinct which strives for ever closer union ; and (*b*) the instinct for destruction, which leads towards the dissolution of what is living."

(Encyc. Brit., XVIII, 673.)

This idea lends added significance to the sexual inversion concerning which we had a good deal to say in Chapter Three, and which found its most complete expression in the mystical " eunuch." Another way of expressing the same notion is frankly to regard the unconscious as the seat of a recessive sex. Traditionally the soul of a man was regarded as feminine, and this comes near to our own conclusion, which has at least the merit of simplicity. Briefly it seems that the physical sex is balanced by an " unconscious " or mystical sex, the two ultimately uniting in the spiritual androgyne. The first part of this idea . . . the unconscious or recessive sex, is quite well known in literature other than psychology, perhaps the best statement of the theme occurring in Leland's *The Alternate Sex*. This strange work is quoted with approval by Havelock Ellis, who himself inclines towards Groddeck's extreme view. It is Groddeck who expresses the full implications of the present theory and boldly asserts as a psychological and observable fact the very state of affairs to which we have been gradually brought by this long analysis of symbols.

" No human being is wholly man, or wholly woman ; every one of us is a woman-man or a man-woman, double-sexed. Man is also not altogether man nor altogether child, but at every age a child-man, child and man inseparably united in one being. It is by male and female that we are brought to life, and everything in us and of us, from the tiniest unitary cell, nay, from the nucleus of that cell to the collective phenomena which we recognise as an individual being, every single part of us is both male and female. Furthermore, at every moment man renews himself, is born again, and is a child, yet all the time he is as old as life itself and can declare : ' Before Abraham was I am ! ' "

(*Exploring the Unconscious*, p. 126.)

We are not concerned at present with more than the simplest statement of this idea . . . that there is a recessive sex ; but it can at least be stated that the logical outcome of the argument as a whole leads to exactly the conclusion so clearly stated by Groddeck. Perhaps the idea will gain even greater clarity with a further quotation, this time from the poet rather than the man of science.

> " My brain I'll prove the female to my soul,
> My soul the father : and these two beget
> A generation of still-breeding thoughts,
> And these same thoughts people this little world
> For no thought is contented."

(SHAKESPEARE : *Richard II.*)

Let us suppose now that the Individual is composed of the three " persons " indicated, a spirit, a soul, and a body, where the first is androgyne and the other two of opposite sex. Then if self-consciousness (derived of spirit) is regarded as the Observer, to borrow a very useful term from Dunne, the subsidiaries may be expressed as M or F for the physical sex and f or m for the " recessive " sex. Then the Individual may be expressed in the usual terms of our equations as under :

Woman, $O::^1 F/m$  Man, $O :: M/f$

The total consciousness of the Individual is thus the sum of the three " persons," but his *self*-consciousness is represented only by the Observer. And the extent or depth of the *self* is *proportionate to the degree of integration between the opposites*. But it must not be forgotten that the equation is dynamic and that " at every moment man renews himself."

And now let us get down to the proverbial " brass tacks." The perfect man, the Christ, has completed the mystical marriage in his own personality, has realised the complete unity of the Observer ; but all lesser men must compromise. Few can even attempt the mystical marriage without undue danger . . . the process must involve a tremendous mental strain, and in any case the conquest of physical sex must precede the conquest of its mental equivalent. Which is another way of saying that marriage and even sexual intercourse is the basis and the beginning of all balanced personality, the first requirement of life, the primary condition for happiness. God is love.

It is a reproach for which the Church will not easily atone that she has confounded physical union with the mystical marriage ; that in the name of love she has sought to separate lovers and at the same time to bind together those who no longer love. Mating, the physical union, is no substitute for marriage, but it is the first and generally necessary step towards the final union which is permanent. Mating and marriage are

---

$^1$ The sign : : should be read, " is the product of the relationship."

not evil and good respectively, they are in the fullest
sense complementary. It is better to love with the
body than not to love at all, and the individual who is
content with mating, who does not aspire always to a
higher and therefore more permanent love relationship,
is neurotic.

The physical act gives a temporary freedom from
desire (in the psychological sense) which is extremely
valuable, but where there is a deeper love the degree of
freedom is proportionately increased. We might express
mating by M/F and marriage by M/F//f/m, a *double* union
which is potentially eternal. This is the relationship
with which the New Testament is concerned, and the
conventional Church morality is a gross misinterpretation. Moreover it is this misinterpretation which is
primarily responsible for the unquiet age in which we
live. All human relations spring from the family, and
the family is in turn based upon the sex relationship.
The consequences of unbalanced sexual morality are
infinite in their capacity for the creation of disunion,
misery, and war.

It should be remembered, however, that our civilisation has already passed through the worst phase of this
materialistic morality. The nineteenth century was
probably the nadir. But it required the Great War to
make any considerable change. Even now it may be
doubted whether the return to sanity is rapid enough
to avoid another war.

But perhaps it is desirable to indicate some of the
*direct* and obvious results of this moral system. The
quotations which follow are taken from Bloch's *Sexual
Life of Our Time*, wherein that eminent doctor cites an
earlier authority, Dr. Gross-Hoffinger, who published at
Leipzig in 1847 *The Fate of Women, and Prostitution in*

*Relation to the Principle of the Indissolubility of Catholic Marriage, and especially in Relation to the Laws of Austria and the Philosophy of Our Time.* . . . . Fortunately the author's style is more concise than the title indicates, and he summarises the results of his investigations as follows :

" Although I have earnestly sought for happy marriages, my search has been to a large extent vain, and I have never been able to satisfy myself that happy marriages are anything but extremely isolated exceptions to the general rule."

In support of this conclusion there are tabulated the main features of one hundred marriages from the three principle strata of society.   Among them there were :

| | |
|---|---|
| Unhappy, about | 48 |
| Indifferent | 36 |
| Virtuous | 1 |
| Unquestionably happy | 15 |
| Virtuous and orthodox | — |

Further classification yielded :

| | |
|---|---|
| Intentionally immoral | 14 |
| Dissolute and libertine | 51 |
| Altogether above suspicion | ? |

And :

| | |
|---|---|
| Wives who were ill owing to the husband's fault | 30 |
| Wives who were ill not owing to the husband's fault | 30 |

From such results as these Gross-Hoffinger makes the following judgments :

" 1. About one-half of all marriages are absolutely unhappy.
  2. Much more than one-half are obviously demoralised.
  3. The morality of the remaining small moiety is preserved only by avoiding questions regarding the husband's faithfulness.

4. Fifteen per cent of all marriages live on the earnings of professional unchastity and procurement.

5. The number of orthodox marriages which are entirely above every suspicion of marital infidelity (assuming the existence of complete sexual potency) is, in the eyes of every reasonable man, who understands the demands Nature makes and the violence of those demands, equivalent to nil. Hence the ecclesiastical purpose of marriage is generally, fundamentally, and completely avoided."

And how much misery derives from the present state of affairs quite apart from marriage! There is the great industry of prostitution with its by-products of disease and degeneracy, and, at one remove, the vast army of neurotics and psychotics, who, as Freud has amply demonstrated, derive primarily from sexual maladjustment. We may recall also the statistics already quoted. . . . Eight times more feeble-minded than consumptives. One person in twenty-two in need of treatment. Four millions in the British Isles who are markedly unbalanced.

In the causes of such maladjustment are included those transferred impulses which are recognised broadly as desire for material possession; love of money for instance, "that odourless, dehydrated filth, which has been made to shine." In the same category are the grosser manifestations of the "will to power"; and it is perhaps permissible to summarise the whole attitude as "sadomasochistic," an attitude which is responsible for all forms of hate, greed, cruelty, and bestiality, from "spoiling" children to chain-smoking, from asceticism to the violation of corpses.

"The best prophylaxis for these paraphilias lies, as I have already said, in education. What society needs is a campaign against envy and jealousy. If we reduce the cases of sado-masochism to one effect, we strike upon jealousy and the preparedness for jealousy.

" That individual is jealous who has not found satisfaction
in love. (Whether physical, transferred or sublimated.) Our
patients are all incapable of love and consumed with desire
for it. They transfer this condition to the entire world about
them. They crave recognition and sympathy and act as if
they had no desire for them. They are all ambitious, but
too weak to carry out their ambitious plans for a great historical mission. Thus envy and jealousy drive them into the
role of the revengeful person and the penitent one. They
feel themselves cheated of their desired happiness and allay
their pain in the pleasure of the wrong they can do themselves
and others. The compulsion of the external world creates
an inner compulsion. Every pressure produces a counter-
pressure." (STEKEL : *Sadism and Masochism*, Vol. II, 460.)

All this is significant in the present chapter chiefly
because it is religion which should play the rôle of the
*balancing power* alike in the life of the individual and of
the community. In default of such an impetus towards
sublimation, all these evils are inevitable. It is even
fair to say that the extent of such evils is the measure of
the failure of religion, which has become divorced from
the very force which is at once its own life and the object
of all living.

A religion of love has been prostituted into the
motherhood of a morality of which the very foundations
are those disintegrative forces whose nature we have
tried to demonstrate. Love has been degraded to desire
. . . " sex-appeal," and the will to sublimation has
become the passion for possession. Small wonder that
there is no vision, and the people perish !

Nor is it any consolation to reflect that the agent
which contributed more than any other to this fearful
state of affairs has been activated throughout by the
highest intellectual motives. Yet it is not just to blame
the Church, for the age creates its own Church, and it

was the materialism of the nineteenth century which produced a materialist Church, a religion blind and deaf even to the obvious results of its own hypocrisy. That Church, like the Sphinx of Œdipus, was a monster and a destroyer. But there is another Sphinx and there is another Church—again the symbol of the dual Mother.

The Harlot Mother of the Antichrist is also the Virgin Mother of the Christ, and the Harlot is merged into the Virgin when the rule of materialism approaches its term. There is no way to the heights save through the depths.

> " Behold now Behemoth which I made with thee ;
> He eateth grass like the ox.
> Lo now, his strength is in his loins,
> And his force is in the muscles of his belly.
> He moveth his tail like a cedar :
> The sinews of his stones are knit together.
> His bones are as tubes of brass ;
> His limbs are like bars of iron.
> *He is the chief of the ways of God.*"
>
> (Job xl, 15–19.)

We might have begun the whole book with this quotation, which states most clearly the significance of the sex-force in its primeval aspect. But desire is only the bottom of a ladder whose rungs carry consciousness upward out of Behemoth, through Jesse and the Song of Songs, until it passes altogether beyond sex in the conception of the mystical androgyne (invert or eunuch), who receives a name "better than of sons or daughters." Thus is born from desire its complement, love. Desire *takes* but love *gives*, and this is the beginning of the conscious Quest until love's ultimate destiny becomes apparent.

> " He that believeth on me, as the scripture hath said, out of his belly shall flow rivers of living water."
>
> (John vii, 38.)

" Whosoever drinketh of the water that I shall give him shall never thirst; but the water that I shall give him shall be in him a well of water springing up into everlasting life."

(John iv, 14.)

The " well " is, of course, the source of libido whose " rock bottom " is Behemoth and which finds Oriental expression as that *serpent* Kundalini, which rises up in the individual until he becomes " radiant and perfect." Discipleship gives way to apostleship and that which was " water " manifests as " tongues of fire "—those same flames whose " phallic nature " was commented upon by Róheim in the course of the Baptism analysis.

Pentecost is that attainment which is the crown of the earthly quest and the earthly " magnum opus " of transmutation, for there consciousness passes beyond mortality.

" For he is our peace who hath made both one,
and hath broken down the middle wall of partition.
Having abolished in his flesh the enmity,
for to make of himself one new man,
so making peace.
And that he might reconcile both unto God
in one body by the cross,
having slain the enmity thereby."

(Eph. ii, 14 ff.)

Christianity is now speaking the same language as the Orient, and when the Cross is viewed as in this profound statement of St. Paul, the Christ is manifest in the symbols of the Buddha. Says the Book of Manu :

" Whosoever remaineth the same in living as in dying, in fortune as in misfortune, whether gaining or losing, in love and in hatred, will be redeemed.

" Whoso nothing pursueth and regardeth nothing of small account, whoso is free from the opposites (nirdvandva), whose soul knoweth no passion . . . he is wholly delivered.

" Whosoever doeth neither right nor wrong, renouncing

JESUS OF NAZARETH 285

the treasure (of good and evil deeds) heaped up in former lives, whose soul is tranquil when the bodily elements vanish away, *whoso holdeth himself free from the opposites, that one is redeemed.*"

(Mahabharata, xiv.)

The Buddhist attitude is transmitted by Sir Edwin Arnold :

" Many a house of life
Hath held me . . . seeking ever him who wrought
These prisons of the senses, sorrow-fraught ;
Sore was my ceaseless strife !
But now,
Thou Builder of this Tabernacle . . . Thou !
I know Thee ! Never shalt thou build again
These walls of pain,
Nor raise the roof-tree of deceits, nor lay
Fresh rafters on the clay ;
Broken Thy house is, and the ridge-pole split !
Delusion fashioned it !
Safe pass I thence . . . deliverence to obtain."

(*Light of Asia*, Bk. VI.)

Perhaps it should be added that the " Builder " is the Great Achitect, and his House is this material life of the " opposites " which it is our destiny as his Sons to " grow out of," as we grow out of childish things ; " to reconcile both unto God," the duality merged into triunity.

And if such lofty symbolism is common to the whole width and depth of humanity, so also is the " symbolism of the unconscious " on those more ordinary levels which are the special study of psychology.

". . . a negro of the Southern States of America dreams in the motives of Grecian mythology, and a Swiss grocer's apprentice repeats in his psychosis the vision of an Egyptian Gnostic."

(JUNG : *Psychological Types*, p. 624.)

Common language derives from a common source in which is the harmony of all contradictions and the mean-

ing of all symbols.  We have tried to demonstrate some
of the intellectual fruit of such symbols, chiefly in
regard to the individual; but the highest flights of
language are fitted for the cosmic rather than the mystic
allegory.  The sublimation which from Stone made
Fire, from Water, Wine, from Behemoth, Christ the
King, carries humanity out of the depths of mortality
into a " new heaven and a new earth."

" And he shewed me a river of water of life clear as crystal
proceeding out of the throne of God and of the Lamb.  In
the midst of the street of it and on either side of the river
was there the Tree of Life. . . . And the leaves of the Tree
were for the healing of nations."               (Rev. xxii, 1–2.)

But why do the nations require healing and what is the
nature of their wound ?

" And I stood upon the sand of the sea and saw a beast
rise up out of the sea, having upon his heads the name of
blasphemy. . . . And power was given him over all kindreds,
and tongues, and nations.
" And all that dwell in the earth shall worship him. . . .
And no man might buy and sell save he had the mark, or
the name of the beast or the number of his name.  And his
number is 666."                                    (Rev. xiii.)

For the individual there is a certain " dark night,"
and for humanity also.  The night is hideous with
tempest, earthquake, terrible beasts, and fire.  But after
these is heard a voice, there is found a treasure, and the
Golden Flower blooms in the Purple Hall of the City of
Jade.
At this time also the Knight of the Quest crosses the
glass drawbridge of the Castle of Souls, and is conducted
to the Hall of Roses in which the Rich King Fisher and

his company are healed by eucharistic magic and the asking of the Question.

All these ideas, however, are included in one, just as the intricate pantheon of Egypt is implicit in the One One. For at the end of the night dawns the day "Omega" when the Unity itself is known.

> "They shall not hurt nor destroy in all my
> holy mountain : and the earth shall be full
> of the glory of the Lord as the waters cover
> the sea."

> "Then the eyes of the blind shall be opened,
> And the ears of the deaf shall be unstopped,
> Then shall the lame man leap as an hart,
> And the tongue of the dumb sing. . . .
> And an highway shall be there, and a way,
> And it shall be called the Way of Holiness ;
> The unclean shall not pass over it ;
> But it shall be for those, the wayfaring men. . . ."

> (Isaiah.)

In that day man recognises his Father at full stature :

> "Thou art Ra-Herakhty, the Divine Youth, Heir
> of Eternity, who begat himself and brought forth
> himself, King of this land, ruler of the Tuat,
> chief of the districts of the Other World,
> who came forth from the water, who emerged from
> Nun, who reared himself and made splendid his
> children."

> (Papyrus of Nekht, Brit. Mus., No. 10471.)

There is no longer Father and Son but undivided Unity, so that Man proclaims not only the identity of his God, but his own identity also :

> "I am the God Atum, I who alone was.
> I am the God Re at his first splendour.
> I am the great God, self-created, God of Gods,
> To whom no other God compares."

" I was yesterday and know to-morrow ; the battle-ground of
Gods was made when I spoke. . . .
My impurity is driven away, and the sin which was in me
is overcome.
I go on my way to where I wash my head in the sea
of the righteous.
I arrive at this land of the glorified
and enter through the splendid portal.
Thou, who standest before me, stretch out to me thy hands.
It is I, I am become one of thee.
Daily I am together with my Father Atum."

(ERMAN : Aegypten, p. 409.)<br>
Quoted more fully on p. 100.

To this tremendous recognition there is a response :

" And let the Spirit and the Bride say, Come.
And let him that heareth say, Come.
And let him that is athirst come.
And whosoever will, let him take of the
waters of life freely."                          (Rev.)

This is the perpetual speech of symbolism. The form
of the words varies, but the unity of their source is
absolute.

Who are the Spirit and the Bride ? Do you remember
the hosting of the Sidhe when Caitilin ni Murrachu
became the bride of Angus Óg ? It is the same story.

A mortal peasant girl, she had first felt the desire for
Pan. He came to her among the bracken on the misty
Irish hills, and she went with him gladly, dancing to
his pipes. So she became the harlot-mother and the
half of her destiny was accomplished. Desire, however,
leads on to love, and one day the god of love, Angus Óg,
came to the cave of Pan and asked that the girl should
choose between them.

So Caitilin went with Angus to his Dûn in the land

of Faëry. The peasant girl is now also the Ever-virgin,
the potential Mother of the miraculous Son. So there
is the greatest hosting of the Sidhe that there can ever
be, all the peoples of the ever-living gathering on the
hill-tops in the bright dawn to honour the Spirit and the
Bride.

  " ' My beloved,' said he, ' we will go on a journey to-day.'
  ' My delight is where you go,' said Caitilin.
  ' We will go down to the world of men . . . from our
quiet dwelling among the hills to the noisy city and the mul-
titude of people. This will be our first journey, but on a time
not distant we will go to them again, and we will not return
from that journey, for we will live among our people and be
at peace.'
  ' May the day come soon,' she said.
  ' When my son is a man he will go before us on that
journey,' said Angus, and Caitilin shivered with a great
delight, knowing that a son would be born to her.
  ' Then Angus Óg put upon his bride glorious raiment, and
they went out into the sunlight.' "

And the sign of their journey is, of course, the same
sign, the Spirit and the Bride, combined as they are in
the potential Mother of the Christ. So the focus of the
hosting is Dana, Mother of the Gods, steadfast for ever.
Dana and Caitilin, the Absolute and its personification,
are the inspiration of the song of attainment which is
now therefore primarily the Mother's Song.

"Come to us, ye who do not know where ye are . . . ye
who live among strangers in the houses of dismay and self-
righteousness. Poor, awkward ones ! How bewildered and
bedevilled ye go ! Amazed ye look and do not comprehend,
for your eyes are set upon a star and your feet move in the
blessed kingdoms of the Shee. Innocents ! in what prisons
are ye flung ? To what lowliness are ye bowed ? How are
ye bound between the laws and the customs ? The dark
people of the Fomor have ye in thrall ; and upon your minds

they have fastened a band of lead, your hearts are hung with iron, and about your loins a cincture of brass impressed, woeful ! Believe it, that the sun does shine, the flowers grow, and the birds sing pleasantly in the trees. The free winds are everywhere, the water tumbles on the hills, the eagle calls aloud through the solitude, and his mate comes speedily. The bees are gathering honey in the sunlight, the midges dance together, and the great bull bellows across the river. The crow says a word to his brethren, and the wren snuggles her young in the hedge. . . . Come to us, ye lovers of life and happiness. Hold out thy hand . . . a brother shall seize it from afar. Leave the plough and the cart for a little time : put aside the needle and the awl. . . . Is leather thy brother, O man ? . . . Come away ! come away ! from the loom and the desk, from the shop where the carcases are hung, from the place where raiment is sewn and the place where it is sewn in darkness : O bad treachery ! Is it for joy you sit in the broker's den, thou pale man ? Has the attorney enchanted thee ? . . . Come away ! For the dance has begun lightly, the wind is sounding over the hill, the sun laughs down into the valley, and the sea leaps upon the shingle, panting for joy, dancing, dancing, dancing for joy. . . .

" Down to the city they went dancing and singing ; among the streets and the shops telling their sunny tale ; not heeding the malignant eyes and the cold brows as the sons of Balor looked sideways. And they took the Philosopher from his prison, even the Intellect of man they took from the hands of the doctors and lawyers, from the sly priests, from the professors whose mouths are gorged with sawdust, and the merchants who sell blades of grass . . . the awful people of the Fomor."

(JAMES STEPHENS : *The Crock of Gold*.)

There is only one speech in symbolism, and though it be grave or gay, there is but a single root idea behind it all. I could not have cited a greater contrast than this Irish fairy-tale against the distant thunder of Egyptian ritual, yet they hold a melody in common, under different keys. Perhaps to complete the metaphor we may contrast them both against the quotation which follows, surely the great " C Major " of all such silent music.

" I am Alpha and Omega, the Beginning and the Ending, that which was, and which is, and which is to come, the Almighty.

" He that hath an ear let him hear what the spirit saith.

" To him that overcometh I will give to eat of the hidden manna, and will give him a white stone, and in the stone a new name written which no man knoweth save he who receiveth it.

" He that overcometh I will confess his name before my Father and before his angels.

" To him that overcometh I will give to eat of the Tree of Life which is in the midst of the Paradise of God.

" He that overcometh shall not be hurt of the second death.

" To him that overcometh and keepeth my works unto the end, to him will I give power over all nations : even as I received of my Father. And I will give him the morning star.

" To him that overcometh I will grant to sit with me in my throne, even as I overcame and am set down with my Father in his throne.

" He that overcometh I will make a pillar in the temple of my God, and he shall go out no more : and I will write upon him the name of my God and the name of the city of my God : and I will write upon him my own new name."

# CHAPTER ELEVEN

## THE INTUITIVE APPROACH

" We should not pretend to understand the world only by the intellect; we apprehend it just as much by feeling. Therefore the judgment of the intellect is, at best, only half the truth, and must, if it be honest, also come to an understanding of its inadequacy."

(JUNG : *Psychological Types*, p. 628.)

IN the Introduction I made it clear that in no sense do I claim intuition, least of all that faculty in myself, as either necessarily without error or necessarily " evidential." On the other hand it does seem to transcend the limits of intellect at least occasionally, and there is no doubt in my own mind that the present synthesis is derived from an intuitive perception wherein all the fundamentals required for the intellectual interpretation were somehow compressed into " feeling." The process has probably been analagous to that recognised occasionally in musical composition which is presented to the composer in the first instance " in a flash." To reduce that " flash " to terms of written music may involve the production of a long symphony, all of which is " felt " to have been in some mysterious way present in the original inspiration.

I am inclined to think that intuitive perception is more common than is generally supposed, but that it is seldom recognised because of its vagueness and the difficulty of reducing such preception to intelligible terms. It is also unfortunate that even intense intuitive experience tends to be forgotten very rapidly in the same way that a dream, which was vivid immediately upon waking, somehow disappears even within the next few minutes. Altogether it is a hopeless case for scientific investigation, and seems likely to remain so until subjects can be found who will produce the faculty to order. In my own case, for instance, there was an intense experience which I suppose may be labelled mystical for lack of a better term. In spite of the intensity there was nothing which the mind could take hold of; the most that might be transmitted in words is a sense of certainty concerning the purpose and destiny of life. There was no vision, not even a symbol, and yet consciousness seemed to have been turned inside out. Immediately afterwards, for perhaps an hour, one walked in a dream as though beauty had revealed herself in the world for the very first time. It was inconceivable that the feeling could ever fade, much less disappear.

Yet in a few weeks, not only had the rosy haze dispersed, but even the memory had faded. A little later and the most that one could say was : " Well, I know that I did feel that certainty, even if it breaks every rule of experience and every cannon of common sense." One was even able to explain the whole thing away ; the ghostly experience being reduced to a mere practical joke played upon consciousness by the unconscious.

That experience has never been repeated, and the tendency is to regard it with growing incredulity in spite of the impossibility of explaining it away. The only evidence in its favour is arrived at by the sort of analysis of which I have here included a typical example. This particular piece was written two years before the experience, but nevertheless represents both the result of our argument and the sense of certainty already mentioned.

As for the stages by which the "hunch" was eventually expressed in words, the initial steps were mentioned in the Introduction and the remainder are recorded here. But it must not be supposed that I am able with one per cent inspiration to avoid the full ninety-nine per cent perspiration which are proverbially demanded before practical results are achieved.

In the analysis of my poems I followed the method employed by Dr. Jung in his classic work on the " Miller phantasies," where he showed that young lady's aspiration, even the " longing of the moth for the sun," to be libidinous, in the orthodox sense of that term. Presumably I expected to get some results along the same lines, but naturally hoped to vindicate my character; so between these differing viewpoints there was no clear idea at the back of my mind. . . . I was to all intents and purposes unbiased.

Nevertheless, the analyses were quite sufficiently " successful " to make it evident that I was just as much a sex-ridden hypocrite as Miss Miller. I should probably have left the matter there had the poems belonged to anyone but myself, but pride insisted upon an attempt to find an explanation. Pride said it was ridiculous to reduce one's highest ideals to a desire for incest, whatever the psychologists might hold.

Nor did the opposition come entirely from pride : it was clearly a problem of no ordinary interest that confronted me. On the one hand the sexual analysis was psychologically justified . . . I had to admit that; while over and above that analysis I continued to believe in a higher significance for the states of mind from which the verses were derived.

After a great deal of trial and error, there was developed a method of analysis which accepted the sex symbols as corresponding to abstract terms, such, for instance, as the desire for incest being equivalent to the longing for immortality, while more detailed correspondences were worked out for the various factors contributing to that longing or desire. Thus the erect penis could be read abstractly as corresponding to "aspiration" or the "*will* to immortality," while the womb became the "sacrifice" involved in such aspiration and will. These meanings being additional to and by no means instead of the orthodox readings.

There is no need to particularise minutely since most of these symbols have already been dealt with at one time or another; for instance, the "fluid of Ra," and the "blood" of Isis, castration, inversion, and the ambivalence of the Mother.

But although it was clear that there was a meaning which was "supersexual," I was still a long way from using this new meaning with any degree of accuracy. First I went through the poems again, this time making two analyses, one in sexual terms and the other in "mystical" terms. Then the results were reduced to order by modifying the sense of particular symbols as seemed to be required for the underlying harmony of the whole series. This harmony revealed a progressive set of ideas which culminated in the phrase " consummate duality," a statement which was meaningless at the time it was written, but which later appeared as the germ of the present theory . . . the idea of the equations of " triunity."

Perhaps it will be worth while to make an example of

a short poem which will not expose me unduly.  It was
written without any particular quality of inspiration in
March, 1934.

> " Beyond this vibrant matter and above
>     The dust-blind groping of our human brain,
>     Shackled by physics in a sandstorm twilight,
>     An agate corridor depends,
>     A smooth perspective blackness,
>     As a telescope reversed.
>
> " Yet infinite afar reflection glows,
>     A vivid atom-point of light,
>     Pregnant with a new intensity
>     Of flowing colour and abundant life."

Let us take the physical analysis first, adopting the
attitude which a psychoanalyst would employ if the
poem had been written by one of his patients whom he
knew fairly well.  The first word he would regard as
significant is, of course, " pregnant," and he would
conclude immediately from the general tone of the piece
that the basis of it is a *desire for escape*, to get out of this
cold, hard world into a place where there are no more
unpleasant realities.  In that he is obviously correct.

The question then arises as to how the escape is to be
expressed.  What or who can give such an escape?
Death perhaps, and yet it is unlikely that the analyst
would accept the word.  He would almost certainly
pick out the " agate corridor " and its " smooth, per-
spective blackness." These ideas, together with
" pregnant " can mean only one thing.  The patient
wants to go back to the Mother. . . . At this point the
analyst will smile happily.  It is the Œdipus complex
again.  In fact the case is peculiarly clear, for the poem
obviously describes the mother womb, that " corridor "
by which the patient came into the world and which

is now so " infinite afar." Probably the analyst would say as much to the patient, and would receive all the confirmation he required. Certainly the patient felt at times that he was helpless . . . too weak to grapple with life, but it had never occurred to him that he wanted to go back to the mother. Of course the analysis is perfectly reasonable, one can't imagine anything much more peaceful and protected than an unborn baby ; but that is not quite the same thing as accusing a grown man of a desire for incest, albeit in the depths of the unconscious.

To this the analyst would reply that the patient has no cause for worry, that he has now recognised his desire for escape, which is a most important step in the right direction. The next is to find a new outlet for the libidinous energy which is now finding expression in the incest wish. A transference must be arranged. The patient might be advised to adopt a positive sex attitude, to find a mistress or marry. He might also be advised to give up dreaming and poetry, which seem only to intensify the desire for escape, and take up instead some occupation which would require a positive attitude that would leave him little time or energy for dreaming.

Such a solution would, of course, be correct, *so far as it went*. The patient would no doubt be much comforted and the budding neurosis effectively countered. If all went well, a permanently balanced attitude would emerge ; the patient would be reasonably contented with his niche in life. . . . But he would be cured also of his *aspiration*, and the advice which enabled him to find contentment might also have turned an artist into an artisan. This, as I see it, is the normal success of psychoanalysis. . . . Consider now the mystical content of the poem.

The patient is trying to find something—" groping,"

a *positive* attitude. For what is he groping? Evidently for "light" which is "above" matter. The idea of limitations imposed upon consciousness by incarnation are elaborated with the aid of an almost conventional picture of the structure of matter, where the gyrating atoms are compared to grains of sand. So it is the *extension of consciousness* for which the patient is striving. . . . His "escape" when seen thus is not negative but positive, the *complement* of that arrived at by the physical analysis.

The analyst's task is now to determine which of the two attitudes is dominant and to advise the patient in such a way as to balance them. Neurosis will result just as certainly from an over-mystical as from an over-physical attitude.

But in any case the advice will differ in one vital respect from that resulting from the purely physical analysis. The channels of transference will now have to be secondary considerations as compared with the primary necessity of developing the quality of (balanced) aspiration. It would be dangerous to tell the patient to concentrate exclusively upon the mystical side of his nature, but it would be absurd to try and stifle it altogether. Admittedly the patient who is permitted to continue this "quest" is not likely to reach the solid contentment which would have been his had the analysis taken only the physical into consideration. But there is such a thing as "divine discontent."

> "What is he but a brute
> Whose flesh has soul to suit,
> Whose spirit works lest arms and legs want play?
> To man, propose this test—
> Thy body at its best,
> How far can that project thy soul on its lone way?
>                     (ROBERT BROWNING.)

The task of the analyst then is not solely to arrange for transference, but also to ensure a progressive sublimation ; this makes all the difference, to my mind, between a positive and a negative analysis. Modern psychotherapy seems to be predominantly destructive for that very reason ; it is content with transference. At the same time our " mystical " analyst would certainly point out that the quickest way to become unbalanced is to neglect to keep one's feet firmly planted on earth. The more one's head is in the clouds, the more necessary is attention to the other extremity. Learned tomes testify that even this modern generation is too modest to take proper care of its " feet," too " nice " to be natural. But our analyst would not be content with " mating," he would emphasise the psychological ideal of *marriage*, its permanence, and its dependence upon the proper recognition of " recessive " sex.

We are now, perhaps, looking too far ahead, and it will be as well to illustrate one of Freud's analyses for comparison with that just given.

" His next thought was the general reflection that the conception of heat had always impressed him, that heat was the most important thing in the universe, the source of life and so on.

" This remarkable attitude of quite a prosaic young man certainly needed some explanation, so I asked him to continue his associations.

" The next thought was a factory stack which he could see from his bedroom window. He often stood of an evening watching the flame and smoke issuing out of it, and reflecting on this deplorable waste of energy. Heat, flame, the source of life, the waste of vital energy issuing from an upright hollow tube . . . it was not hard to divine from such associations that the ideas of heat and fire were unconsciously linked in his mind with the idea of love, as is so frequent in symbolic thinking, and that there was a strong masturbation complex present, a conclusion that he presently confirmed."

(*Psychopathology of Everyday Life*, p. 291.)

It would certainly be surprising if there were no masturbation complex, especially if the young man's aspiration was thwarted by his environment so that the " vital energy," in default of sublimation, was directed downwards. Many psychologists now hold that no normal human being is devoid of some such complex, since masturbation, in one form or another, is almost inescapable. But such considerations are hardly germane to the main point at issue, which is to emphasise the extension of analysis which takes place when the symbols are read mystically as well as physically. In the present case, for instance, the very fact that the patient is a young man suggests that he is ambitious, that he wants to " set the Thames on fire." In fact he wants to be like the tall chimney which everyone notices, and which so impresses him with the idea of *virility*. In other words this young man's attitude is quite opposite to that of our first patient, who was by no means dominant in his physical attitude towards the world. On the contrary he wanted to escape from the world. It was a tunnel (agate corridor) which he chose as his symbol, the very opposite of the tall chimney.

Knowing nothing about Freud's patient, it would be obviously impertinent to go further, except perhaps to point out the mystical association of heat with love which is recognised as the " source of life " in the dictum " God is love." It seems at least probable that this young man was full of affection to which there seemed to be no response; therefore instead of affection the medium of his expression became desire, hence lust. Then, finding that there was still no response; the lust became introverted and an autoerotic neurosis developed.

Here again it would not be sufficient to re-direct physical love into heterosexual channels (they have no great advantage over autoeroticism as such), which would be the normal object of psychoanalysis. In order to make the most out of the patient his energies should be re-directed towards the *aspiration* (sublimation) of which the flaming chimney was a fit symbol.

But we have said enough about the symbol in psychology and nothing at all about its increasing significance in other fields. Almost unnoticed the symbol is creeping into almost every department of human relations. It saturates science and the arts, and inspires all those strange movements which seem at first sight so bewildering ; impressionism, surrealism, poetry based upon subconscious association. When compared to the very *literal* attitude of the last century, this cult of symbolism attains the stature of a revolution. Even politics are not immune. What extraordinary power surrounds the new cults of Swastica and Fasces, the Hammer and Sickle !

No discussion of intuition is complete without some reference to prophecy, its most mysterious form ; not that there is any intention of building up a " case " for such prediction. The main argument is closed, and what remains are to be regarded as " notes in passing " ; no more than suggestive of some of the lines of enquiry which have been ignored.

When Count Leo Tolstoy, the great novelist, approached his end in the autumn of 1910, he is said to have dictated the " spiritual outlines " of the future from " an almost trancelike condition." The bulk of his message hardly concerns us, but one section is of peculiar interest. I quote here from the version given in *The Story of Prophecy*, by H. J. Forman :

" It is the light of symbolism that shall outshine the torch of commercialism. In place of polygamy and monogamy of to-day there will come a *poetogamy*, a relation of the sexes based fundamentally upon the poetic conceptions of life. Life is evolution and evolution is development from the simple to the more complicated forms of the mind and body."

What strikes me particularly is that the word " poetogamy " and the " poetic conceptions of life " are almost meaningless without the concept of the unconscious. The word symbolism, as understood prior to the psychological discoveries, must have been almost completely devoid of significance, at least in Europe. As for the rest, at least Tolstoy saw the broad sweep of world affairs through a period of active war, which he predicted for 1913, to a period of cultural chaos. " The relation between man and woman is accepted as a prosaic partnership of the sexes. Art has become realistic degeneracy. Political and religious disturbances have shaken the spiritual foundations of all nations." The period of chaos gives place in its turn to a time when, in the middle of the century, " God, soul, spirit, and immortality will be molten in a new furnace, and I see the peaceful beginning of a new era."

Of course prophecy is the most difficult of all the intuitions to value correctly, but for that very reason I have brought forward this example. The Tolstoy prophecy is intuitive vision in the grand manner, made with every circumstance which could contribute to its authority. Yet in many respects it is clearly and seriously at fault. There was to be a United States of Europe by 1925 with only four potential enemies, the Anglo-Saxons, the Latins, and the Slavs. A Mongolian Slav was to be responsible for the destruction of monotheism in favour of pantheism. There was to have been a civil rather than a military Napoleon, a writer or journalist who would dominate Europe from 1915 to 1925. It might be suggested that the whole time-table is late, that the " journalist " Napoleon is Hitler, and the Mongolian only biding his time ; but even so the fact remains that the prophecy is wrong. And yet what are we to make of Tolstoy's anticipation of this symbolism whose emergence is already obvious. Though we are not accustomed to employ the actual word " symbolism " there can be no doubt but that it is a dominating cultural feature of the age. Was it intuition that Tolstoy had ? In this respect at all events it can hardly have been guesswork. Then why was much of the vision incorrect ? What were the limits of intelligent anticipation ? Certainly it is necessary to treat all claims of vision with very great reserve.

To anyone who has even a nodding acquaintance with the literature of the unconscious it must be surprising that intuition . . . supposing such a faculty to exist, can ever get through the elaborate defences of consciousness. Every one of us deceive ourselves perpetually. To find a moment devoid of promptings from the deeper mind is rare indeed, as anyone can prove by the simple expedient of learning to watch the trend of his own thought and to analyse it without pity. It is not too much to say that very many people are little more than automata kept moving by chains of conditioned reflex; their passions, their opinions, their emotions are not independent judgments but the resultant from a series of equations . . . from wishes and fears in the dark recesses of the unconscious. Whenever the focus of conscious thought becomes blurred, there is a rush of repressed ideas to the surface ; or, alternatively, a seeming blank, while the censor holds back the unruly crew. Small chance for intuition when there is so much competition for the narrow stage of the conscious mind !

Another aspect of the problem is suggested by Oriental mysticism, which seems to be based on the recognition of these very factors. It is always emphasised that the greatest difficulty and even danger[1] is in store for the mind which sets out to realise its own true nature, the Self. Whatever the particular system, the greatest weight of authority is behind the assertion that the disciple must free himself from illusion, from the opposites ; and that he cannot know the Self until his mind is freed from all these extraneous ideas, which are the products of automatic reactions, dictated by the constitution of the Self's vehicles, the body and the soul. In proportion as such ideas are conquered, so does consciousness expand. The first stage is the freedom from the grosser material attachments, then comes freedom from passion ; passion merges into desire in all its myriad forms, the " desire for the presence of the loved and the absence of the unloved " : but already the disciple is beyond the ordinary run of mortals. At some point in his freeing from desire dawns the intuitive recognition of his identity and destiny, the first stage of the progressive unfoldment of the Self.

Practical mysticism, whether Eastern or Western, recognises the great gulf which separates this ideal sequence from the grim see-saw battles to which even the lives of the genius and the saint bear witness ; but

[1] Compare the following in respect of psychoanalysis : " Looking back, I can count up a long series of highly gifted analysts who have voluntarily departed from this life. . . Occupation with analysis is a great danger. It is a handling of sharp weapons which may easily turn against the analyst." (W. STEKEL : *Sadism and Masochism*, Vol. I, p. 126.)

the ideal remains nevertheless, being one thing only under all the veils of sectarian expression—the progressive evolution of consciousness.

Perhaps the most elaborate symbolic ritual ever designed to hinge upon these ideas is that of *The Tibetan Book of the Dead*. There the dead man is represented as being " set face-to-face " with all the symbols of consciousness, from the highest absolute to the lowest depths of materialism. Somewhere between the two extremes he finds that with which he is naturally in sympathy, his own wavelength as it were, and he is promptly absorbed in it for the further pursuit of his destiny whatever that may be ; to attain Buddhahood, to rest in heaven, to be born again a king or a beggar, to writhe in hell, or even to reincarnate in some animal. The ritual represents the dead as witnessing a tremendous pageant of gods and demons, *all of which he must recognise as the products of his own mind*. He is prevented from so recognising by the degree of his " attachment " (desire) which, in spite of his *knowledge*, will tend to bind him to that level in which he has lived. Thus the dead man is alternately awed and terrified by apparitions, until at last comes that which he has loved on earth. This he is able to recognise, and to it he returns in due course.

Let me quote from two of the fourteen " days " during which this weird pageant unrolls. I choose the first and the last, but invert their order. The priest (still alive on earth) is addressing the dead man.

" O nobly-born, if one recognise not one's own thought-forms, however learned one may be in the Scriptures, although practising religion for a kalpa,[1] one obtains not Buddhahood. If one recognises one's own thought-forms, by one important art and by one word, Buddhahood is obtained.

" If one's thought-forms be not recognised as soon as one

[1] A " day of Brahma," 4,320,000,000 years.

dieth, the shapes of Dharma-Rāja, the Lord of Death, will shine forth. . . . The largest of the bodies of Dharma-Rāja, Lord of Death, equalling the heavens (in vastness); the intermediate, Mt. Meru; the smallest, eighteen times one's own body, will come filling the world systems. They will come having their upper teeth biting the nether lip; their eyes glassy; their hairs tied on top of the head; big-bellied, narrow-waisted; holding a (karmic) record-board in the hand; giving utterance from their mouth to sounds of 'Strike! Slay!', licking (human) brain, drinking blood, tearing heads from corpses, tearing out (the) hearts: thus will they come, filling the worlds.

"O nobly-born, when such thought-forms emanate, be thou not afraid, nor terrified; the body which thou now possessest being a mental body of (karmic) propensities, though slain and chopped to bits, cannot die. Because thy body is, in reality, one of voidness, thou needest not fear. The (bodies of the) Lord of Death, too, are emanations from the radiances of thine own intellect."

(EVANS-WENTZ : *The Tibetan Book of the Dead*, p. 147.)

Notice that the wretched man who is confronted with the Lord of Death has previously failed to recognise any higher principle, hence his miserable fate. Had he only been sufficiently " free " to recognise the earlier and higher Gods there would have been no need to interview the Devils. But he who minds the Devil's children must sooner or later meet their Mother, just as he who harbours the divine Son will also meet His Father; which, in the case of the Tibetan system, is the Buddha Amitābha.

Here then is the " setting face-to-face " which may occur immediately after death :

"After the expiration hath completely ceased, press the nerve of sleep firmly; and a lama, or person higher or more learned than thyself, impress in these words, thus :

" 'Reverend Sir, now that thou art experiencing the Fundamental Clear Light, try to abide in that state which now thou art experiencing.'

" And also in the case of any other person, the reader shall set him face-to-face thus :

" ' O nobly-born (so-and-so), listen. Now thou art experiencing the Radiance of the Clear Light of Pure Reality. Recognise it. O nobly-born, thy present intellect, in real nature void, not formed into anything as regards characteristics or colour, naturally void, is the very Reality, the All-Good.

" ' Thine own intellect, which is now voidness, yet not to be regarded as the voidness of nothingness, but as being the intellect itself, unobstructed, shining, thrilling, and blissful, is the very consciousness, the All-Good Buddha.

" ' Thine own consciousness, not formed into anything, in reality void, and the intellect, shining and blissful—these two —are inseparable. The union of them is the Dharma Kāya state of Perfect Enlightenment.

" ' Thine own consciousness, shining, void, and inseparable from the Great Body of Radiance, hath no birth, nor death, and is the Immutable Light—Buddha Amitābha.' "

(Op. cit., p. 96.)

The foregoing illustrations probably make the Oriental attitude tolerably clear, yet, in spite of the underlying similarity between West and East, our task can hardly be called complete without a more detailed reference to one of the Western systems of symbols. . . . I mean the traditional symbols as opposed to the psychological. For obvious reasons the Kabalah takes pride of place, and I will accordingly confine my last few remarks to that ancient inheritance, of which the very basis is the progressive ascent of consciousness from the material to the utter abstraction of the Boundless Light, Ain Soph Aur ; which might well be *personified* as Amithāba to emphasise correspondence with the Eastern system.

It is even more interesting, in view of our own essentially practical arrangement of the three equations, to find that the Kabalah recognises three primary *levels* having each three Terms mutually related in the way which I have expressed as " triunity," the basic sexual relationship of two opposites and their integration. Thus the Kabalistic " Cosmic *level* " is the " Supernal Triangle," the Mystic and Physical *levels* having their corresponding " triangles."

Owing to this triangular arrangement the Third Term is placed in the centre, so that on the famous Tree of Life the three Pillars are arranged with the " opposites " flanking the central " pillar of equilibrium." Thus from Kether, the Crown, depend the Cosmic opposites, represented as male and female upon the pillars of Mercy and Severity. Beneath them the *mystical* opposites of Geburah and Chesed in turn derive the sexual opposites, the forces of desire, Hod and Netzach, which are directly linked with the materialistic principle, the Harlot Mother, otherwise Malkuth, who occupies the lowest place on the central pillar as the Creating Father occupies the highest.

Between these two is that Son whom we recognise as the Triple Christ. In the Kabalah he is Tiphareth and occupies the centre of the Pillar of Equilibrium. He is the pivot about which turns the entire universe, and is recognised under three familiar titles, being at once the Child, the Sacrifice, and the King.

But it is no part of my business to go even superficially into the countless relationships of the various principles (Sephiroth) on the Tree. It seems sufficient to note that Otz Chiim transmits in considerable detail the same knowledge which is on one hand the basis of the Tibetan ritual just described, and on the other corresponds with our own rude system, the child of the youngest science of modernity. In spite of disguises there is only one fundamental system, one destiny, one road.

" For God created man to be immortal and made him in the image of His own eternity."

(Wisdom ii, 23.)

———————

# POSTSCRIPT

## THE VISION OF A PSYCHIATRIST

"SO long as the world is sick, there will be sick people. Every step which we take toward freedom, inner and outer freedom, diminishes the number of parapathies.[1] If society wants to have healthy members it must first become healthy itself. How far we are from this ideal! Social epidemics, which manifested themselves so frightfully in the World War, are not yet exterminated. The Torch of Hatred still casts its lurid glow over this world, and love of one's neighbour remains a fiction of which only the noble-hearted long and dream. As in the Christian religion the sadistic component has found its way into the picture of suffering for all mankind under the cruel symbol of the Crucified, so our whole social life, together with its glorious progress, is undermined with envy and hate. This social sadism, whatever it may be called, and however it may be manifested, shows us what an enormous number of individual sadists there are. A grievous admission! Everyone should recognise first how deeply the primal reactions are rooted in him before he condemns a sick person who summarises the unhappiness of his times in a sexual misdemeanour.

"The greatest group murderers are the state and society. When society shall once cease murdering and destroying, the morning sun of righteousness will arise upon poor and rich, the evil conditions of society will be removed; then also will all the paraphilias[2] of cruelty vanish. . . .

"Only the unhappy are cruel! Mankind has lost the art of being happy. Because parents and teachers are unhappy they beat their children. Because we are harassed, we harass others. Because we suffer, we make others suffer.

[1] Neuroses.                    [2] Perversions.

" Diseases are the manifestation of our times. What could we expect after the great surge of hatred of the war ? The watchword, ' Hate toward hatred ! ' would be futile. For hate ends no struggle ; it creates further hatred. The religion of love toward one's neighbour has failed in its ideal task because it has combatted with hatred those who believed differently. Only love can attain victory over hatred ! Not until we understand hatred and unearth its deeper roots can we make it harmless. To know all is to forgive all. The hater must learn that his hate is a displacement of individual problems upon social ones ; he must recognise the pathological character of his asocial position and, knowing it, overcome it. This mighty task, in which all religions have failed, analysis will one day accomplish. Freud once made the pessimistic statement that analysis after his death would dwindle to nothing because the world would not endure the truth. I am not so pessimistic. I believe that an analysis purified from all errors and dross will bring a new world philosophy. It will surely transform humanity and rend aside the tissue of lies which now conceal man's true countenance.

" All of the world's unhappiness arises from lies. Our entire system of education and our conduct of life are reared upon deception. We are unable to bear the truth because we have not been educated to the truth.

" Yet one thinks of a time when the analytic truths will become the possession of all. Defects in education will disappear ; man will learn to know simply the one thing : how one may be happy and enjoy life without robbing one's neighbour of happiness and joy in life.

" . . . Analysis will show us the way to overcome the fear upon which our civilisation is built and how man may construct a world of love in which there shall be but one penalty : remorse for having done wrong, and one atonement : the victory of good over evil."

(DR. WILHEM STEKEL, *Sadism and Masochism*,
Vol. II, p. 460 ff.)

# APPENDIX

## TYPICAL EQUATIONS

In theory it is possible to recognise seven Terms on each of
the three *levels*, i.e. Dual Father, Dual Mother, Triple Son.  Here
the primary concern is to suggest the fundamentals only, and so
a minimum of words are used.

| SOURCE | **1** FATHER | **2** MOTHER | **3** SON |
|---|---|---|---|
| Alchemy | Sun | Moon | Star |
|  | Gold | Silver | Fire |
|  |  | Earth | Salt |
|  |  |  | Stone |
|  |  |  | Elixir |
|  |  |  | Tincture |
| America | Ipalnemohuani | Chicomecohuatl | Centeotl |
| Central | Sun | Centeotl | Quetzalcoatl |
|  |  | Teteonann | Kukulcan |

(*Centeotl is the maize spirit and Virgin of
Tulan, thus both Mother and Son.*)

| SOURCE | FATHER | MOTHER | SON |
|---|---|---|---|
| America North | Guitche Manito | Wenonah | Hiawatha |

*Vide Jung:* The Psychology of the Unconscious.

| SOURCE | FATHER | MOTHER | SON |
|---|---|---|---|
| Asia Minor | Anu | Hea | Bel |
|  | Baal-Ammon | Baalat | Tammuz |
|  | Dagon | Anaitas | Gilgamesh |
|  | Shamash | Ate | Adonis |
|  | Marduk (?) | Astarte | Attis |
|  | Moloch | Astoreth | Oannes |
|  | Mithra | Istar |  |
|  |  | Atagastis |  |
|  |  | Ma (Greece) |  |
|  |  | Mama (Sumeria) |  |
|  |  | Cybele (Phrygia) |  |
|  |  | Tanit (Moon) |  |
|  |  | Sin ,, |  |

(*Most of the Mothers are dual.*)

| SOURCE | 1 FATHER | 2 MOTHER | 3 SON |
|---|---|---|---|
| | *Jehovah* | | *Jonas* |
| | Iнон | | *Joshua* |
| *Britain* | " *Ceugant* " | *Keridwen* | *Arthur* |
| | {*Light*} | | *Perceval*, etc. |
| | {*Sun*} | | *Galahad* |
| *Buddhism* | *Amitābha* | *Gökarmo* (?) | *Chenrazee* |
| | *Suddhodana* | *Maya* | *Siddarta* |
| | (*King*) | (*Queen*) | (*Prince*) |
| | | | *Gautama Buddha* |
| *Celtic* | *Dagda* | *Dana* | *Lugh* |
| | *Angus Óg* | *Brigid* | *Llew* |
| | (*love*) | | *Cuculain* |
| *China and Japan* | *Yang* | *Yin* | *Kwanyin* |
| | *In* | *Yo* | *Shen I* |
| | *Izanagi* | *Izanami* | *Susa-no-o* |
| *Christianity* | *Alpha and Omega* | | |
| | *Lord God* | *Virgin* | CHRIST {*King* / *Sacrifice* / *Child* / *Icthus*} |
| | *Joseph* | *Mary* | *Jesus* |
| | | | *Son of Man* |
| | | | *Heir of God* |
| *Classical Antiquity* | *Zeus* | *Juno* | *Hermes* |
| | *Jupiter* | *Demeter* | *Mercury* |
| | *Abraxas* | *Maia* | *Apollo* |
| | | *Latona* | *Orpheus* |
| | | | *Bacchus* |
| | *Hera* | | *Dionysus* |
| | *Hecate* | | *Hercules* |
| | *Typhon* | | *Jason* |
| | *Medusa* | | *Perseus* |
| | *Laius Sphinx* | *Jocasta* | *Œdipus* |

(The Heroes have usually a divine Father and human Mother.)

| *Egypt* | *Tem* | *Nu-Nut-Mut* | *Khepera* |
|---|---|---|---|
| | *Ra* | *Isis* | *Osiris-Horus* |

| SOURCE | 1 FATHER | 2 MOTHER | 3 SON |
|---|---|---|---|
| Hindu | Bhrama | Vishnu Vishnu/Siva Kali (Preserver/Destroyer) | Krishna |
| Masonry and Rose Croix | Doric Tat Jachin | Ionic Tathu Boaz | Corinthian |
| Kabalah | Kether (Crown) | Marah (Sea) Ama/Aima (Fertile/Sterile) | TIPHARETH { King Sacrifice Child |
| Persia | Ahura-Mazda | Ormuzd/Ahriman (Light/Darkness) | Zoroaster |
| Scandinavia | Odin | Freya-Frigga | { Balder Beowulf |
| Abstractions | Vertical Circle Male Spirit Consciousness | Horizontal Square Female Matter Unconscious | Cross Triangle Androgyne Man Self-conscious |

# BIBLIOGRAPHY

ABBOT, J.  *The Keys of Power* (Indian Symbolism).
ADAMS, M.  *The Book of the Master* (Egyptian Religion).
ADLER, A.  *Practice and Theory of Individual Psychology.*
          *Problems of Neurosis.*
          *Science of Living.*
          *Social Interests.*
À KEMPIS.  *Imitation of Christ.*
ARNOLD, SIR EDWIN.  *The Light of Asia.*

BAGNALL, O.  *Origin and Properties of the Human Aura* (Physics).
" BARDASS " pub. Welsh MSS. Society (o.p.).
BERDAEV, N.  *The Destiny of Man.*
          *Freedom and the Spirit.*
BERGSON, H.  *Creative Evolution.*
BESANT, A.  *Esoteric Christianity.*
BESTERMAN and CROWLEY.  *The Mystic Rose.*  2 vols.  (Anthropology.)
BLAVATSKY, H. P.  *The Secret Doctrine.*  2 vols.
BLOCH, I.  *The Sexual Life of Our Time.*
BLUM, LÉON.  *Marriage.*
BREND, W. A.  *Sacrifice to Attis.*
BRIDGES, ROBERT.  *The Spirit of Man.*  (Anthology.)
BROCKINGTON.  *Mysticism and Poetry.*
BROWN, S. J.  *The World of Imagery.*
BRUNNER, E.  *The Philosophy of Religion.*
BUDGE, SIR E. A. W.  *From Fetish to God in Ancient Egypt.*
          *Amulets and Superstitions.*
          *Cleopatra's Needles.*
          *The Queen of Sheba.*
BULLEY, M.  *Art and Understanding.*
DE BURGH.  *Towards a Religious Philosophy.*

CABELL, J. B. *Figures of Earth.* (Fiction.)
　　　　*Domnei.* (Fiction.)
CALVERTON and SCHMALHAUSEN. *Sex in Civilisation.*
CARREL, A. *Man the Unknown.* (Physiology.)
CARTER, HOWARD. *The Tomb of Tut-Ankh-Amen.* 2 vols.
CATHERINE OF SIENA, The Dialogue of
CHAPMAN, D. *Matter, Myth, and Spirit.*
CLELAND, H. F. *Our Prehistoric Ancestors.*
CONAN DOYLE, SIR A. *History of Spiritualism.* 2 vols.
COPLESTON, R. S. *Buddhism.*
CRILE, G. *The Phenomena of Life.*
CROW, C. *The Master Kung.*
CURTIS, L. *Civitas Dei.* 3 vols.

DAVIDSON and ALDERSMITH. *The Great Pyramid.*
DICKINSON and BEAL. *A Thousand Marriages.*
DUNNE, J. W. *The New Immortality.*
　　　　*The Serial Universe.*
　　　　*An Experiment with Time.*

EAGLE, A. *The Philosophy of Religion versus the Philosophy of Science.*
ELLIS, HAVELOCK. *Studies in the Psychology of Sex.* 4 vols.
　　　　*The Task of Social Hygiene.*
*Encyclopædia Britannica.* XIV ed.
EWER. *A Survey of Mystical Symbolism.*

FERENCZI. *Sex in Psychoanalysis.*
FLÜGEL, J. C. *The Psychology of Clothes.*
FORTUNE, D. *The Mystical Qabalah.*
FRAZER, SIR J. *The Golden Bough.*
　　　　*Folklore in the Old Testament.*
　　　　*Belief in Immortality.*
　　　　*Totemica.*
FREUD, S. *The Interpretation of Dreams.*
　　　　*Psychopathology of Everyday Life.*
　　　　*Civilisation and its Discontents.*
FULLER, SIR B. *Etheric Energies.*

GARDINER. *The Chester Beatty Papyri No.* 1. (The Contendings of Horus and Set.)

GIBSON, A. B. *The Philosophy of Descartes.*
GOETHE. *Faust.* (Trans. Bayard Taylor.)
GOLDBERG, B. Z. *The Sacred Fire* (Sex and Religion).
GRANT, J. *Winged Pharaoh.* (Fiction.)
GRANT, MALCOLM. *A New Argument for God and Survival.*
GRODDECK, G. *The Unknown Self.*
        *The Book of the It.*
        *The World of Man.*

HALL, M. *Man the Grand Symbol.*
        *Symbolical Philosophy.*
HANNAY. *Rise, Decline, and Fall of the Roman Religion.*
HARTMANN, F. *Magic.*
HEATH, S. *The Romance of Symbolism.*
HOLLINGWORTH, H. L. *Abnormal Psychology.*
HOWEY, M. O. *The Encircled Serpent.*
HULME and WOOD. *Ancient Egypt Speaks.*
HULME, F. E. *Symbolism in Christian Art.*

INMAN. *Ancient Faiths and Modern.*

JAMES, H. *The Story of Prophecy.*
JOAD, C. E. M. *The Testament of Joad.*
JONES, G. *Welsh Folklore and Folk Customs.*
JUNG, C. J. *The Psychology of the Unconscious.*
        *Psychological Types.*
        *Modern Man in Search of a Soul.*
JUNG and WILHELM. *The Secret of the Golden Flower.*

KENYON, T. *Witches Still Live.*
KRAFFT-EBING. *Psychopathia Sexualis.* 2 vols.

LAUBSHER, B. J. F. *Sex, Custom, and Psychopathology.*
LAWRENCE, D. H. *Apocalypse.*
        *Collected Poems.*
LEADBEATER, C. L. *The Hidden Side of Things.*
        *The Inner Life.*
        *The Other Side of Death.*
LELAND, C. G. *Aradia. The Gospel of the Witches.*
        *The Alternate Sex.*

LEUBA, J. H.  *The Psychology of Religious Mysticism.*
LEVI, ELIPAS.  *Transcendental Magic.*
LODGE, SIR OLIVER.  *Beyond Physics.*
LONG, M. F.  *Recovering the Ancient Magic.*

McDOUGALL, W.  *An Outline of Psychology.*
              *The Character and Conduct of Life.*
MEARS, I. and L. E.  *Creative Energy* (Tao).
MITCHELL, J. M.  *Hinduism Past and Present* (o.p.).
MYERS, F. W. H.  *Human Personality and its Survival.*  2 vols.
*Myths.*  Series published by Harrap.  14 vols.
    „       „      „ Gresham.  6  „

NIETZSCHE, F.  *Thus Spake Zarathustra.*
             *Ecce Homo.*
             *Beyond Good and Evil.*

OESTERREICH, K.  *Occultism and Modern Science.*
OLIVER, C. W.  *The Extension of Consciousness.*
           *Oxford Book of English Mystical Verse.*
OUSPENSH, P. D.  *A New Model of the Universe.*

PALMSTIERNA, E.  *Horizons of Immortality.*
DU PREL, C.  *Philosophy of Mysticism.*  2 vols.

RAPPOPORT, A. S.  *Myth and Legend of Ancient Israel.*  3 vols.
REINACH.  *Orpheus* (*Comparative Religion*).
RÓHEIM, G.  *The Riddle of the Sphinx.*
           *Animism and the Divine King.*

SHORTER, A. W.  *The Egyptian Gods.*
SIMPSON, SIR J. Y.  *British Archaic Sculpturings.*
SINCLAIR, R.  *Metropolitan Man.*
SMITH, WHATLEY.  *The Measurement of Emotion.*
SPENCE, L.  *The Mysteries of Britain.*
Spinoza, the Philosophy of.  (Trans. Elwes.)
STEKEL, W.  *Sadism and Masochism.*  2 vols.
         *Sexual Aberrations.*  2 vols.
         *Bisexual Love.*
STEPHENS, J.  *The Crock of Gold.*  (Fiction.)

SUMMERS, M.  *History of Demonology and Witchcraft.*
*A Popular History of Witchcraft.*
*The Geography of Witchcraft.*

UNDERHILL, E.  *Mysticism.*

WAITE, A. E.  *The Brotherhood of the Rosy Cross.*
*The Holy Grail.*
*The Quest of the Golden Stairs.*  (Fiction.)
*The Secret Tradition in Freemasonry.*
WELLS, H. G., and G. P.  *The Science of Life.*
WENTZ, W. Y. E.  *The Tibetan Book of the Dead.*
WILD, K. W.  *Intuition.*
WILDE, OSCAR.  *Salome.*
WILLIAMSON, W.  *The Great Law.*  (Theosophy.)

YEATS, W. B.  *Collected Poems.*
YEATS, W. B., and SHREE PUROHIT SWAMI.  *The Ten Principal Upanishads.*

# INDEX

Skopzi, 74
Son. (*See* Consummator and Christ)
Spear, 177 ff.
Sphinx, 11, 12, 144, 248 ff. (Œdipus), 255, 257
Stekel, 98, 281–282, 304, 309 ff.
Stone (symbol), 166 ff.
Summers, 40
Sun, 210 ff.

T

Taboo, 18, 28 ff., 76 (marriage)
Tao, 78, 176
Thebes, 22, 122, 247, 257
Time, 99–100, 267–268
Tjet, 192
Tobit, 30
Transmutation, 176, 284
Trees (symbols), 104, 116–117, 127, 205 (Egypt)
Truth, 129
Tuatha da Danaan, 162 ff.
Tyndale, 45

U

Unity, 92
Uzzah, 14, 159, 170

V

Venus (Bearded), 70
Venus of Willendorf, 63
Virgin, 218, 266, 289; Virgin-Harlot, 138, 144, 194, 244, 253, 283, 288
Virgin Mary, 184, 237 (titles), 273–274

W

Waite, A. E., 167 ff., 180–181, 186
Wine (Cult), 160
Witchcraft, 142, 144
Word, the, 43, 45, 60, 92, 97, 98–99, 106, 196, 260–261

Y

Yoga, 97

Z

Zoroaster, 21